DEVELOPMENTS IN GENRE BETWEEN POST-EXILIC PENITENTIAL PRAYERS AND THE PSALMS OF COMMUNAL LAMENT

Society of Biblical Literature

Academia Biblica

Saul M. Olyan,
Old Testament Editor

Mark Allan Powell,
New Testament Editor

Number 7

Developments in Genre between
Post-Exilic Penitential Prayers and
the Psalms of Communal Lament

Developments in Genre between Post-Exilic Penitential Prayers and the Psalms of Communal Lament

Richard J. Bautch

Society of Biblical Literature
Atlanta

Developments in Genre between Post-Exilic Penitential Prayers and the Psalms of Communal Lament

Copyright © 2003 by the Society of Biblical Literature

All rights reserved. No part of this work may be reproduced or transmitted in any form or by any means, electronic or mechanical, including photocopying and recording, or by means of any information storage or retrieval system, except as may be expressly permitted by the 1976 Copyright Act or in writing from the publisher. Requests for permission should be addressed in writing to the Rights and Permissions Office, Society of Biblical Literature, 825 Houston Mill Road, Atlanta, GA 30329, USA.

Library of Congress Cataloging-in-Publication Data

Bautch, Richard J.
  Developments in genre between post-exilic penitential prayers and the psalms of communal lament / by Richard J. Bautch.
    p. cm. — (Academia Biblica ; no. 7)
  Includes bibliographical references and index.
  ISBN 1-58983-047-4 (pbk.)
  1. Atonement (Prayer)—Judaism. 2. Sin (Judaism) 3. Judaism—History—Post-exilic period, 586 B.C.-210 A.D. 4. Bible. O.T. Isaiah LXIII, 7-LXIV, 11—Criticism, interpretation, etc. 5. Bible. O.T. Ezra IX, 6-15—Criticism, interpretation, etc. 6. Bible. O.T. Nehemiah IX, 6-37—Criticism, interpretation, etc. I. Title. II. Series: Academia Biblica (Series) (Society of Biblical Literature) ; no. 7.
BM645.A8 B38 2003b
221.6'63—dc22
                    2003017087

07 06 05 04 03   5 4 3 2 1

Printed in the United States of America
on acid-free paper.

IN MEMORIAM

Dorothy Marie Bautch
and Richard Bernard Bautch,
my parents

CONTENTS

ACKNOWLEDGMENTS ix
TABLES xi
ABBREVIATIONS xiii

CHAPTER 1: A FORM-CRITICAL APPROACH TO THE
POST-EXILIC PRAYERS OF PENITENCE 1
   1.1   Introduction 1
   1.2   Scholarship on Prayer 6
   1.3   The Scholarly Context of This Study 8
   1.4   The Form-Critical Method of Hermann Gunkel 13
   1.5   Additional Considerations of Methodology 17
   1.6   Intertextuality in the Sixth and Fifth
         Centuries B.C.E. 18
   1.7   The Dating of Select Prayers and the Psalms
         of Communal Lament.. 24

CHAPTER 2: ISA 63:7–64:11—AN ANOMALOUS PSALM
OF COMMUNAL LAMENT 29
   2.1   Text 29
   2.2   Text-Critical Issues and Notes.. 31
   2.3   Form-Critical Inventory of Isa 63:7–64:11 35
   2.4   Form-Critical Analysis of Isa 63:7–64:11 37
   2.5   The Context of Isa 63:7–64:11 41
   2.6   The Confession of Sins 48
   2.7   Deuteronomistic Theology 55
   2.8   Conclusion: *Sitz im Leben* 61

CHAPTER 3: EZRA 9:6–15—LAW AND LITURGY 65
   3.1   Text 65

3.2	Text-Critical Issues and Notes	66
3.3	The Context of Ezra 9–10	69
3.4	Form-Critical Inventory of Ezra 9:6–15	72
3.5	Form-Critical Inquiry I: Ezra 9:6–15 and the Communal Laments	73
3.6	Form-Critical Inquiry II: Ezra 9:6–15 and the Levitical Sermon	80
3.7	Form-Critical Determination: Ezra 9:6–15 a Mixed Genre	83
3.8	*Sitz im Leben* of Ezra 9:6–15	84
3.9	Ezra 9:6–15 and Deuteronomic Law	86
3.10	Excursus: The Authorship of Ezra 9:6–15	91

CHAPTER 4: NEH 9:6–37—A TRANSFORMATION OF THE COMMUNAL LAMENT ... 101

4.1	Text	101
4.2	Text-Critical Issues and Notes	104
4.3	Context: Neh 7:5–10:40	106
4.4	Structural Analysis: Neh 9:6–37	109
4.5	Form-Critical Inquiry: Neh 9:6–37 and the Psalms of Communal Lament	116
4.6	Neh 9:6–37: *Sitz im Leben*	121
4.7	Neh 9:6–37 and Pentateuchal Sources	125
4.8	Conclusion	135

CHAPTER 5: THE FORM-CRITICAL LEGACY OF THE COMMUNAL LAMENT IN THE HELLENISTIC AND ROMAN PERIODS ... 137

5.1	Introduction	137
5.2	Structural Transformations Related to the Petition	138
5.3	The Confession of Sin: A Lexical Typology	146
5.4	Literary and Theological Summation	159
5.5	Manner and Tone: Prophecies of Warning	161
5.6	*Sitz im Leben*	165
5.7	Conclusion	171

BIBLIOGRAPHY ... 173
AUTHOR INDEX ... 183
SCRIPTURE INDEX ... 187

ACKNOWLEDGMENTS

I am grateful to the many people who have supported my writing and publishing the dissertation that follows. Leigh Andersen and Saul Olyan, editors for the Society of Biblical Literature, have been most encouraging as they have guided my writing into print. The production of this book has been supported as well by St. Edward's University, which generously provided me with research funds during the dissertation's final stages. I also thank Alison Koen, a student at St. Edward's, for her skilled work typesetting the pages electronically.

I am indebted to the theology faculty at the University of Notre Dame, who taught me so very much through the course of my doctoral studies. I have a deep debt of gratitude to my dissertation committee. Through their critical engagement, Joseph Blenkinsopp, Hindy Najman, Eugene Ulrich and James VanderKam brought me to refine my ideas and to express them with clarity. I am especially grateful to Joseph Blenkinsopp, who directed the dissertation. While subjecting my work to his probing mind, he provided unfailing support and, in difficult moments, good cheer.

My family helped me immeasurably as the dissertation was conceived, researched and written. For their support, I thank my sisters as well as the Daniels family and the Coblentz family. I have not the words to thank the one person who has contributed the most to this dissertation as a loving wife and as a committed colleague in the field of biblical studies. Kelley Coblentz Bautch helped me to think through my data and to build arguments with them. Sensitive and constant, her spirit has been an inspiration to me. This study on prayer and the return to God is a result of all her help and encouragement.

This book is dedicated to the memory of my parents, Dorothy Marie Bautch and Richard Bernard Bautch.

TABLES

1. Omissions (>), additions (+) and variants (=) of Isa 63:7–64:11 in the principal ancient texts 33

2. Form-critical structure of the psalms of communal lament 36

3. Form-critical comparison of the psalms of communal lament and Isa 63:7–65:12 48

4. Omissions (>), additions (+) and variants (=) of Ezra 9:6–15 in the principal ancient texts 68

5. Omissions (>), additions (+) and variants (=) of Neh 9:6–37 in the principal ancient texts 105

6. Sequence of events in the historical accounts of Israel included in the Hebrew Bible 112

7. Form-critical structure of the psalms of communal lament 118

ABBREVIATIONS: JOURNALS, PERIODICALS, SERIES AND MAJOR REFERENCE WORKS

AB	Anchor Bible
ATANT	Abhandlungen zur Theologie des Alten und Neuen Testaments
BA	*Biblical Archaeologist*
BDB	*A Hebrew and English Lexicon of the Old Testament*
BJS	Brown Judaic Studies
BWA(N)T	Beiträge zur Wissenschaft vom Alten (und Neuen) Testament
BZ	*Biblische Zeitschrift*
BZAW	Beihefte zur Zeitschrift für die alttestamentliche Wissenschaft
CBQ	*Catholic Biblical Quarterly*
CBQMS	Catholic Biblical Quarterly Monograph Series
DJD	Discoveries in the Judaean Desert
DNTB	*Dictionary of New Testament Background*
EJ	*Encyclopedia of Judaism*
EncJud	*Encyclopaedia Judaica*
ExpTim	*Expository Times*
FOTL	Forms of the Old Testament Literature
GKC	*Gesenius' Hebrew Grammar*
HAT	Handbuch zum Alten Testament
HS	*Hebrew Studies*
HUCA	*Hebrew Union College Annual*
ICC	International Critical Commentary
Int	*Interpretation*

JBL	*Journal of Biblical Literature*
JJS	*Journal of Jewish Studies*
JNSL	*Journal of Northwest Semitic Languages*
JSOTSup	Journal for the Study of the Old Testament: Supplement Series
JSPSup	Journal for the Study of the Pseudepigrapha: Supplement Series
JTS	*Journal of Theological Studies*
KAT	Kommentar zum Alten Testament
KBL	*Lexicon in Veteris Testamenti libros*
LCL	Loeb Classical Library
LSJ	*A Greek-English Lexicon*
NCB	New Century Bible
OBT	Overtures to Biblical Theology
OTP	*Old Testament Pseudepigrapha*
OTL	Old Testament Library
RB	*Revue Biblique*
RGG	*Religion in Geschichte und Gegenwart*
SBLDS	Society of Biblical Literature Dissertation Series
SBLEJL	Society of Biblical Literature Early Judaism and Its Literature Series
SBLMS	Society of Biblical Literature Monograph Series
SSN	Studia semitica neerlandica
STDJ	*Studies on the Texts of the Desert of Judah*
STR	Studies in Theology and Religion
TDOT	*Theological Dictionary of the Old Testament*
TLOT	*Theological Lexicon of the Old Testament*
TLZ	*Theologische Literaturzeitung*
Transeu	*Transeuphratène*
VTSup	Supplements to Vetus Testamentum
WBC	Word Biblical Commentary
WMANT	Wissenschaftliche Monographien zum Alten und Neuen Testament
WTJ	*Westminster Theological Journal*
ZAW	*Zeitschrift für die alttestamentliche Wissenschaft*

1

A FORM-CRITICAL APPROACH TO THE POST-EXILIC PRAYERS OF PENITENCE

1.1 Introduction

Recognizing that repentance involves a radical change of behavior and a firm commitment to God's will, one rabbinic commentary praises those who have sinned and repented and extols them above even those who have never sinned (*b. Ber.* 34b).[1] The commentary in question contains another tractate (*b. San.* 43b) describing repentance as a harbinger of the world to come, and elsewhere in the passage it is said that repentance also harks back to human origins, where it was one of the seven things God made before creation. These and other passages suggest that the rabbis idealized the repentant sinner and accorded repentance itself a transcendent character.[2] The high estimation of

---

[1] *b. Ber.* 34b reads: "In a place where penitents stand even the wholly righteous cannot stand." The translation is from the *Hebrew-English Edition of the Babylonian Talmud* (ed. M. Simon and I. Epstein; London: Soncino, 1960), 2.34b. Luke 15:7 similarly esteems the repentant sinner. An even earlier example of the repentant sinner idealized in Jewish thought is found in Philo, who ranks repentance second only to sinlessness but holds that the latter "belongs to God alone or possibly a divine man." Philo implies that among humans, repentance is a preeminent value (ἡ ἀγαθός). *"De Virtutibus,"* pp. 162–305 in *Philo VIII* (LCL 341; ed. F. H. Colson; Cambridge, Mass.: Harvard University Press, 1939), 270.

[2] The hypothesis stands on additional evidence, such as *Pesiqta de Rab Kahana* 23, redacted in Galilee ca. the fifth century. According to Lou Silberman, the redactor "took those items that suited his theme, the acquittal of man and most particularly of Israel on *Rosh Ha-shanah*, this reflecting the acquittal of Adam on the day of his creation and anticipating an eschatological redemption, the new being of man, in the new or renewed

repentance is not original to the rabbis. It emerged from Second Temple Judaism,[3] where repentance flourished and the confession of sin became a hallmark of post-exilic piety. Indeed, the confession of sin became one of the best attested prayer forms during the period of the Second Temple.

Five features distinguish Second Temple prayer that is rooted in the confession of sin: a functional efficacy, a communal dimension, a set of structuring conventions, a ceremonial context and an intertextual character. Each feature merits elaboration and comment.

Functional Efficacy. Penitential prayer involved the pray-er in a process of repentance or תשובה, which involves a turning *from* evil and a turning *toward* good.[4] We may consider the efficacy of *teshuvah* in terms of its cause and its effect. A cause was verbal confession, examples of which abound in later biblical literature and are examined in this dissertation. In antiquity, however, verbal confession does not come under discussion until the time of the rabbis, whom we must briefly consult. The rabbis referred to verbal confession as וידוי. In *Leviticus Rabbah,* for example, *viddui* and *teshuvah* are distinct but closely related in the manner of cause and effect.[5] The interplay of *teshuvah* and *viddui* is elsewhere affirmed by the rabbis.[6]

---

creation, to occur on the same day." The temporal coincidence of creation and judgment illustrates the trans-historical character of forgiveness in the rabbinic treatise. See "A Theological Treatise on Forgiveness: Chapter Twenty-Three of *Pesiqta de Rab Kahana,*" pp. 95–107 in *Studies in Aggadah, Targum and Jewish Liturgy* (ed. J. J. Petuchowski and E. Fleischer; Jerusalem: Magnes Press, 1981), 106.

[3] We hold the view associated with Joseph Heinemann and others that there was continuous development in Jewish liturgical thought throughout antiquity, from early stages with prayer in the form of creative compositions to the final, set formulations of prayer texts that postdate the fall of the Second Temple by several centuries. Thus, rabbinic sources can provide important data about Second Temple prayer. For example, Heinemann notes that "statutory" or communal, fixed prayer was regarded by the sages as עבודה, divine service or worship. He concludes, "It becomes evident that prayer was regarded as עבודה, in a manner analogous to the sacrificial cult, not only in the period following the destruction of the Second Temple, but even during the period of the temple itself, the only difference being that, in the temple period, prayer did not take the place of sacrifices but rather paralleled and complemented them." Later in his discussion, Heinemann adds that repentance or תשובה is another rabbinic concept that finds expression in the liturgy of the Second Temple period. See his *Prayer in the Period of the Tanna'im and the Amora'im: Its Nature and Its Patterns* (Jerusalem: Magnes, 1966), 15, 31.

[4] On the development of the Hebrew word תשובה, from the root for "return," see Jacob Milgrom's "Repentance," *EncJud* 14:73.

[5] "[A person] should say: 'I confess all the evil I have done before Thee; I stood in the way of evil; and as for all [the evil] I have done, I shall no more do the like; may it be Thy will, O Lord my God, that Thou shouldst pardon me for all my iniquities, and forgive me all my transgressions, and grant me atonement for all my sins.'" *Lev. Rab.* 3:3. The translation is from the *Midrash Rabbah Leviticus* (ed. M. Simon and H.

Extending the rabbis' legacy, Maimonides yoked together verbal confession and *teshuvah;* he begins his treatise on repentance stating that if one transgresses a command of the Torah, "when he repents and turns back from sin, it is his duty to confess before the Lord."[7] Brought to prominence in the post-exilic period, verbal confession became an enduring hallmark of Jewish prayer and a perennial trigger for repentance.

The penitential prayers effected כפרה, God's forgiving and actually removing sin in a manner analogous to when one atones for sin by sacrificing, giving alms, suffering oppression, practicing obedience or fasting. In the Second Temple period, the public, communal confession of sin expressed both one's return to God and the forgiveness of sins commonly associated with atonement, although the two functions would later be differentiated and distinguished in rabbinic thought.

Communal Dimension. While effecting the expiation of an individual's sins, penitential prayer after the Exile expressed a distinctive perspective that set the individual in solidarity with a national history marked by moral failure. A significant number of first-person plural pronouns and verbal suffixes established the communal character of the prayer. Such grammatical elements expressed the prayer's communal dimension. In this regard, not to be overlooked is the cultic background of prayer that pervades the Hebrew Bible. Henning Graf Reventlow notes that cultic unity is connoted in the term קהל or community. The notion of קהל, he contends, has fostered a solidarity of sufferers who, as the people of God, could confront shattering experiences.[8] Those suffering even the perceived absence of God had a serviceable recourse in prayers of communal lament such as Isa 63:7–64:11, one of the primary sources for this dissertation. A modern footnote to this matter derives from A. I. Kook, who taught that while *teshuvah* atones for an individual's misdeeds, it also helps to revive the nation of Israel and bring eternal redemption to the whole world.[9] The communal dimension of repentance, Kook thought, benefited both the world globally and Israel particularly.

Structuring Conventions. Most prayers of repentance in the Second Temple period reflected a self-conscious use of literary conventions relating to the lament form. The prayers employed conventions such as the lament, the

---

Freedman; trans. J. Israelstam; London: Soncino, 1939), 37.

[6] See also *m. Yoma* 1.3, 3.8, 4.2, 6.2 and *b. Yoma* 86a,b. Citations of the *Mishnah* are from *Mishnah* (ed. C. Albeck; Tel Aviv: Dvir, 1959).

[7] He proceeds to interpret Num 5:6 as requiring a confession *in words* [emphasis added], and indicates that the confession is a "positive command." Maimonides, *The Book of Knowledge from the Mishneh Torah of Maimonides* (trans. H. M. Russell and J. Weinberg; New York: KTAV, 1983), 109.

[8] *Gebet im Alten Testament* (Stuttgart/Berlin/Cologne/Mainz: Kolhammer, 1986), 304–6.

[9] Abraham Isaac Kook, *Orot* (trans. B. Naor; Northvale, N.J./London: Aronson, 1993), 212–14.

petition and the confession of sin. Moreover, prayer became the vehicle for relatively new conventions such as the recital of national history. A national history marked by moral failure became a standard element of post-exilic penitential prayer. Thus, this dissertation will study conventions used to structure penitential prayer after the return from exile.

A focus will be language as an ingredient of literary convention. In the pre-exilic period there were distinct words for confessing sins (חטא), iniquities (עון), and transgressions (פשע), and the verbal roots were not synonymous.[10] Yet in the post-exilic period, language sometimes became stereotyped and formulaic with the result that its meaning, and that of the convention, can only be determined indirectly. For example, after the exile the roots חטא, עון, פשע were routinely combined in a single expression and in this process became vague clichés. As a result, in post-exilic texts these expressions must be interpreted primarily in light of parallel phrases and contexts.[11]

Ceremonial Context. We have noted that the prayers of repentance had a communal character derived in part from the milieu of the cult. As effects of the cult, the prayers incorporated significant cultic *realia* such as specific prayer times, be these hours in a given day or festal dates on the calendar. For example, we shall later discuss apparent connections between יום כפורים and the liturgical gatherings reported in Nehemiah 8 and 9. Such an association links penitential prayer to a national observance as well as to the cult.

After the exile the cult was in flux; as its form was being renewed, not everything could be restored.[12] In this time of change, prayer developed into a form of religious activity that was increasingly autonomous from the cult. The development is expressed in the relationship between prayer and sacrifice; a "shift in emphasis away from sacrifice and toward prayer" suggests that prayer grew in popularity as that of sacrifice waned in the Persian, Hellenistic and Roman periods.[13] Although the exact relationship between post-exilic prayer and the cult is open to debate,[14] prayer in this period developed into a form of

---

[10] See Rolf Knierim, *Die Hauptbegriffe für Sünde im Alten Testament* (Gütersloh: Gerd Mohn, 1965), 229–34.

[11] Alan Avery-Peck has observed: "While the distinctions ... in the meanings of the biblical terms [פשע, עון, חטא] used for sin are important, it must also be clear that in later biblical and post-biblical texts these terms frequently are used to refer to sin in general. The distinctive connotations attributable to their root meanings and to their original uses often times appear to have been lost, so that in later contexts the words simply function as synonyms." "Sin in Judaism," *EJ* 1320–32; esp. 1323.

[12] Yehezkel Kaufmann observes that the ark, the Urim and Thummim, and the anointing oil were not restored. *The Religion of Israel: From Its Beginnings to the Babylonian Exile* (trans. M. Greenberg; New York: Schocken, 1972), 184.

[13] This point is made by Joseph Blenkinsopp in "The Second Temple as House of Prayer," pp. 109–22 in *"Où demeures-tu?" La Maison depuis le monde biblique* (ed. J. C. Petit; Quebec: Éditions Fides, 1994), 110.

[14] Among scholars of prayer in the Second Temple period, its degree of

religious activity that was increasingly less dependent upon the cult. While the penitential prayers were invariably associated with a ceremonial context, the context was not reducible to the cult.

Intertextual Character. In the period of the Second Temple, many prayers of repentance had a dimension of intertextuality that will be elaborated later in this chapter. In short, the religious thought of earlier generations surfaced in these prayers and was subject to rearticulation. In many cases, episodes of misfortune and disaster are recalled as evidence that God punishes the people's rebellion before offering them forgiveness. The belief in divine retribution typically associated with the Deuteronomistic History (Dtr) is affirmed by these prayers, which also particularize certain aspects of the retribution. In the literature of prayer, an "acceptance of the rightness of divine judgment" distinguishes the prayers of lamentation composed after the exile[15] from their pre-exilic counterparts and suggests that the later prayers are the product of intertextual developments within the Deuteronomistic system of thought.

With these five features in view, this dissertation will undertake a critical study of public, communal confession in early Second Temple Judaism, with a focus on three biblical exemplars from the sixth and fifth centuries. The prayers in question are Isa 63:7–64:11, Ezra 9:6–15 and Neh 9:6–37. The study will be diachronic in nature because its goal is to identify developments in genre. Specifically, we seek to cite and discuss continuities in form between the psalms of communal lament and the penitential prayers of the post-exilic period. While the psalms of communal lament are the study's primary point of reference, we will also examine other literary forms that have influenced the penitential prayers, such as the prophetic warning.[16] Like the communal laments, the

---

independence from the cult remains at issue. Israel Knohl and Esther Chazon limit prayer's autonomy from the sacrificial cult. Knohl envisions the temple as a series of concentric circles in order that an inner circle for priestly service is linked to an outer circle where people recite folk prayers. See his "Between Voice and Silence: The Relationship Between Prayer and Temple Cult," *JBL* 115 (1996): 17–30; esp. 23. Chazon recognizes that Ezra 9:5, Dan 9:21, Jdt 9:1 and Acts 10:30 all refer to prayer outside the temple at the time of the daily, afternoon sacrifice. Nonetheless, she concludes: "[These sources] indicate that prayers said at the temple remained on its periphery both geographically and culticly." See her "When Did They Pray? Times for Prayer in the Dead Sea Scrolls and Associated Literature," pp. 42–51 in *For A Later Generation: The Transformation of Tradition in Israel, Early Judaism, and Early Christianity* (ed. R. A. Argall, B. A. Bow and R. A. Werline; Harrisburg, Pa.: Trinity, 2000), 47–48.

[15] As Peter Ackroyd writes, "The type of the psalm of lamentation, with its apparent complaints at the silence and inactivity of the deity, is turned into its obverse—though this is in reality part of that psalm form—in which the acceptance of the rightness of divine judgment is in itself an anticipation of what may follow." *Exile and Restoration: A Study of Hebrew Thought of the Sixth Century B.C.* (Philadelphia: Westminster, 1968), 77.

[16] For an introductory overview of the prophetic warning in psalmic literature, see

prophetic warning is a form whose origins are pre-exilic but whose influence extends to the Jewish prayers of penitence composed after the return from Babylon. While the history of literary forms provides the primary focus of this dissertation, our study deals with various issues of prayer as it is documented in the Hebrew Bible and discussed by modern scholars. In fact, scholarship on prayer constitutes the initial segment of background to this dissertation.

1.2 Scholarship on Prayer

In the century most recently concluded, the tradition of scholarship on prayer is found primarily within discussions of theology in the Hebrew Bible. Discussions in the first three decades of the century were often keyed to the history-of-religions approach to studying the Hebrew Bible. The approach equated prayer with sacrifice and often subordinated the former to the latter; prayer itself was a peripheral concern that is related to the psalter and sacrificial practices.[17] Prayer's intrinsic value was to be recognized by subsequent generations of biblical scholars.

The first of these generations was that of Walter Eichrodt and Gerhard von Rad. For these scholars, prayer found in the Hebrew Bible is a distinct response to God as sovereign Lord. In Eichrodt's view, Israel affirms God's dominion through prayer, just as a vassal would recognize the superiority of his king.[18] Eichrodt's higher estimation of prayer stops short of giving prayer a place of primary importance in the relationship between God and God's people. Rather, for Eichrodt and his generation, nothing compares with God's initiative, expressed in covenantal promises[19] or historical deeds.[20] Only in the following generation is prayer considered a primary datum of Israelite religion. Von Rad attempted to analyze prayer in terms of a schematic said to reflect Israel's historical development. Prayer would be judged largely by its place in biblical history, with eighth century material from the period of classical prophecy held in high regard. Von Rad took a less sanguine view of lament-based prayers

---

W. H. Bellinger, Jr., *Psalms: Reading and Studying the Book of Praises* (Peabody, Mass.: Hendrickson, 1990), 90–91.

[17] An example is *Hebrew Religion: Its Origin and Development*, by W. O. E. Oesterley and T. H. Robinson, whose treatment of prayer proper is cursory indeed. See W. O. E. Oesterley and T. H. Robinson, *Hebrew Religion: Its Origin and Development* (London: SPCK, 1930).

[18] Walter Eichrodt, *Theology of the Old Testament* (OTL; 2 vols.; Philadelphia: Westminster, 1961–7 [1933–9]), 1:175.

[19] Ibid., 1:419–24.

[20] Historical deeds constitute the *Entfaltung der alttestamentlichen Zeugnisinhalte* or "unfolding of the witness of the Old Testament" in the theology developed by Gerhard von Rad, who notes the difficulty in locating a center to these events. *Theologie des Alten Testaments* (2 vols.; Munich: Chr. Kaiser Verlag, 1968–1969 [1957]), 1:128.

composed during and after the exile.[21] Von Rad's judgment that these prayers reflect empty piety removed from the fundamental core of Yahwism retains few if any adherents, and in fact prayer patterned on the lament form may now be seen as a catalyst for theological activity after the return from exile.

The generation after that of Eichrodt and von Rad brought prayer even more to the fore of theology based upon the Hebrew Bible. Claus Westermann established the dialectical model that maintained a primary focus on God's initiatives but considered the human response to God, prayer, to be of no less importance.[22] Westermann and those scholars who employ his model may be credited with the balanced recognition of the divine and human perspectives as both are found in the biblical material on prayer. Moreover, Westermann recognized the diversity of modes within human prayer and identified praise and lament as the two categories into which all modes fall.[23] In Westermann's model, lament has positive valuation as the uniquely human response to loss and disaster. Such a view of prayer and of lament in particular departs from von Rad's critique based on a linear view of Israelite history. While Westermann also discusses the periodization of prayer,[24] in his work no stage is denigrated and the post-exilic models of note, such as Ezra 9 and Nehemiah 9, are recognized for integrating poetry with prose. Similarly noted is the shift in the prayers from lament to the confession of sin.[25]

The humanistic perspective on prayer in the Hebrew Bible reveals that authors used various literary conventions to generate prayerful responses to providential events, including disaster that resulted in the loss of national sovereignty. While maintaining the importance of God's initiative in human history, Westermann and scholars under his influence draw attention to the responsive nature of prayer. Prayer as response in the post-exilic period based itself upon history and patterned itself upon earlier Israelite literature. Alongside the formal conventions that gave structure to the received writings, the sources informing these writings and imparting to them an explicitly religious character also influenced the composition of post-exilic prayer. Prominent among these sources were the Deuteronomistic History and the priestly writings found in the Pentateuch. The presence of pre-exilic and exilic source material in post-exilic prayers of penitence elicited much interest among biblical scholars writing in the final decade of the past century.

---

[21] Ibid., 1:403–4.

[22] In Claus Westermann's view, the theology of the Hebrew Bible is the direct effect of the interrelationship between God and humankind. *Elements of Old Testament Theology* (Atlanta: John Knox, 1982), 153–54.

[23] Ibid., 156. See also *Praise and Lament in the Psalms* (Atlanta: John Knox Press, 1981), 154.

[24] *Elements of Old Testament Theology*, 153–74.

[25] Ibid., 165–213.

1.3 The Scholarly Context of this Study

For most of the twentieth century, studies of Isa 63:7–64:11, Ezra 9:6–15 and Neh 9:6–37 reflected various methodologies and a range of exegetical concerns keyed to historical, literary and religious *realia*.[26] That is to say, until ten years ago, the interest in these penitential prayers was piecemeal and heterogeneous. On the whole, this body of carefully conducted yet inconclusive scholarship underscored the need for sustained investigation into this prayer type.

In the last ten years, there have appeared a number of studies of Neh 9:6–37 that examine and evaluate the sources and literary traditions that inform this prayer. It would be a misnomer to classify these studies as tradition criticism, which refers to the study of the history of oral traditions during their period of transmission. Current studies focus on motifs and similar units of tradition that figure prominently in the prayer's composition. Thus, the studies recall the practice of *Traditionsgeschichte,* the analysis of a tradition in a late stage of its transmission with attention to compositional techniques, patterns, motifs and purposes. Harking back to Ivan Engnell, the scholar most prominently associated with *Traditionsgeschichte*,[27] the more recent studies in this vein have broad implications. In these studies, the analysis of sources and literary traditions extends beyond those in Neh 9:6–37 and considers comparable prayers of the post-exilic era, including Isa 63:7–64:11 and Ezra 9:6–15. For the scholars in question, the applicability of this type of *Traditionsgeschichte* is not

---

[26] Commentaries that combine the approaches of literary and historical criticism include: Peter Ackroyd, *I & II Chronicles, Ezra, Nehemiah* (London: S.C.M. Press, 1973); L. W. Batten, *A Critical and Exegetical Commentary on the Books of Ezra and Nehemiah* (ICC; Edinburgh: T & T Clark, 1913); Joseph Blenkinsopp, *Ezra-Nehemiah: A Commentary* (Philadelphia: Westminster, 1988); F. C. Fensham, *The Books of Ezra and Nehemiah* (Grand Rapids, Mich: Eerdmans, 1982); Kurt Galling, *Die Bücher der Chronik, Esra, Nehemia* (Göttingen: Vandenhoeck & Ruprecht, 1954); Wilhelm In der Smitten, *Esra; Quellen, Überlieferung und Geschichte* (SSN 15; Assen: Van Gorcum, 1973); Ulrich Kellermann, *Nehemia; Quellen, Überlieferung und Geschichte* (BZAW 102; Berlin: Töpelmann, 1967); Jacob Myers, *Ezra, Nehemiah* (AB 14; Garden City, N.Y.: Doubleday, 1965); Wilhelm Rudolph, *Esra und Nehemia samt 3* (HAT 20; Tübingen: J. C. B. Mohr [Paul Siebeck], 1949); R. N. Whybray, *Isaiah 40–66* (NCB; Grand Rapids, Mich.: Eerdmans, 1981); Claus Westermann, *Isaiah 40–66* (OTL; Philadelphia: Westminster, 1969).

[27] Engnell's method is based on a denial of pre-exilic sources that admits only a post-exilic, priestly redaction of the Pentateuch later joined to the Deuteronomistic History. The method is described as "patternistic" because it is keyed to "culture-morphological" and "cult-morphological" unities in the Old Testament and in ancient Near Eastern literature. See his "Methodological Aspects of Old Testament Study," pp. 13-30 in *Congress Volume : Oxford 1959* (VTSup 7; ed. G. W. Anderson et al.; Leiden: E. J. Brill, 1960), 18-19.

limited to one prayer; rather, it is understood as an effective means of studying the corpus of penitential prayer from the post-exilic period.

A critical survey of settings and themes adduced from several prayers informs Carl Anderson's 1987 doctoral dissertation, "The Formation of the Levitical Prayer of Nehemiah 9."[28] Comparing Neh 9:6–37 to Ezra 9:6–15, Dan 4:1–9 and Neh 1:5–11, Anderson concludes that the group forms "a new genre [the post-exilic penitential prose prayer] which best expressed the nation's contrition and penitence."[29] Given the uniqueness of each prayer in question, a common genre is implausible, as we will argue in the concluding chapter of this dissertation. On the other hand, Anderson does well to document the fact that Neh 9:6–37 contains a significant amount of Dtr phraseology. Although his treatment of Dtr as a source is not especially trenchant, Anderson initiates the trend in recent scholarship to examine the sources and literary traditions behind Neh 9:6–37 and related prayers of repentance.

A dissertation similar to that of Anderson was published by Volker Pröbstl in 1997 under the title *Nehemia 9, Psalm 106 und Psalm 136 und die Rezeption des Pentateuchs.*[30] The title indicates that Pröbstl has designated a group of later prayers for study. Like Anderson, Pröbstl precedes his source-critical analysis with an investigation of the *Gattung* of Neh 9:6–37. Pröbstl concludes that the sources and traditions behind the prayer are intertwined to the extent that their respective origins may not be identified definitively; he nonetheless dates Neh 9:6–37 to the late fourth or early third century B.C.E.[31]

Paralleling Pröbstl's study in several respects, the revised dissertation of Mark Boda was published in 1999 as *Praying the Tradition: The Origin and Use of Tradition in Nehemiah 9.*[32] Boda devotes a chapter to the prayer's form-critical nature, which is said to represent a "tradition of prayer" analogous in type to a *Gattung*,[33] before pressing on to the source-critical investigation. In this matter, Boda identifies in Neh 9:6–37 a Dtr foundation that was supplemented and superseded by material from Priestly/Ezekelian circles.[34] He dates the prayer to a point in the sixth century B.C.E. contemporary with the prophecy of Zechariah.[35] The date is one of the earliest proposed for Neh 9:6–37, and there are grounds to challenge it. [36] In a subsequent article, Boda has

---

[28] Carl Anderson, "The Formation of the Levitical Prayer of Nehemiah 9," Th. D. Dissertation, Dallas Theological Seminary, 1987.

[29] Ibid., 109.

[30] Volker Pröbstl, *Nehemia 9, Psalm 106 und Psalm 136 und die Rezeption des Pentateuchs* (Göttingen: Cuvillier Verlag, 1997).

[31] Ibid., 103–5.

[32] Mark Boda, *Praying the Tradition: The Origin and Use of Tradition in Nehemiah 9* (BZAW 277; Berlin/NewYork: Walter de Gruyter, 1999).

[33] Ibid., 41.

[34] Ibid., 62–6.

[35] Ibid., 189–95.

[36] Boda dates Neh 9:6–37 in the sixth century based on its inclusion of the priestly

provided additional support for his position that Neh 9:6–37 was contemporary with the prophecy of Zechariah and, in fact, has demonstrated that the prayer antedated the prose sermons of Zechariah (Zech 1:1–6; 7:1–8:23) and influenced them significantly.[37]

A broad treatment of penitential prayer appeared in 1998 with the publication of Rodney Werline's *Penitential Prayer in Second Temple Judaism: The Development of a Religious Institution.*[38] The book is derived from Werline's dissertation written under George Nickelsburg, and its agenda is primarily source-critical: "To show that authors of penitential prayers reinterpret penitential traditions for their respective traditions."[39] Like Anderson and Boda, Werline maintains that the formative source for post-exilic prayers of penitence is the Deuteronomistic History, and he adds that Deuteronomy 4 and 28–30 "introduce the terminology, ideas and ideology of repentance" into the penitential prayer of Second Temple Judaism.[40] In his analysis of Deuteronomistic effects, Werline underscores "tension" in a composition. For example, he asserts that Isa 63:7–64:11 stands at a point of tension between lament and confession of sin, and that the prayer in Ezra 9 is distinguished by a tension between hope and despair.[41] Werline considers the prayers' form-critical aspects, but unlike Anderson and Boda he holds that the penitential prayers of the Second Temple period cannot be said to constitute a distinct genre or *Gattung.*[42]

Form-criticism is even less prominent in Judith Newman's *Praying by the Book: The Scripturalization of Prayer in Second Temple Judaism.*[43] Published in 1999 as the revision of a doctoral dissertation written under James Kugel, *Praying by the Book* delivers an exhaustive study of the interpretive use of

---

source. The dating is questionable in that P, as a pentateuchal source, is to be located in the fifth century or later, after the emergence of the Aaronide priesthood to which P uniquely refers (Lev 8: 1–13, 10:1–3; Num 3:1–13, 16:1–50). On the emergence of the Aaronide Priesthood in the biblical record, see Joseph Blenkinsopp, "The Judaean Priesthood during the Neo-Babylonian and Achaemenid Periods: A Hypothetical Reconstruction," *CBQ* 60 (1998): 25–43.

[37] Mark Boda, "Zechariah: Master Mason or Penitential Prophet," pp. 49-69 in *Yahwism After the Exile* (STR 5; ed. B. Becking and R. Albertz; Assen: Royal Van Gorcum, 2003), 49-69.

[38] Rodney Werline, *Penitential Prayer in Second Temple Judaism: The Development of a Religious Institution* (SBLEJL 13; Atlanta: Scholars Press, 1998).

[39] Ibid., 6.

[40] Ibid., 12–13.

[41] Ibid., 41–53, esp. 52.

[42] "... the prayers appear in a sundry of literary genres—historical narratives, apocalypses, sectarian literature, and a letter. ... As my interpretations of the prayers indicate, the authors of the prayer come from disparate circumstances." Ibid., 194.

[43] Judith Newman, *Praying by the Book: The Scripturalization of Prayer in Second Temple Judaism* (SBLEJL 14; Atlanta: Scholars Press, 1999).

scriptural sources in the composition of Neh 9:6–37 and other post-exilic prayers. Specifically, Newman examines "scripturalization" understood as "the reuse of biblical texts or interpretative traditions to shape the composition of new literature."[44] Her chapter on Neh 9:6–37 inventories and analyzes its many allusions to earlier biblical traditions, interpretations and citations. Her conclusions are of a source-critical nature, and she stresses that the prayer has drawn on the priestly source in addition to the Deuteronomistic material.[45]

While oriented primarily to *Traditionsgeschichte,* the scholarship we have reviewed reflects the importance of form criticism. Most of these studies include a treatment of form criticism that complements the primary inquiry into the sources and traditions that a given prayer has adopted. One rationale for combining form criticism and source criticism lies in the fact that determining the *Gattung* to which a prayer belongs can clarify issues of sources and traditions. As Boda remarks, "[Determining the *Gattung*] highlights the elements in the passage that may have nothing to do with the tradents of the prayer but rather with the liturgical conventions of the *Gattung*."[46] By providing an in-depth treatment of the literary form in post-exilic laments, the present dissertation is a resource to the increasing number of scholars involved in *Traditionsgeschichte* as the study of traditions and sources in prayers of lament.[47]

Furthermore, there is intrinsic value to studying the post-exilic prayers of lament by means of form criticism, understood as inquiry into the genre and setting of a text. Scholars have begun to raise questions of genre and setting with regard to the final form of a biblical text as it was established in the Achaemenid era. That is, the form-critical agenda is being reconstituted so that inquiries into genre and setting might advance our knowledge less of a text's historical origins and more of its literary evolution. Specifically, form critics focus on "the larger literary corpora created by... redaction back to any prior discernible stages in their literary history."[48] An example of this effort is Ehud Ben Zvi's commentary on Micah, which explores the social setting not of the historical Micah in the eighth century B.C.E. but rather of the post-exilic scribes based in Judah who created the book of Micah to understand better God's word

---

[44] Ibid., 12–13.

[45] Ibid., 115.

[46] *Praying the Tradition,* 18.

[47] In turn, this dissertation incorporates the insights of the above scholars because an awareness of sources and their use can be critical to understanding a prayer's formal arrangement and logic.

[48] This programmatic statement appears in each volume of the series "The Forms of the Old Testament Literature," edited by Rolf Knierim, Gene Tucker and Marvin Sweeney. Because the volumes provide form-critical analysis of every biblical book according to a standard methodology, the series represents the current state of form-critical studies. Ehud Ben Zvi, *Micah* (FOTL 21b; Grand Rapids, Mich.: Eerdmans, 2000), xii.

addressed to them and their contemporaries.[49] To press this inquiry, Ben Zvi employs the questions of genre, setting and intention. In comments upon the manner of form criticism that Ben Zvi employs, Michael Floyd notes that the "literary nature" of the object under study comprises more than the text's rhetorical patterns and includes broader phenomena such as the sociology of reading in the ancient world.[50] Furthermore, Floyd suggests that there is an emerging practice of form criticism attuned to the post-exilic period, with the scope and depth of this practice as yet undetermined. The practice, exemplified by Ben Zvi's commentary on Micah and the series to which it belongs, does not aim to valorize form criticism as a methodology. Rather, it reasserts claims by Hermann Gunkel and the history-of-religion movement about the fundamental importance of genre and setting for understanding an ancient text. Similarly, genre and setting are the primary concerns of this dissertation as it inquires into the prayers of communal lament composed after the exile in Judah and its environs.

Thus, the intellectual foundation of this dissertation may be called form criticism in the following sense. While providing a form-critical inventory of post-exilic laments, this dissertation investigates form-critical issues related to genre development and considers their theoretical implications. Moreover, the dissertation moves systematically from an examination of a prayer's literary form to a consideration of its setting or context. Specifically, there is inquiry into each prayer's manner and tone as well as its setting in life or *Sitz im Leben*. Ultimately, this dissertation is an intensive form-critical exercise that compares Isa 63:7–64:11, Ezra 9:6–15 and Neh 9:6–37 with the genre of communal lament. The exercise is informed methodologically by the initiatives of Gunkel and those who have refined his work. Scholars today would rightly question a study that employs form-criticism derived singularly from Gunkel's *Einleitung in den Psalmen*.[51] Such is not the case here. Rather, Gunkel's precepts and principles are retained and revised in accord with subsequent advances in form-critical method and in the study of the psalmic genres.

---

[49] Ibid., 5. Elsewhere, on p. 9, Ben Zvi states: "It is most significant that the book of Micah ... develops a substantial gap between, on the one hand, the world of actual production and consumption of the book of Micah..., and, on the other hand, the world described in these books. The gap shapes an image of particular and foundational periods in Israel's past as substantially different from what was experienced by the literati responsible for these writings and their transmissions."

[50] Michael Floyd, "Basic Trends in Form-Critical Study of Prophetic Texts" (paper presented at the annual meeting of the SBL, Nashville, 19 November 2000), 5–8.

[51] Hermann Gunkel, *Einleitung in die Psalmen: Die Gattungen der religiösen Lyrik Israels* (ed. J. Begrich; Göttingen: Vandenhoeck & Ruprecht, 1933).

1.4 The Form-Critical Method of Hermann Gunkel

In *Einleitung in die Psalmen,* Hermann Gunkel stipulates three criteria that must be met in order to establish a *genre* of truly comparable texts, such as the psalms of the communal lament.[52] The order in which Gunkel presents the three criteria does not imply a descending priority. First, the poems in question must belong to or derive from a specific cultic occasion, that is, a common *Sitz im Leben.* Second, the poems must evince a common manner and tone that derive from the *Sitz im Leben* or could easily be related to it. Finally, the poems must employ a common language that is related to their form. The last point is the most fundamental: truly comparable literary structures must issue in comparable expressions. Gunkel's tripartite focus on the psalms' generic structure is arguably the most elementary aspect of his form-critical approach to understanding the psalms.

Applying his method to the psalms of communal lament, Gunkel generates a listing of the elements that constitute the communal lament. This datum represents common language that is related to form, the third focus noted above. Gunkel's list includes the complaint, the petition, self-reproaches with motivational effects, and the assurance of help.[53] Gunkel locates these elements in entire psalms, sections of psalms in mixed genres, psalmic fragments included in other genres, psalms in narrative texts, and psalms in the writings (such as the Book of Job). In thus listing the elements of the communal lament with reference to a range of psalm types, Gunkel both observes the standard for genre division of the psalms proper and adduces from elsewhere in the Hebrew Bible examples of poetry that strengthen his conclusions. A primary goal of this dissertation is similarly to demonstrate how the lament's form-critical elements are attested in verse and prose outside the psalter. Specifically, we will study elements such as lament, petition and especially the confession of sin in post-exilic prayers of penitence. The ultimate goal is to establish and comment upon the form-critical affinities that exist between the later prayers and that genre represented by the earlier psalms.[54]

Gunkel's second major contribution comes with regard to *Sitz im Leben,* which he considers to be a complex matter in the case of the laments. In work prior to his *Einleitung,* Gunkel argues that the lament of the individual originated in a cultic ceremony but most strongly reflects its subsequent setting,

---

[52] Gunkel discusses his criteria for a genre in the first chapter of *Einleitung in die Psalmen,* 22–24.

[53] Ibid., 125.

[54] The goal's articulation is indebted to Northrop Frye, who holds, "The purpose of criticism by genres is not so much to classify as to clarify... traditions and affinities [that exist between a work and its genre], thereby bringing out a large number of literary relationships that would not be noticed as long as there were no context established for them." *Anatomy of Criticism* (Princeton: Princeton University Press, 1957), 248.

a circle of pious lay persons.[55] Gunkel recognizes that the "I" psalms of lament have their basis in cult; he reconstructs a healing rite where the sick man goes to a sanctuary and there sacred acts take place, after which the man is either absolved (as in Ps 51:9) or professes his innocence. In Gunkel's view, this is an ancient expiation rite. He adds, however, that the cult's songs evolved into spiritual songs not attached to the cult, and that the latter are the precursors of many of the psalms in the psalter. Specifically, the individual laments are said to be furthest from the cult, genetically, and to show only occasionally remnants of the original *Sitz im Leben* (as in Ps 51:7). These laments more prominently reflect the secondary (now primary) *Sitz im Leben* of the pious lay circle.[56] Thus, Gunkel understands Israel's laments to arise principally in association with a lay collective that was removed from the cult.

Gunkel's view of the matter clashes with that of Sigmund Mowinckel, who on the one hand admits that the biblical laments—both individual and communal—reflect the priority of personal prayer over that of the cult.[57] The cult, however, remains a constitutive part of the biblical laments' composition, in Mowinckel's view.[58] Concurring with Mowinckel, this dissertation presumes continuity between the prayers of lament and cultic activities such as offering sacrifice. Historically, the lament was connected with the *todah* or thanksgiving sung in the great congregation and accompanied by sacrifice.[59] Analogously, the communal or individual confession of sin was connected with the sacrifices for guilt (אשם) and sin (חטאה).[60] Because these correspondences were subject to development and change, we will judge on a text-by-text basis the extent to which literary and liturgical features in a post-exilic prayer of lament justify our associating the prayer with a ceremonial *Sitz im Leben*.

While Gunkel and Mowinckel have debated *Sitz im Leben* and other historical issues surrounding the laments,[61] their theological differences center on eschatology. Gunkel claims that both the communal and individual laments conclude with assurances of help in order to provide an eschatological focus. The claim leads Gunkel to include the laments and other psalms in a trajectory

---

[55] "Die Psalmen," *RGG* 4:1609–27.

[56] Ibid.

[57] See his *The Psalms in Israel's Worship* (New York: Abingdon, 1967 [1964]), 2:17. On *Sitz im Leben* and other issues, Gunkel's *Einleitung* served as his considered response to Mowinckel's *Psalmenstudien*, which had appeared ten years earlier in 1923.

[58] Mowinckel proposes a new evaluation of the cult comprising temple singers influenced by temple prophets. Ibid., 2:25.

[59] Ibid., 2:21.

[60] Blenkinsopp, "The Second Temple as House of Prayer," 111.

[61] These historical issues include the identification of enemies who cause the distress. Contra Mowinckel's view that the enemies are magicians, Gunkel introduces other literature, namely Job, to interpret the enemies (Job's friends) as bereft of any magical power. In general, Gunkel argues that in psalms of lament the enemies are real people.

extending from prophecy, the trajectory's basis, to early Christian texts that culminate in the future reign of God. Unduly influenced by messianic thought and Christianity, Gunkel's high estimation of prophetic matter in the lament psalms is indeed suspect. This dissertation will take a different approach to showing how prophecy is reflected in the communal laments and in subsequent prayers modeled on the laments. The prayers in our study reflect prophecy not in terms of eschatology but rather in terms of warning. The warning in question is exemplified in prophecies of misfortune found in Amos, Micah and Ezekiel (Amos 7:16, Mic 2:6, Ezek 21:2,7).

Scholars who were contemporaries of Gunkel subjected his claims to critique and modification. Subsequent generations have extended the process. For example, Robert Wilson has noted confusion in Gunkel's view of *Sitz im Leben*. Specifically, Wilson has shown that when Gunkel defines "setting in life," he conflates two discrete points of reference, "the original setting of the language of a genre, and the setting in which the genre is actually used."[62] Wilson implies that one's notion of *Sitz im Leben* must at times be two-dimensional. Wilson's critique is important to this dissertation because it suggests that prophetic functions such as warning may originate in a decidedly prophetic context but subsequently be attested in a cultic context.[63] In this case, the corrective to Gunkel lends plausibility to our views about the prophetic warning.

Furthermore, whereas Gunkel assumed that psalmic conventions and individual works had been accurately transmitted orally over a period of several centuries, Robert Culley has studied and catalogued those formulas and formulaic phrases in the psalms that give evidence of oral transmission.[64] Although Culley's catalog includes only six examples from the psalms of communal lament, in three of these cases certain language corresponds significantly with expressions in the prayers we shall study.[65] Conclusions based on the correspondences, however, will be drawn conservatively as Culley notes that repeated phrases and formulas in certain psalms *might* be indicative of traditional language, *possibly* with an origin in oral, formulaic composition. Furthermore, Culley notes that a high percentage of oral formulaic language in a psalm is not definitive evidence of oral composition because traditional

---

[62] Robert Wilson, *Prophecy and Society in Ancient Israel* (Philadelphia: Fortress, 1980), 11.

[63] Wilson notes, "The original setting of the language of a genre *may not* be the same as the setting in which the genre is actually used. In the case of prophecy, the social matrix of prophetic language and the social location of prophetic activity may not be identical. A prophet who delivers oracles in the temple court may not employ speech forms that originated in the temple." Ibid.

[64] Culley's investigation of oral style and oral poets is titled *Oral Formulaic Language in the Biblical Psalms* (Toronto: The University of Toronto Press, 1967).

[65] The language is found in Pss 77:19; 79:10 and 80:15. Ibid., 72, 77, 83.

language "does not disappear from a poetic tradition the moment oral formulaic composition ceases to be practiced."⁶⁶ Nonetheless, Culley provides both rationale and criteria for our judging the extent to which literary and liturgical features in a post-exilic prayer of lament may be traced back through an oral tradition to a ceremonial *Sitz im Leben* associated with the pre-exilic psalms of communal lament.

More recently, Gunkel's work has elicited less interest in *Sitz im Leben* or oral tradition while spurring new conceptual initiatives. Interest now centers on construing anew the relationships between psalmic genres. This broader reaction to Gunkel is typified by Claus Westermann's study of psalmic lament and praise, which has in turn influenced Walter Brueggemann to craft several innovative articles.⁶⁷ Current scholarship does not dispute the most basic findings of Gunkel and Mowinckel, such as the list of elements that constitute the communal lament. In fact, in his 1984 study *Psalmody and Prophecy*, W. H. Bellinger Jr. presents the psalms of lament as comprising an invocation, lament, petition, motivation(s), certainty of a hearing and vow.⁶⁸ His schema is essentially that of Gunkel and Mowinckel. In a more far-reaching study, Henning Graf Reventlow builds his 1986 study of Old Testament prayer on the findings and insights of Gunkel and Mowinckel. In this work, Reventlow's methodological commitments are in no way naïve, because his was one of the voices that twenty years earlier first signaled the limitations of form criticism.⁶⁹ The substance of Reventlow's view is that prayer in the Old Testament emerges from a cultic background and that Israelite piety is best attested in the psalter, whose cultic character is self-evident. Reventlow understands the psalter to comprise several genres, including the lament, which in later prayers such as Ezra 9:6–15 and Neh 9:6–37 has been altered to emphasize repentance rather than protest.⁷⁰ Reventlow and Bellinger show that the projects of Gunkel and Mowinckel remain serviceable to scholars and may act as a credible basis for the study at hand.

We adopt Gunkel's positions in light of subsequent advances in form-critical method and in the study of the psalmic genres. Thus, the seminal issue, genre, is understood as a matter of *Gattungsgeschichte*,⁷¹ in keeping with this

---

⁶⁶ Ibid., 14 and 22, 112–16.

⁶⁷ Westermann's project is found in *Praise and Lament in the Psalms*; Brueggemann's work includes "The Costly Loss of Lament," pp. 98–111 in *The Psalms in the Life of Faith* (ed. P. D. Miller; Minneapolis: Fortress, 1995).

⁶⁸ *Psalmody and Prophecy*, (JSOTSup 27; Sheffield: JSOT Press, 1984), 22–24.

⁶⁹ Reventlow's assessment of form criticism is included in "Der Psalm 8," *Poetica: Zeitschrift für Sprach- und Literatur Wissenschaft* 1 (1967): 304–32. His position is later cited in James Muilenburg's "Form Criticism and Beyond," *JBL* 88 (1969): 4.

⁷⁰ Reventlow, *Gebet*, 275–81.

⁷¹ *Gattungsgeschichte* is the analysis of the literary genre's historical origin, development, and death or transmutation into another literary or mixed genre. It may be contrasted with *Gattungsforschung*, the study of literary genres.

dissertation's interest in *Sitz im Leben* and the larger historical context as a datum of literary development. Specifically, this dissertation construes the communal lament as a genre not in the sense of a closed and theoretical construct that accounts for every element of the prayer type, but as a range of literary conventions shared by the speaker and the hearer who are together inscribed in a socio-historical context.[72] Form criticism thus allows us "to ask what, in a given text, constituted the communication event between writer and readers, between speaker and listener in a typical way ... to ask how the typical factors related to one another and how the typical and the unique interact."[73] The dissertation's discussions of genre incorporate recent theoretical advances from disciplines outside of biblical studies.[74] These advances, like the approach of *Gattungsgeschichte*, stress the dynamic and interactive features of genre.

1.5 Additional Considerations of Methodology

It is important to recognize that the manner in which genre bears upon the prayers in this study is not univocal. First, the texts can show a form-critical resemblance to various genres in addition to that of the psalms of communal lament. Gerhard von Rad has shown that the levitical sermon has imparted Deuteronomistic form and content to certain speeches in Chronicles (e.g. 2 Chr 20:5–12), and Otto Plöger has advanced von Rad's work.[75] Specifically, Plöger has observed that not only the Chronicler's (hereafter C) speeches but certain of his prayers derive from Dtr's hortatory discourse.[76] An example of one such prayer is Neh 9:6–37. Plöger notes the prayer's affinities with both the psalms,

---

[72] See Roy Melugin, "Muilenburg, Form Criticism, and Theological Exegesis," pp. 91-100 in *Encounter with the Text: Form and History in the Hebrew Bible* (ed. M. Buss; Philadelphia: Fortress, 1979), 94.

[73] Rolf Knierim, "Old Testament Form Criticism Reconsidered," pp. 42–71 in *Reading the Hebrew Bible for a New Millennium: Form, Concept and Theological Perspective* (SAC; ed. W. Kim et al.; Harrisburg, Pa.: Trinity, 2000), 71; repr. from *Int* 27 (1973).

[74] See Alastair Fowler, *Kinds of Literature: An Introduction to the Theory of Genres and Modes* (Cambridge, Mass.: Harvard University Press, 1982); Heather Dubrow, *Genre* (London: Methuen, 1984); Tzvetan Todorov, *Genres in Discourse* (Cambridge: Cambridge University Press, 1990).

[75] Gerhard von Rad, "The Levitical Sermon in I and II Chronicles," pp. 267–80 in *The Problem of the Hexateuch and Other Essays* (New York: McGraw-Hill, 1966), 272; Otto Plöger, "Reden und Gebete im deuteronomistischen und chronistischen Geschichtswerk," pp. 35–49 in *Festschrift für Günther Dehn zum 75. Geburstag* (ed. W. Schneemelcher; Neukirchen-Vluyn: Neukirchener Verlag, 1957), 35–49.

[76] Plöger makes a distinction between C and the historian of Dtr on the grounds that the former employs prayers more than he employs speeches to punctuate an important period of history. "Reden und Gebete," 44.

specifically Psalm 78, and with contemporary sermonic prayers (Ezra 9:6–15).[77] Both types of literature have influenced the prayer in Neh 9:6–37, Plöger implies. His analysis of Ezra 9:6–15 is more cursory, but his interpretive categories continue to be helpful in specifying this text's genre. In chapter three of this dissertation, an analysis of Ezra 9:6–15 concludes that the prayer represents a mixed genre.

Second, from a form-critical viewpoint the texts in this study are not in a pristine state and are at times fraught with complications. The three principal prayers for study resemble the psalms of communal lament inexactly and depart from the *Gattung* in significant ways. James Muilenburg describes this phenomenon positively in judging that the "imitations" of another *Gattung,* the covenant lawsuit, exhibit a diversity of forms and styles.[78] The imitations, in his view, are composed with "consummate skill."[79] A less sanguine view would hold that the genre is in disintegration and that the exempla are form-critically flawed. Any deficiencies, however, exist not in a text or the genre, but in the resourcefulness of scholars to use form criticism in the analysis of a text whose structure departs from that of established models.

Muilenburg does not call for an end to form-critical study, and he challenges scholars to apply the methodology appropriately when working with a text of mixed genre or otherwise poor form-critical definition. Moreover, he calls for recognizing such "imitations" as literary achievements composed by creative tradents. Thus, a goal of this dissertation is to articulate how these prayers have been influenced by conventions operative in the psalms of communal lament while acknowledging their artful departure from those conventions. A related goal is to describe the process by which composers appropriated the form-critical legacy of the communal laments, in the post-exilic period and as well in later phases of the Second Temple period. An important first step toward this goal will be to consider the practice of transmitting traditions in the period after the exile. Specifically, we must indicate the senses in which the term "interpretation" is and is not accurately descriptive of the composition of penitential prayers in the sixth and fifth centuries B.C.E.

1.6 Intertextuality in the Sixth and Fifth Centuries B.C.E.

A monograph dealing with intertextuality in the sixth and fifth centuries B.C.E. is much needed. Intertextuality, as it influenced the composition of penitential prayers, comprises interpretation and other literary procedures of a less self-conscious nature. At present, intertextuality in this period is often misrepresented in scholarship that exaggerates the manner and degree of interpretation operative in the ancient texts.

---

[77] Ibid., 45.
[78] Muilenburg, "Form Criticism and Beyond," 5.
[79] Ibid.

Opinions in this regard often refer to interpretive practices that have been superimposed onto composition in the sixth and fifth centuries but actually are in evidence only several centuries later.[80] The appeal to studies that focus on the second and first centuries is understandable given the history of scholarship. The term "rewritten Bible" was introduced by a specialist in intertestamental literature, and there have appeared several learned studies of interpretive composition in the second and first centuries B.C.E.[81] These studies thus supply insights that may *or may not* correlate to the sixth and fifth centuries, a period whose interpretive composition should be studied independently. Lester Grabbe has stressed the difference between interpretation in the post-exilic period and that of later centuries.[82] He critiques those who discuss fifth-century literature in terms of interpretive practices that can be documented only centuries later. He also disputes the claim that interpretive practices became conspicuous in Jewish literature as early as the post-exilic period,[83] a rejoinder that must be challenged

---

[80] Werline's *Penitential Prayer in Second Temple Judaism* surveys penitential prayers from 586 B.C.E. to 70 C.E. The book's premise that confessional prayer is a hermeneutical exercise in reinterpreting religious traditions is drawn directly from intertestamental studies and proves effective in Werline's analysis of penitential prayers from this time. Less effective is Werline's reading the penitential prayers of much earlier eras, i.e. the Persian Period, as hermeneutical. The earlier prayers require a reading more consonant with the diverse *realia* of post-exilic Judea, and establishing such a context is one objective of this dissertation. See *Penitential Prayer in Second Temple Judaism*, 46, 192. A specific example of using intertestamental literature as the basis for understanding post-exilic scriptural interpretation is found in J. Gerald Janzen's study of Neh 9:8. Janzen suggests that the verse reflects the composer's exegesis of Genesis 22, and in support he cites exegesis of the Akedah in Jub. 17:18, Wis 44:20, and 1 Macc 2:52. From the later texts Janzen deduces a tradition that reads Neh 9:8 as referring to the Akedah and suggests solely on these grounds that Neh 9:8 not only belongs to the tradition but initiated it. "Nehemiah 9 and the Aqedah," (paper presented at the annual meeting of the SBL, New Orleans, 25 November 1996).

[81] Geza Vermes begins speaking of inner-biblical exegesis as "rewritten Bible" in *Scripture and Tradition in Judaism: Haggadic Studies* (Leiden: Brill, 1961), 95, 124–26. In his wake, scholars of the intertestamental literature have produced several important studies. James Kugel treats the analysis of interpretive motifs and their exegetical origins in several of his works, notably *In Potiphar's House: The Interpretive Life of Biblical Texts* (San Francisco: HarperCollins, 1990), 247–70; Michael Fishbane provides a comprehensive study of exegesis found in scripture in *Biblical Interpretation in Ancient Israel* (Oxford: Clarendon Press, 1985), 91–277. Exegetical composition keyed to the fulfillment of prophecy flourished at Qumran and elsewhere, and the principles for such interpretation at Qumran are elaborated by William Brownlee in *The Midrash Pesher of Habakkuk* (SBLMS 24; Missoula: Scholars Press, 1979).

[82] Grabbe holds that scholars should be cautious about assuming that the Torah's completion was quickly followed by a "rapid development" of the exegetical approach to Torah. *Ezra-Nehemiah* (London/New York: Routledge, 1998), 195.

[83] Ibid.

in light of Chronicles, a thoroughgoing re-interpretation of the Deuteronomistic History.[84] *Contra* Grabbe, the indications are that select modes of interpretation were current after the exile, and that these modes are a partial indicator of intertextuality at this time. Intertextuality, as it influenced the composition of penitential prayers, comprised interpretation and other literary procedures. A complex phenomenon, intertextuality was based upon five principles.

The re-use of scripture was undertaken with attention to form as well as content. We have reviewed a segment of recent scholarship that focuses on literary traditions in Israel's worship. The contemporary focus parallels the study of sources by scholars earlier in the last century. Source criticism is typified by Julius Wellhausen, whose investigations into worship were eventually broadened by scholars such as Hans-Joachim Kraus. Kraus affirms Wellhausen's emphasis on sources, or content, while calling for an investigation of worship that also considers the form-critical elements underscored by Gunkel and especially Mowinckel.[85] This dissertation gives credence to Kraus's view that form supplements content in the composition of biblical prayer. That which is transmitted is defined by both its form and content. For example, the effects of the prophetic warning in Neh 9:6–37 and other prayers relate to both its form and content. Contrary to Sara Japhet's view that the post-exilic prophet who preaches reform has no ties to classical prophecy,[86] we shall see in chapter four that the warning function in post-exilic prophecy reflects earlier forms that have undergone evolution. Specifically, Neh 9:6–37 reflects warning based on the *rib*-form,[87] a structure that in turn implies a pre-exilic situation of prophetic reproof.

The re-use of scripture is based upon an internal logic and consistency. In *Rewriting the Bible: Land and Covenant in Postbiblical Jewish Literature*, Betsy Halpern-Amaru suggests that when the reinterpretation of a scriptural text includes a theological dimension, the version is "systematically developed and internally consistent" according to a certain "inner logic."[88] This appears to be the case with the post-exilic prayers of penitence as they are based upon the psalms of communal lament. Certain laments draw attention to an element dominant in their construction. In turn, the dominant element allows one to characterize the psalm both structurally and theologically. Noting that sin is not

---

[84] Chronicles reinterprets, most notably, Dtr's emphasis on the Sinai covenant as the election of all Israel and substitutes the election of David, who stands at the center of C's history.

[85] Hans-Joachim Kraus, *Worship in Israel: A Cultic History of the Old Testament* (Richmond, Va.: John Knox, 1965 [1954]), 20–24.

[86] *The Ideology of the Book of Chronicles and Its Place in Biblical Thought* (Frankfurt: Peter Lang, 1989), 187.

[87] See Pierre Buis, "Notification de jugement et confession nationale," *BZ* nf 11 (1967): 204.

[88] Betsy Halpern-Amaru, *Rewriting the Bible: Land and Covenant in Postbiblical Jewish Literature* (Valley Forge, Pa.: Trinity, 1994), 4.

frequently confessed in the communal laments of the psalter, Mowinckel concludes, "Actually in very many psalms the motive of penitence is not *dominant*."[89] (Emphasis added.) Similarly, Westermann remarks upon the confession of trust: "In some psalms the confession of trust is so *dominant* that it is possible to speak of a 'psalm of trust for the people.'"[90] (Emphasis added.) Most recently, Boda has compared the Book of Lamentations and penitential prayer thus: "In both the *dominant form* of request is for divine recognition of distress."[91] (Emphasis added.) Mowinckel, Westermann and Boda invoke a concept of the dominant in analyzing various prayers of communal lament, although their references to the concept are neither systematic nor self-conscious.

Outside of biblical studies, the concept of the dominant has been elaborated more explicitly. It is judged "one of the most crucial, elaborated and productive concepts in Russian Formalist Theory," to cite Roman Jakobson.[92] Jakobson defines the dominant as "the focusing component of a work of art: it rules, determines, and transforms the remaining components." He concludes, "It is the dominant which guarantees the integrity of the structure."[93] After the exile, the psalms of communal lament evince a new dominant element, the confession of sin. When the confession of sin is added to the genre's repertoire, the genre changes substantively and *is dominated* by the penitential element newly introduced. The causes as well as the effects of this transformation are a central concern of this dissertation, which will analyze the confession of sin in each of the major, post-exilic prayers of penitence.

Although it is an inner logic that relates to both the theological consistency and the formal structure of a given prayer, the confession of sin is itself defined by developments outside the ambit of prayer. The confession of sin serves primarily as the reflex of repentance in a theological sequence of sin-punishment-repentance-salvation. The sequence represents a type of retribution theology that is prominent in the Deuteronomistic History, particularly in the book of Judges.[94] For this reason, the theology embedded in the books of Dtr

---

[89] *The Psalms in Israel's Worship*, 1:214.

[90] *Praise and Lament in the Psalms*, 55. See also p. 210, where Westermann identifies the confession of sin as the motif that comes to dominate Psalm 74.

[91] Mark Boda, "The Priceless Gain of Penitence: From Communal Lament to Penitential Prayer in the 'Exilic' Liturgy of Israel," (paper presented at the Annual Meeting of the SBL, Denver, 17 November 2001), 8.

[92] Roman Jakobson, "The Dominant," pp. 82–87 in *Readings in Russian Poetics: Formalist and Structuralist Views* (ed. L. Matejka and K. Pomorska; Cambridge, Mass.: The MIT Press, 1971), 82.

[93] Ibid.

[94] Blenkinsopp, *Ezra-Nehemiah: A Commentary*, 306. The Dtr formulation of Judg 2:11–23 is easily distinguished from, for example, the priestly compendium of misdeeds in Lev 26:3–45.

will be an important point of reference in our analysis of the confession of sin that is dominant in post-exilic penitential prayer.

Given the prominence of genre and generic elements in the composition of penitential prayer, an author's conscious interpretation of a scriptural source will be secondary. The composer's conscious interpretation of source texts as well as the full range of his authorial intentions are secondary in the sense suggested by Wimsatt and Beardsley in their essay "The Intentional Fallacy." They address the footnotes that a modern author might attach to a work of poetry or fiction, and they contend that such data are not "external indexes to the author's intention."[95] The notes, Wimsatt and Beardsley lead one to conclude, are analogous to the knowledge of a biblical author's intentions that might be gained through exegesis.[96] Thus, if a biblical author's interpretations and intentions enter the discussion, that authorial data constitutes a secondary or tertiary level of meaning. This approach to a text that engages a prior text is close to Judith Newman's concept of scripturalization as the observable re-contextualization of identifiable scriptural language, without regard to the author's intentions.[97]

On occasion, a composer of prayer has to all appearances borrowed directly from a psalm of communal lament and perhaps transformed the original language for a theological end. In such a case, which is relatively rare, borrowing is not simply the use of common language or ideas; the composer has worked from an extant text. This is the case with certain expressions of lament in the prayer of Isa 63:7–64:11. One may establish links between Isa 63:11, 15 and 64:1 and the psalms of communal lament based on oral formulas.[98] The formulas, as catalogued by Culley,[99] support a claim that the recurrence of language in the prayer is an identifiable, intentional reference to a source text. The criterion of oral formulation supports such a claim in the manner of the allusive and stylistic criteria that Benjamin Sommer has introduced to establish literary dependence among the prophets.[100] Nonetheless, it bears repeating that

---

[95] W. K. Wimsatt and M. C. Beardsley, "The Intentional Fallacy," pp. 945–51 in *Critical Theory Since Plato* (ed. H. Adams; Orlando: Harcourt, Brace, Jovanovich, 1992), 951.

[96] Ibid.

[97] Newman, *Praying by the Book*, 13.

[98] Formulaic parallels exist between Isa 63:11 and Ps 79:10, Isa 63:15 and Ps 80:15, and Isa 64:1 and Ps 77:19.

[99] Culley identifies the formulas found in Pss 77:19; 79:10 and 80:15 in his *Oral Formulaic Language*, 72, 77, 83.

[100] Sommer identifies and analyzes in Second Isaiah an ongoing practice of alluding to earlier texts, both prophetic and otherwise. He specifies the prophet's typical patterns of allusion (reversal of earlier prophecies, reprediction of earlier prophecies, fulfillment of earlier prophecies, and typological linkages), as well as the stylistic features (the split-up pattern, sound play, word play, and identical word order) that allow one to characterize an allusion as a direct borrowing rather than simply the use of common

documentable direct influence is quite rare in the prayers under study, and a precise account of the composer's attention to sources or broader intentions is not of primary concern.

Interpretation that transforms the structure of an earlier prayer has the potential to transform the ritual universe of meaning as well. Presuming that liturgy is generative of social meaning, we may posit a ritual universe that envelops the post-exilic prayers of penitence. This universe is transformed when the psalms of communal lament and the mores implicit in them are reformulated in the composition of later prayers that are patterned upon the psalms. That the text and its "universe" are transformed is underscored by Michael Fishbane, who credits certain prayers on sacrifice in the rabbinic literature with transforming the sacrificial cult into a ritual of fasting.[101] Brought to completion in the rabbinic literature, this transformation begins with the exilic and post-exilic emphasis on fasting that is reflected directly in the prayers of the period.[102]

At times the prayers of penitence provide a window on the historical context in which they arose. In the Persian period, the advent of a new king might bring shifts in policy toward the satrapies; in turn, the shifts might elicit a reaction from those affected by the policies. For example, the persons in Yehud responsible for the biblical account of Ezra's mission (Ezra 7:1–10:44; Neh 8:1–18) express support for the Persian king in both programmatic statements and in prayer.[103] The texts in question may be extending *renewed* support to the Persian throne under Artaxerxes I (465–423 B.C.E.), who channeled resources to his western border to stymie incursions there by Egypt and Greece. In addition to

---

language or ideas. See his *A Prophet Reads Scripture: Allusion in Isaiah 40–66* (Stanford: Stanford University Press, 1998), 32–72.

[101] Fishbane cites Rav Sheshet's prayer about fasting (*b. Berk.* 17a) as a witness to the transformation in question. *The Exegetical Imagination: On Jewish Thought and Theology* (Cambridge, Mass.: Harvard University Press, 1998), 4. Similarly, this dissertation will show that prayers such as Nehemiah 9 have affinity with the penitential liturgy that arose at the onset of the exile when a Temple-based rite of atonement was no longer available.

[102] Specifically, the act of self-affliction in Neh 9:1 reflects the ethos of יוֹם כִּפּוּרִים, whose injunction to "afflict yourselves" (וְעִנִּיתֶם אֶת נַפְשֹׁתֵיכֶם) Lev 16:31; 23:27,32; Num 29:7) is a technical term for fasting in the priestly law. The prayer's injunction to fast transforms a ritual universe that has been predicated on literal sacrifice.

[103] The programmatic statement is found in Ezra 7:26a: "Whoever will not obey the law of your God and the law of your king, let judgment be strictly executed upon him." As Samuel Balentine notes, the "and" in the first clause "envisions two *complementary* authorities that exercised power in Yehud: YHWH, the God of the ancestors, and the Persian emperor." *The Torah's Vision of Worship* (OBT; Minneapolis: Fortress, 1999), 41. Of the prayers considered in this dissertation, Ezra 9:6–15 is the most conciliatory toward the the overlords of Yehud, the kings of Persia. Ezra 9:9 reads in part, "(God) has extended to us his steadfast love before the kings of Persia, to give us a respite for rebuilding the house of our God."

these protections, Artaxerxes reestablished royal support of local cults by using local leaders with religious position and influence over the populace.[104] The support, a custom that had directly benefitted the Jerusalem temple and its priests since the time of Darius (522–486 B.C.E.), had been curtailed by Artaxerxes' predecessor, Xerxes (486–465 B.C.E.). Xerxes had reversed the policy of funding of local cults to pay for his attacks upon Greece, which drained his imperial treasury.[105] The renewal of support under Artaxerxes corresponds with the mission of Ezra and has perhaps shaped the biblical account of the mission in modest ways.

1.7 The Dating of Select Prayers and the Psalms of Communal Lament

To determine the manner of interpretation in the post-exilic prayers of repentance as well as the prayers' generic development over time, this dissertation uses methods that presuppose a historical-critical approach to the Bible. Specifically, the method is keyed to the use of form-criticism and the relative dating of forms connected with the psalms of communal lament. These forms are found in the lament psalms themselves as well as in the post-exilic prayers of penitence, whose structure is based on that of the communal lament. By demonstrating the greater antiquity of the psalms of communal lament, we will establish with plausibility that they influenced subsequent prayers of penitence in matters such as the lament, the petition, the confession of sin and similar categories of form.

For the purposes of this dissertation, the communal laments are represented by psalms 44, 74, 78, 79 and 80.[106] That is, among the psalter's communal laments, these five psalms most clearly reflect the form-critical pattern identified by Gunkel and Mowinckel.[107] On other grounds, namely superscription, four of these psalms may be grouped with the psalms of Asaph, whose full complement includes psalms 50 and 73–83. The study of the Asaphite psalms has focused

---

[104] Jon Berquist discusses Artaxerxes' renewal of imperial support for the Yehud in *Judaism in Persia's Shadow: A Social and Historical Approach* (Minneapolis: Fortress, 1995), 108.

[105] On Xerxes' denial of imperial funding for the Jerusalem Temple, see Albert Olmstead, *History of the Persian Empire: Achaemenid Period* (Chicago: University of Chicago Press, 1948), 235–37.

[106] The listing includes Psalm 78, which is regularly classified as a wisdom psalm. Psalm 78 is like a communal lament, however, in that it relates the people's distress when they are separated from God. Moreover, in this psalm as in the communal laments the people do not acknowledge their own sin as contributing to their alienation. And like most of the communal laments that I have indicated, Psalm 78 is an Asaphite psalm that is undoubtedly pre-exilic.

[107] See Mowinckel, *The Psalms in Israel's Worship*, 1:193–219. Both Gunkel and Westermann complemented their form-critical studies of these psalms with tradition-historical investigations, to be seen presently.

less on form and more on content,[108] which often is specified in terms of pentateuchal traditions. A recent study in this vein by Michael Goulder dates the Asaphite psalms to the final quarter of the eighth century B.C.E.[109] Goulder's dating is roughly consistent with Gunkel's view that the Asaphite psalms were a cultic collection used by a group of temple singers.[110] Mowinckel as well dated most of the Asaphite psalms to a time before or at the exile.[111] In light of this dating, it appears that the Asaphite psalms were sufficiently established to influence the later composition of post-exilic prayers of penitence such as Nehemiah 9.[112]

Pentateuchal traditions are a key to dating Neh 9:6–37. The traditions of both the priestly (P) source and Dtr figure significantly in the composition of Neh 9:6–37, and scholars increasingly are confirming P's influence upon the prayer. Chapter four of this dissertation examines the relative influence of P and Dtr on this text, and at present only the implications for dating are of import. Earlier in this chapter we noted that P, as a pentateuchal source, may be dated to the fifth century or later, after the emergence of the Aaronide priesthood to which P frequently refers (Lev 8: 1–13, 10:1–3; Num 3:1–13, 16:1–50). That is, had the Aaronide priesthood prominent in P existed before the exile, it should have been attested in scripture from that period.[113] The virtual silence as to the Aaronide priesthood in books such as Deuteronomy and Ezekiel thus supports a post-exilic dating of both P and texts that bear its stamp, such as Neh 9:6–37.[114]

In chapter three we will demonstrate on literary grounds that the composition of Ezra 9:6–15 took place within perhaps 20 years of Ezra's mission, dated to 458 B.C.E. In dating Ezra's mission we accept the notice of

---

[108] Noting the formal diversity that pertains among the Asaphite psalms as a whole, K.-J. Illman holds that their commonality is to be observed in terms of content rather than form. See his *Thema und Tradition in den Asaf-Psalmen* (Abo: Abo Akademi, 1976), 7–8.

[109] Michael Goulder, *The Psalms of Asaph and the Pentateuch: Studies in the Psalter, III* (JSOTSup233; Sheffield: Sheffield Academic Press, 1996).

[110] Gunkel, *Einleitung*, 440–49.

[111] Mowinckel, *The Psalm's in Israel's Worship*, 2.93–97.

[112] See Peter Ackroyd, *The Chronicler in his Age* (JSOTSup 101; Sheffield: Sheffield Academic Press, 1991), 102.

[113] In the pre-exilic and exilic literature, priests are represented as Levites (Deut 18:6–8; 2 Kgs 23:8,20) and Zadokites (Ezek 44:6 ff, cf. 2 Kgs 23:9). It is noteworthy that Deuteronomy nowhere mentions Aaronides, and cites Aaron only to criticize his role in the incident of the golden calf (9:20).

[114] In dating the Aaronide elements found in P to the post-exilic period, one may allow that other elements derive from an earlier time. A model for the mixed dating of P is offered by Israel Knohl, who speaks of a pre-exilic portion of P, the priestly Torah, which evinces a schematic, measured, restrained style; includes a limited amount of narrative; casts law in linguistic structures while foregoing hortatory motive clauses; and concludes with Leviticus 10. See his *Sanctuary of Silence: The Priestly Torah and the Holiness School* (Minneapolis: Augsburg Fortress, 1995), 106–8.

Ezra 7:7–8 as accurate and historical, *contra* John Bright, who emends the text and dates the mission to 428 B.C.E.[115] Our dating also differs from those who interpret Ezra 7:7–8 as referring to the *second* king Artaxerxes, whose dates would require Ezra's mission to occur in 398 B.C.E.[116] In accepting the traditional dating, we give weight as well to the biblical order that places Ezra before Nehemiah, whose mission dates to 445 B.C.E. If the final redactor of the Ezra and Nehemiah material were working shortly after their time, it is unlikely that he would have forgotten their correct order.[117]

Language conspicuous of pentateuchal sources as well as the Deuteronomistic history provide the key to dating the prayer in Isa 63:7–64:11. The analysis of the prayer presented in chapter two indicates three strata of Dtr terminology correlating roughly to the pre-exilic, exilic and post-exilic periods. First, a Deuteronomic stratum not later than the seventh century is found in the first lament, Isa 63:15–19a.[118] The other lament, Isa 64:9–10, corresponds to the second stratum, from the sixth century, which is Deuteronomistic. This stratum reflects the trauma of the exile and it is typified by the confession of sin (64:4b–6). Also in this stratum is the individual's vow of confidence (64:7–8) as marked by the increasingly pronounced (familial) piety of the time. As well, the prayer's conclusion (64:11) corresponds to this stratum. Third, a Dtr stratum that is clearly post-exilic lies behind the historical section (63:7–15) and the call for an epiphany (63:19b–64:4a). While the former continues to reflect familial piety, both sections include language otherwise conspicuous of pentateuchal formation. As with Neh 9:6–37, the presence of pentateuchal elements considered to be post-exilic allows for dating Isa 63:7–64:11 subsequent to the communal laments in the psalter.

In the following chapters this dissertation will refine the dates of the three post-exilic prayers of penitence that are under study. We will conclude that all are from the late sixth or fifth centuries B.C.E., and that less than a century separates the latest from the earliest. This dating is consistent with the view of Marvin Sweeney, who argues that the final form of Isaiah served to support the reforms of Ezra and Nehemiah.[119] Sweeney points to evidence such as Isaiah's view of "the nations" coinciding with those lands added to the Persian Empire and Isaiah's references to "the righteous" and "the wicked" appearing in Nehemiah 9 with the same denotations of those persons who observe or do not

---

[115] See his *History of Israel* (Philadelphia: Westminster, 1981 [1959]), 391–402.

[116] See Norman Snaith, "The Date of Ezra's Arrival in Jerusalem," *ZAW* 63 (1951): 53–66.

[117] This point is brought out by David Clines in *Ezra, Nehemiah, Esther* (NCB; Grand Rapids, Mich.: Eerdmans, 1984), 16–24.

[118] A later mode of familial piety in 63:16,17b suggests these verses are secondary.

[119] Marvin Sweeney, *Isaiah 1–39* (FOTL 16; Grand Rapids, Mich.: Eerdmans, 1996), 52–54.

observe the covenant.[120] Sweeney indicates a common agenda among the three books. He provides additional grounds for dating as roughly contemporaneous the latest material in Isaiah, including Isa 63:7–64:11, and the books of Ezra and Nehemiah as they contain the penitential prayers Ezra 9:6–15 and Neh 9:6–37.

In introducing this section on dating, we appealed to methods that presuppose a historical-critical approach to the Bible. The use of form criticism and the relative dating of forms connected with the psalms of communal lament is indeed important, as is the use of source criticism and the provisional dating of those sources and traditions found in the Pentateuch. The sources establish the tentative timeline upon which we may locate both the psalter's examples of the communal lament and their iterations in the penitential prayers of the post-exilic era.

---

[120] Ibid., 52, 54.

2

ISA 63:7–64:11—AN ANOMALOUS PSALM OF COMMUNAL LAMENT

2.1 Text[1]

63:7 I will recall the LORD'S covenant deeds, the LORD'S praises,
According to all that the LORD has requited us and great goodness to the house of Israel,
Which he has requited to them according to his mercies and his great covenant love.
63:8 For he said, "Surely they are my people, children who will not be untrue";
And he became their savior. 63:9 In all their distress,
It was no messenger or angel but his presence that saved them;
In his love and compassion he redeemed them,
He lifted them up and carried them all the days of old.
63:10 But they were obstinate and grieved his holy spirit,
Such that he turned against them as an enemy and he fought against them.
63:11 But he remembered days of old, (remembered) Moses and his people.
Where is the one bringing up from the sea the shepherds of his flock?
Where is the one placing his holy spirit in their midst,
63:12 Causing his glorious arm to go at the right hand of Moses
And parting the sea before them to make for himself an everlasting

---

[1] Translations at the beginning of a chapter are the author's. In the case of Isa 63:7–64:11, the text is rendered as poetry according to the three- and two-stress cola that characterize virtually every verse. Verses are numbered according to MT. LXX divides the final verse of chapter 63 into 63:19 and 64:1, thus designating twelve verses in chapter 64.

name?

63:13 He has been leading them through the depths; like a horse in the desert, they do not stumble.

63:14 Like cattle in the field go down, the spirit of the LORD gives us rest.

Thus you led your people to make for yourself a glorious name.

63:15 Look down from the heavens and see, from your height of holiness and glory.

Where is your zeal and your might?

Your welling of emotion and your sympathy are withheld from me.

63:16 For you are our father,

Though Abraham does not know us and Israel does not recognize us.

You, LORD, are our father; "our Redeemer from of old" is your name.

63:17 Why do you, LORD, cause us to err from your ways (and) harden our hearts from fear of you?

Turn for the sake of your servants, the tribes of your inheritance.

63:18 For a short while your holy people had possession; our adversaries have desecrated your sanctuary,

63:19 We have long been those "you did not rule over" and "your name was not spoken of them."

Oh that you would rend the heavens (and) come down, that the mountains would tremble before you,

64:1 As fire kindles brushwood (and) brings water to a boil,

So that your name be known to your adversaries—the nations will tremble before you.

64:2 When you do awesome deeds that we do not expect, you come down, the mountains tremble before you.

64:3 And from of old no one has heard or given ear,

No eye has seen any God except you acting on behalf of those waiting for him.

64:4 You visit the one who rejoices and the one who does righteousness; they remember you in your ways.

Behold, you grew angry, we have sinned; we are forever (implicated) in them, and we shall be saved?

64:5 We have all become like the unclean person, and all our righteous deeds like a soiled garment;

And we have faded like a leaf, all of us, and like the wind our iniquities carry us away.

64:6 There is no one calling upon your name, no one rousing himself to take hold of you,

For you have hidden your face from us, and made us to melt by means of our iniquities.

64:7 And now, LORD, you are our father.

We are the clay, and you are our potter; we are all the work of your hand.

64:8 Be not excessively angry, Lord, and do not remember iniquity forever.

Behold, consider, we are all your people. 64:9 Your holy city has become a wilderness;

Zion has become a wilderness, Jerusalem has become a desolation.
64:10 The house of our holiness and glory where our fathers praised you
Has been burned by fire, and all our precious things have been destroyed.
64:11 On top of these things, will you absent yourself, Lord? Will you be
silent and afflict us excessively?

2.2 Text-Critical Issues and Notes

The Hebrew text of the Book of Isaiah that is available in MT has been extremely well preserved, as shown by certain of the Qumran manuscripts. 1QIsa^b is remarkably similar to MT,[2] and 4QIsa^b is comparable to MT orthographically;[3] neither manuscript is later than the first century C.E. The two manuscripts indicate MT's stability over centuries and commend it as the basis of our study. Additionally, the discovery of 1QIsa^a has elicited text-critical discussion that bears upon our study.[4]

While 1QIsa^a reflects the wording of MT, it is generally argued to be reflective of a distinctive textual tradition.[5] That is to say, 1QIsa^a is dissimilar from the traditional text that MT shares, although this difference does not constitute a separate and materially different *interpretive* tradition.[6] The difference between MT and 1QIsa^a is such that variants in the latter do not constitute a novel text that changes the meaning of a verse over and against the consensus interpretation reflected in MT. This is true for Isa 63:7–64:11, which

---

[2] "[The manuscript] is often described as virtually identical with the MT. But there are more than a hundred differences in orthography and more than another hundred textual variants, mostly minor." Eugene Ulrich, "Isaiah Scrolls," *DNTB* 552. 1QIsa^b is available in *The Dead Sea Scrolls of the Hebrew University* (ed. E. L. Sukenik; Jerusalem: Magnes Press, 1955), 42–60.

[3] 4QIsa^b is available in *Discoveries in the Judaean Desert* 15 (ed. E. Ulrich et al.; Oxford: Clarendon Press, 1997), 17–43.

[4] See 1QIsa^a in *The Dead Sea Scrolls of St. Mark's Monastery* Vol. 1 (ed. M. Burrows; New Haven: ASOR, 1950).

[5] "A comprehensive and thorough examination [orthography, pronunciation, morphology, vocabulary, syntax and even proper nouns] will... prove that 1QIsa^a reflects a later textual type than the Masoretic text." E. Y. Kutscher, *The Language and Linguistic Background of the Isaiah Scroll* (*STDJ* 6; Leiden: Brill, 1974), 2–3. Additionally, Frank Moore Cross, while providing no analysis of Isaiah, states that 1QIsa^a exhibits no "tendency toward" MT, whose Babylonian provenance accounts for its textual character. See his "The History of the Biblical Text in Light of Discoveries in the Judaean Desert," pp. 177–95 in *Qumran and the History of the Biblical Text* (ed. F. M. Cross and S. Talmon; Cambridge, Mass.: Harvard University Press, 1975), 186.

[6] A distinctive *interpretational* tradition has been argued by Shemaryahu Talmon, who identifies at least seven verses in which 1QIsa^a replicates MT with slight variation but provides a novel reading. Talmon's sampling of data is not broad enough to support his claims, which I have otherwise tested and found to be intriguing but not wholly persuasive. See his "DSIa as a Witness to the Ancient Exegesis of the Book of Isaiah," pp. 116–26 in *Qumran and the History of the Biblical Text*.

is represented in two Qumran manuscripts, 1QIsa^a and 4QIsa^b. In these manuscripts there are three omissions, six additions and 14 variants. Invariably, these changes clarify meaning rather than change it; they involve transposing words (63:9,17), adding conjunctions (63:10,16; 64:9), changing number (63:15,17,18; 64:10) and other minor alterations to facilitate the text's reception. In this vein, even the more substantial variants (63:13; 64:1,5) aim to clarify opaque expressions rather than to coin new ones. In more than a few cases, variants in 1QIsa^a coincide with those in LXX (63:10,15,17; 64:1,5).

The text-critical parallels between 1QIsa^a and LXX have been studied by Joseph Ziegler, who claims that the two texts share a common textual tradition, over and against that of MT.[7] This is the case only inasmuch as LXX, like 1QIsa^a, represents not a new tradition at the level of meaning but rather an attempt at a faithful translation that would be intelligible to a Greek-speaking audience. With Isa 63:7–64:11, LXX contains five omissions, three additions and 27 variants. Many of the variants are minor and result from adding a conjunction (64:5,9) and changing tense (63:10) or number (63:15,18; 64:9,10). More numerous are variants that reflect an attempt to clarify a difficult expression (63:11,12,15,18; 64:1,5) done often with a view to improving the narrative by harmonizing words in a given verse (63:14,15; 64:1,3,4,6). In three such cases our translation follows LXX over MT: "no messenger or angel but his presence" (63:9); "in his midst" (63:11); "holy city" (64:9). The other ancient versions provide text-critical data that "is not entirely negligible but is nevertheless much less than that of LXX [and Qumran]."[8] The data appears in full in Table 1.

---

[7] "Eine stattliche Anzahl von Varianten konnte notiert werden, die in LXX Qu gegen M überstimmen. Diese Übereinstimmung besagt aber nicht, dass überall die Vorlage LXX die gleiche hebr. Lesart wie Qu hatte." Joseph Ziegler, "Die Vorlage der Isaias-Septuaginta (LXX) und die erste Isaias-Rolle von Qumran (1QIsa^a)," *JBL* 78 (1959): 59.

[8] Whybray, *Isaiah 40–66*, 44.

TABLE 1

OMISSIONS (>), ADDITIONS (+) AND VARIANTS (=) OF ISA 63:7–64:14 IN THE PRINCIPAL ANCIENT TEXTS

(No symbol preceding an entry indicates agreement with MT;
"Other translations" not always applicable)

V.	MT	LXX	Qumran (1QIsaᵃ unless otherwise noted)	Other Translations Targum (T) Vulgate (V)
63:7	ורב טוב לבית ישראל	= κύριος κριτὴς ἀγαθὸς τῷ οἴκῳ Ισραηλ	ורב טוב לבית ישראל	= et secundum multitudinem misericor- diarum suarum (V)
63:7	גמלם	= ἐπάγει ἡμῖν	= נגמאלם	
63:9	ומלאך פניו	= ἀλλ' αὐτὸς κύριος	ומלאך פניו	
63:9	וינטלם וינשאם	ἀνέλαβεν αὐτοὺς καὶ ὕψωσεν αὐτοὺς	= וינשאם וינטלם	
63:10	הוא נלחם בם	+ καὶ αὐτὸς ἐπολέμησεν αὐτούς	+ והוא נלחם בם	
63:11	משה עמו	>	מושה עמוא	
63:11	המעלם	> ὁ ἀναβιβάσας	> המעלה	
63:11	רעי צאנו	= τὸν ποιμένα	רועי צואנו	רעה (T)
63:11	בקרבו	= ἐν αὐτοῖς	בקרבו	
63:12	מוליך לימין משה זרוע תפארתו	= ὁ ἀγαγὼν τῇ δεξιᾷ Μωυσῆν	מוליך לימין משה זרוע תפארתו	
63:12	לו	αὐτῷ	>	
63:13	בתהמות	διὰ τῆς ἀβύσσου	= בתומות	
63:14	רוח יהוה תניחנו	= κατέβη πνεῦμα παρὰ κυρίου καὶ ὡδήγησεν αὐτούς	רוח יהוה תניחנו	= ductor eius fuit (V)
63:15	וגבורתך	= ἡ ἰσχύς σου	= וגבורתכה	
63:15	המון מעיך ורחמיך	+ ποῦ ἐστιν	המון מעיך ורחמיך	

63:15	אלי התאפקו	= ὅτι ἀνέσχου ἡμῶν	אלי התאפקו	
63:16	יכירנו	= ἐπέγνω	= הכירנו	
63:16	אתה	σύ	הואה +	
63:17	למה תתענו יהוה	τί ἐπλάνησας ἡμᾶς κύριε	= למה יהוה תתענו	
63:17	שבטי נחלתך	τὰς φυλὰς τῆς κληρονομίας σου	= שבט נחלתך	
63:18	ירשו	= κληρονομήσωμεν	= ירש	
63:18	עם קדשך	= τοῦ ὄρους τοῦ ἁγίου σου	עם קודשך	
63:19	מעולם	= ἀπ' ἀρχῆς	מעולם	= quasi in principio (V)
63:19	נזלו	= τακήσονται	נזלו	= defluerent (V)
64:1	המסים	= κηρός	= עמס ים	
64:1	מים	= τοὺς ὑπεναντίους	לצריכה +	
64:2	לא	>	>	
64:2	ירדת	>	ירדתה	
64:3	לא 2°	= οὐδὲ	= ולא	
64:3	למחכה לו	= τοῖς ὑπομένουσιν ἔλεον	למחכה לו	
64:4	את שש	>	את ש[ש]	
64:4	בדרכיך יזכרוך	= τῶν ὁδῶν σου μνησθήσονται	בדרכיהכ יזכורוכה	
64:4	ונושע	= διὰ τοῦτο ἐπλανήθημεν	ונושע	
64:5	וכבגד	= ὡς ῥάκος	= כבגד (1QIsa^a, 4QIsa^b)
64:5	ונבל	= ἐξερρύημεν	= ונבולה	
64:6	מתעורר	= ὁ μνησθείς	מתעורר	
64:6	ותמוגנו	= καὶ παρέδωκας ἡμᾶς	= ותמגנדנו	
64:7	ועתה	καὶ νῦν	= ואתה	
64:8	לעד	= ἐν καιρῷ	= לעת	

64:9	עָרֵי קָדְשְׁךָ	= πόλις τοῦ ἁγίου σου	עָרֵי קוּדְשָׁדָה	
64:9	מִדְבָּר	= ὡς ἔρημος	= כְּמִדְבָּר	
64:9	שְׁמָמָה	= εἰς κατάραν	שׁוּמְמָה	
64:10	הָיָה 2°	ἐγενήθη	= הָיוּ 2°	

2.3 Form-Critical Inventory of Isa 63:7–64:11

The commentaries are virtually unanimous in comparing Isa 63:7–64:11 to the psalms of communal lament.[9] All base their judgments on the recurrence of formal elements. Like certain psalms of communal lament, the prayer in Isaiah comprises a historical section (63:7–14), a lament followed by an appeal (63:15–64:4a), a confession of sin (64:4b–6), and a final appeal that both asserts confidence (64:7–8) and issues a second lament (64:9–10). In terms of content and sequence, the prayer's form-critical repertoire compares well with those established by Gunkel[10] and Mowinckel[11] for the psalms of communal lament:

---

[9] Elizabeth Achtemeier compares the entire composition to the communal lament as found in Pss 44, 74, and 79. Specifically: 63:7–14 (a historical recital) = 44:1–8; 63:15–19 (detailing of the community's present, desperate situation) = 44:9–22; 64:1–12 (petition for help) = 44:23–26. *The Community and Message of Isaiah 56–66* (Minneapolis: Augsburg, 1982), 132. Irmtraud Fischer subdivides the prayer into six sections of *Textgraphik* (63:7–10, 11–14, 15–19a; 63:19b–64:4a; 64:4b–8, 9–11) and compares these to psalms 44, 77–79, 89 and others. *Wo ist Jahwe? Das Volksklagelied Jes 63,7–64,11 als Ausdruck des Ringens um eine gebrochene Beziehung* (Stuttgart: Verlag Katholisches Bibelwerk GmbH, 1989), 32–72, 205–23. Claus Westermann cites points of contact between the prayer in Isaiah and the psalms of communal lament, and he concludes that all that is in the Isaiah text is according to the psalms of communal lament. *Isaiah 40–66: A Commentary*, 386. R. N. Whybray notes that the prayer's four main elements correspond to the psalms of communal lament: the account of Yahweh's past acts of redemption (63:7–14); the appeal to him for help (63:15–64:4a), the confession of sin (64:4b–7), and the renewed appeal that closes the prayer and brings together its themes (64:8–12). *Isaiah 40–66*, 256.

[10] Gunkel, *Einleitung in die Psalmen*, 125.

[11] Mowinckel, *The Psalms in Israel's Worship*, 1:195–219.

TABLE 2

FORM-CRITICAL STRUCTURE
OF THE PSALMS OF COMMUNAL LAMENT

GUNKEL	MOWINCKEL	ISA 63:7–64:11
		Historical Recital (63:7–14)
	Address	Address (63:16)
Complaint	Lament	Lament (63:15–19a)
Petition	Request	Call for an Epiphany (63:19b–64:4a)
Self-Reproaches for Motivational Effect	Statement of Motive	Confession of Sin (64:4b–6)
	Individual's Vow of Confidence	Individual's Vow of Confidence (64:7–8)
	Confidence of Being Heard	
		Lament over Jerusalem (64:9–10)
		Conclusion (64:11)

Gunkel and Mowinckel agree that the core of the communal lament is a petition framed by a complaint and a statement of motive. Isa 63:7–64:11 reflects this ordering with its lament-call for epiphany-confession of sin. Beyond the core, the prayer in Isaiah includes an address and an individual's vow of confidence that further align the prayer with Mowinckel's schema. These are the *prima facie* grounds for listing Isa 63:7–64:11 among the psalms of communal lament, as virtually every commentary does.

This much said, the commentaries part ways. No one designation of the units agrees completely with any other, and the units' sequence is said to approximate, not replicate, that of psalms 44, 74, 78, 79 and 80.[12] These discrepancies are explained somewhat by the nature of psalmic composition, which routinely modifies and rearranges formal elements in psalms of a given type.[13] Nonetheless, the inclusion of Isa 63:7–64:11 among the psalms of

---

[12] These five psalms reflect well the form-critical pattern of the communal lament, as identified by Mowinckel, *The Psalms in Israel's Worship*, 1:193–219. As well, before the final redaction of the psalter these psalms were considered a unit, the psalms of Asaph. Cf. Goulder, *The Psalms of Asaph and the Pentateuch: Studies in the Psalter, III*.

[13] The psalms of communal lament lack a definitive sequence; different items alternate in their order and recur several times. See Mowinckel, *The Psalms in Israel's Worship*, 1:196. Presumably, such customization reflected a psalm's historical circumstances. Cf. Erhard Gerstenberger's discussion of "the unresolved problem of how to evaluate justly the relative proportions of individual creativity and social convention in the process of poetic composition." "The Lyrical Literature," pp. 409–44 in *The Hebrew*

communal lament reflects an inexact and cursory judgment, lacking in both detail and comprehensiveness. To achieve further precision, an analysis of the text is in order.

2.4 Form-Critical Analysis of Isa 63:7–64:11

63:7–14. Historical Recital Focused on God's Benevolence and Guidance: The first section employs Israelite history to celebrate two attributes of God, benevolence and guidance. By goodness, mercy and love, God saves the chosen people. Despite their obstinacy (63:10), God leads them through difficulties and into rest. Unlike those psalms that recite large spans of history (Pss 68, 105, 106, 135, 136), the prayer selects two events to embellish with commentary, crossing the Reed Sea and wandering in the wilderness. In this appropriation of history, Isa 63:7–14 parallels Pss 66:6, 74:12–15, 77:16–20, and 114:3–5.[14] Although distinct from the prayer proper (63:15–64:11), this section intensifies the lament that follows and corroborates its request for God to help the people "as at that (earlier) time."[15]

63:15–19a. Lament: This section also revolves around God, albeit indirectly. God's strength and compassion (63:15) are conspicuous by their absence, while God is at a remove and no longer acting as the people's guide (63:17) and sovereign (63:19a). Abandoned and dispossessed of their sanctuary (63:18), the people join in lament. They consider their wrongdoing (63:17) and ask God to relate to them based on God's identity as redeemer and, especially, father. The contrast between God and the fathers, Abraham and Jacob (63:16), has led to the view that this is a sectarian critique targeting a group of post-exilic Jews.[16] Such a reconstruction, however, is problematic,[17] and another interpretation will be developed in the course of this chapter.

Bible and Its Modern Interpreters (ed. D. A. Knight and G. M. Tucker; Minneapolis: Fortress, 1985), 420.

[14] In the case of these psalms, when a single unit of narration evokes a larger idea, such as divine providence, the *Gattung* is that of *history writing*. The genre is distinct from the *historical work*, a compilation of many such units that results in the accounts of the Deuteronomistic Historian and the Chronicler. In Trito Isaiah, this prayer's first section is an instance of history writing. *RGG* 2:1498,1500.

[15] "Funktion der V 7–14 ist es also – wie auch sonst im Bericht von Jahwes früherem Heilshandeln in der KV – die Klage zu verschärfen und die Bitte zu unterstützen: Jahwe soll helfen wie damals." Johannes Kühlewein, *Geschichte in den Psalmen* (Stuttgart: Calwer Verlag Stuttgart, 1973), 122.

[16] Principally, Paul Hanson: "The holy people who once fulfilled their vocation as 'priests of the LORD' now see their sanctuary taken by their adversaries (possibly reflecting the loss of temple access on the part of the Levites to the Zadokite priestly leadership)." *Isaiah 40–66* (Louisville: John Knox, 1995), 239. He elaborates this view in *The Dawn of Apocalyptic: The Historical and Sociological Roots of Jewish Apocalyptic Eschatology* (Philadelphia: Fortress, 1979 [1975]), 92–94.

63:19b–64:4a. Call for an Epiphany: Although some claim that this passage reflects the divine warrior *topos,* distinctive features of the *topos* are lacking, such as God rising from sleep, routing the foe and choosing a new shrine as a dwelling.[18] The divine warrior *topos* had minimal bearing on the verses here. Their basis is rather the Sinai theophany (Exod 19:16–25) and its *Nachleben* in passages such as Judg 5:4–5, which emphasize God's awesome power and marvelous effects. *Exempla* in this passage include the heavens split asunder and mountains trembling (Isa 63:19). Isa 64:1, about blazing brushwood and boiling water, continues the dramatic imagery and prompted the rabbis to offer instruction about Sinai, its theophanic character and the tension between God's immanence and transcendence.[19] Their work suggests, retrospectively, that the prayer is probing the nature of the divine-human relationship that was revealed at Sinai. When the passage concludes: "No one has heard or given ear, no eye has seen any God except you," the rabbis' interpretive emphasis on immanence and transcendence is corroborated.[20] An appeal and a meditation, this passage raised

---

[17] The fundamental difficulty is that the prayer 63:7–64:11 is offered on behalf of an entire community and not a subgroup therein. The "children of the exile" availed themselves of this prayer and did so inclusively, despite partisan differences. It is offered by and on behalf of "all of us" (כֻּלָּנוּ, 64:5,7,8), specified in 63:17 as "your servants, the tribes of your inheritance," which is to say the *golah* community as a whole. See Joseph Blenkinsopp, "The Servant and Servants in Isaiah and the Formation of the Book," pp. 155–75 in *Writing and Reading the Scroll of Isaiah: Studies of an Interpretive Tradition* (ed. C. Broyles and C. Evans; Leiden/New York/Cologne: Brill, 1997), 167. Many aspects of Hanson's historical reconstruction have come under critique by H. G. M. Williamson, "Isaiah 63:7–64:11: Exilic Lament or Post-Exilic Protest?" *ZAW* 102 (1990): 48–58, and Grace Emmerson, *Isaiah 56–66* (Sheffield: Sheffield Academic Press, 1992), 85–94.

[18] These features are displayed in Ps 78:65–72, Isa 42:13–16, 51:9–11. It is significant that Richard Clifford does not include Isa 63:19–64:4 among the passages of biblical poetry "in which Yahweh with his train comes from his mountain home to aid his people." (*The Cosmic Mountain and the Old Testament* [Cambridge, Mass.: Harvard University Press, 1972], 114–19) Nonetheless, Hanson claims that the "protest group" responsible for this prayer is committed to divine warrior imagery that it has adapted from Deutero Isaiah and made more strident. *The Dawn of Apocalyptic,* 98. Also, Werline asserts a cause-and-effect relationship between the confession of sin and the *topos* of the divine warrior: The confession of sin "leads to arrival of the divine warrior and salvation." *Penitential Prayer in Second Temple Judaism,* 45.

[19] In commenting on Isa 63:19b–64:3, the *Mekhilta of Rabbi Ishmael* focuses on boundaries designed to avert any confusion between the proper realms of God and humankind. The Divine's descent upon Mt. Sinai is explained through the analogy of bedding that is spread over a bedframe. *Mekhilta of Rabbi Ishmael* (ed. J. Z. Lauterbach; Philadelphia: Jewish Publication Society of America, 1976) 2.224.

[20] Methodologically, we agree with Jon Levenson that the aggadah of the rabbis makes explicit and prosaic what is implicit and poetic in the Hebrew Bible. A case in point is Isa 63:18–64:3, for which the rabbis provide the first interpretation and the most

theological issues for its medieval interpreters as well, who read in it a reference to Sinai.[21]

64:4b–6. Confession of Sin: An admission of sin (64:4b) keynotes this section, which elaborates upon the people's wrongdoing in language that is cultic and figurative (64:5). After lamenting the people's lack of initiative, the final verse reports that as God has become hidden to the people, their own iniquity hastens their "melting" or moral diminution. This confession of sin is more involved and direct than those found in the psalms of communal lament, and the difference helps to illustrate this prayer's theology. As well, the confession of sin is important for illustrating how the genre of communal lament undergoes change in this prayer. The genre requires that a motivating element follow the petition, but it is now the confession of sin rather than a generic statement of motive. As a result, the petition gains authenticity as the people admit to their sin and confess their own moral failure. In Isa 63:7–64:11, as in the communal laments, the petition is framed by motivating elements, one of which has become the confession of sin.

64:7–8. The Individual's Vow of Confidence: Returning to the positive, paternal language of 63:16, this section is juxtaposed with the confession of sins. The section aims to mitigate the divine wrath and sin's permanence (64:8), two givens in the preceding confession. The change in tone may be the result of the prayer's use in liturgy, where a vow of confidence infuses the people's lament with praise.[22] This element is not to be confused with the oracle of confidence, a thanksgiving whose strong language is commensurate with a promise that the liturgy's officiant has given on behalf of God.[23] In this section, God's intermediary has not spoken; rather, the speaker's guardedly hopeful language is internal to the prayer.

64:9–10. A Distinct Lament Over Jerusalem: The holy city, Zion/Jerusalem, is said to be in desuetude (64:9), and the temple has been burnt after its precious vessels were plundered (64:10). These events correspond well with a dating of the prayer to 587 B.C.E. or sometime thereafter. As well, given the similarity in description with Isa 1:7,[24] this section could reflect a redactor as late as the third

---

satisfactory. See his *Sinai and Zion: An Entry Into the Jewish Bible* (New York: Harper & Row, 1985), 134, 184.

[21] See Jacob ben Meir Tam, *Sefer ha-yashar le-rabenu Tam: Helek ha-hidushim* (Jerusalem: Sifriyati, 1985 [1959]).

[22] Ps 74:12 is the example cited by Westermann, *The Praise of God in the Psalms* (Richmond, Va.: John Knox, 1965 [1953]), 57.

[23] The oracle of confidence is described by Mowinckel, *The Psalms in Israel's Worship,* 217. The *Gattung* of 64:7 is clearly different; it is that of the (individual's) vow of confidence while the psalm type whence it comes is the *individual* lament. Rainer Albertz, *A History of the Israelite Religion in the Old Testament Period* (2 vols; Louisville: Westminster John Knox, 1994 [1992]), 401.

[24] Isa 1:7: Your land is a desolation, your cities are burned with fire; aliens devour your land right before you, and the desolation is like a foreign overthrow.

century B.C.E. who is focusing on the initial and concluding chapters of the Book of Isaiah.[25] The fact that Jerusalem is redeemed in 1:26–27 does not discount the parallel, which could be based on the imagery of destruction and the fact that those who repent (1:27 וְשָׁבֶיהָ) are integral to the redemption.

64:11. Conclusion: Asking whether the LORD will remain absent and silent so as further to oppress the people, this signature to the prayer echoes 63:15. Such echoes are common from 64:7 forward, and on this basis some commentators take the final four verses together as a conclusion.[26] What is important, however the conclusion is construed, is that prayer ends with no oracle of reassurance, as is customary in this genre. The prayer elicits no response and instead puts two questions to God. The second question concerns the duration of affliction; the first and more despairing invokes the relationship between the people and their God now silent and absent.

An analysis has clarified that the prayer's principal concern is strain placed upon the people's relationship with God when instability and vulnerability come to characterize the covenant. The people thus petition God to visit them anew as God once did at Sinai, and the request is literally framed by lament and confession, according to the conventions of the lament genre. Specifically, the people lament that God has become distant as they suffer the consequences of their sin, which they readily confess. Set in a position of prominence, the confession is more involved and direct than those found in the psalms of communal lament, a difference that helps to establish this prayer as atypical of the genre.

Thus, the prayer is modeled on the communal laments, with certain form-critical modifications, such as the confession of sin. Further modifications to the communal lament can be seen in terms of the call for vengeance and the oracle of confidence. Both were omitted, somewhat understandably, by a people whose capital city had once been sacked and whose God seemed distant. The omissions were conspicuous when the prayer was later included with the Isaiah material, and editors dealt with the issue of missing elements by way of the prayer's context, Isaiah 63–65. In the book's final form, the call and oracle were displaced, not omitted, from the psalm of communal lament.

2.5 The Context of Isa 63:7–64:11

---

[25] Paul Volz allows that Trito Isaiah includes material from as late as the Hellenistic Age based on his reading of the reference to Gad and Meni (65:11). *Jesaja II* (KAT; Leipzig: A. Deichertsche, 1932), 284. Odil Steck places the final redaction later yet, in the first quarter of the third century B.C.E. "Zu jüngsten Untersuchungen von Jes 56:1–8, 63:7–66:24," pp. 229–65 in *Studien zu Tritojesaja* (BZAW 30; Berlin/New York: de Gruyter, 1991), 241–42.

[26] See n. 8 on R. N. Whybray.

That Isa 64:11 is not an oracle of confidence but a despairing set of questions creates significant problems, one of which is that a standard element, the oracle of confidence, is unaccounted for. More fundamentally, without the oracle the lament achieves no resolution to the problem of God abandoning the people; the prayer stops short of any real closure. An example of what the lament lacks is found in Psalm 69, an individual's plaint that concludes with six consoling verses arising from the assurance that "the LORD hears the needy, and does not despise his own who are in bonds." (69:33) Other examples of the oracle of confidence are Pss 108:13, 144:12–15 and, among the psalms of communal lament, 79:13. R. N. Whybray notes that in Joel 2 the liturgy of lamentation concludes with an oracle of confidence in which God's promises of a full harvest and enemies vanquished are issued in the first person (2:19–20).[27] Indeed, the oracle is to be seen as God personally sending assurance through an intermediary at the cult. In its classic form, the oracle is an act of divine speech in direct address that recognizes the people's lament, provides assurance and indicates some basis for the assurance, either God's continuing in relationship with the people or God's planning to help and deliver them, as in Joel 2:19–20.[28] In Isa 63:7–64:11, God neither recognizes the people's plight nor responds with credible assurance, rendering the entire prayer "nearly scandalous in its skepticism" among the national laments.[29] God's apparent indifference to the people's plea is a theological problem of no small order.

A specious solution is to read Isa 64:7 as an oracle of confidence: "And now, LORD, you are our father. We are the clay, and you are our potter; we are all the work of your hand." Rainer Albertz, however, has demonstrated that the verse, like 63:16, is a *confession* of confidence that really belongs to the *individual* lament (see footnote 23). Isa 64:7 lacks the properties of an oracle of confidence and exemplifies, rather, the trend toward personal piety at the time of the exile. Here and elsewhere the relationship with God finds its analogy in familial ties, not history, as God is invoked as parent—father (Deut 32:6b, Jer 3:4,19) and mother (Isa 46:3, 49:15, 66:13).[30] Although personalized piety will have an important place in the study of Isa 63:7–64:11, it helps little in the matter at hand, the oracle of confidence.

Comparative study is of little help as Trito Isaiah presents no other situations leading to an oracle of confidence. Deutero Isaiah, on the other hand, has numerous examples as Joachim Begrich pointed out in his seminal article

---

[27] Whybray, *Isaiah 40–66*, 226.
[28] Patrick Miller thus defines and describes the "salvation oracle" in *They Cried to the Lord: The Form and Theology of Biblical Prayer* (Minneapolis: Fortress, 1994), 266.
[29] Fischer, *Wo ist Jahwe?*, 276. Her view is endorsed by Steck, "Zu jüngsten Untersuchungen von Jes 56:1–8, 63:7–66:24," 241.
[30] Albertz, *A History of the Israelite Religion*, 403.

"Das priesterliche Heilsorakel."[31] Begrich concludes that the oracle's historical basis was the national cult, where a *priestly* oracle was in place until the time of the exile. Thereafter, this same oracle came under the auspices of the prophet who changed its tone to that of a pronouncement. Begrich credits sixth-century prophets with the aesthetic expansion of a formula; he shows that liturgical formulae gave rise to variations of the same, at least in this *Gattung* during and after the exile. In the case of Isa 64:11 and the oracle of confidence, an expansion of sorts has occurred with the resolution to the lament displaced to the next section, Isa 65:1–7.[32]

Scholars have posited a connection between 64:11 and the following verses at least since Aage Bentzen identified 64:11–65:1 as a "question-answer" literary device.[33] The most involved work on the issue, by Odil Steck, understands both the lament (63:7–64:11) and the following two chapters to represent the final redaction of the book of Isaiah. Steck holds that the final redaction is a response to an earlier form of the prayer. He understands the later work to be a more far-reaching reply to the prayer than was possible roughly a decade earlier when the prayer originated as part of the penultimate redaction. The final redactors, Steck claims, composed chapters 65 and 66 according to the five-part sequence of statements found in the preceding prayer.[34] While Steck's claim is overstated (see footnote 34), there is substance to it. Moreover, Steck's position underscores the gravity and complexity of the theological problem that arises from the absence of a reply in 64:11. Steck is most accurate in that the following chapter or chapters contain "a reply which connects the prayer's different aspects while taking a more differentiated perspective ... by making reference to statements from the whole book of Isaiah, from God's mouth, which are in fact consoling and restricting at the same time."[35] Steck reconstitutes the oracle of confidence on the supposition that at least parts of chapters 65 and 66 are relating issues from the prayer (63:7–64:11) to the book of Isaiah as a whole.

---

[31] Joachim Begrich, "Das priesterliche Heilsorakel," *ZAW* 52 (1934): 81–92, especially 87.

[32] While 65:1–16a form a unity, 65:1–7 can be taken as a section complete in itself. C. Westermann, *Isaiah 40–66: A Commentary*, 399.

[33] Aage Bentzen, *Introduction to the Old Testament* (Copenhagen: G. E. C. Gads, 1948–49), 2:108.

[34] Steck relies largely on catchwords in proposing that five sections, four of which are about an evildoer (65:1–7, 8–12, 13–25; 66:1–4) and one about pious works (66:5–24), are "exactly" in the sequence of statements of the preceding prayer while referring "exactly" to a change of address in the prayer. In unnecessarily arguing for such form-critical precision, Steck overstates his case. "Tritojesaja Im Jesajabuch," pp. 361–406 in *The Book of Isaiah Le Livre D'Isaïe: Les Oracles et leurs Relectures Unité et Complexité de l'Ouvrage* (ed. J. Vermeylen; Leuven: Leuven University Press, 1989), 396.

[35] "Eine Antwort, die an verschiedene Aspekte dieses Gebets anknüpft und sie verschiedener Hinsicht auch über die Tempelbaufrage hinaus unter Bezugnahme auf Aussagen im ganzen vorgegebenen Jesajabuch aus Gottes Mund klärt, und zwar tröstend und einschränkend zugleich." Ibid., 396–97.

Prescinding from Steck, we focus upon 65:1–7 as the core of the response to the prayer.

Isa 65:1–2 begins the lament's resolution inasmuch as it is direct, divine speech that establishes God's willingness to provide an oracle of assurance, "to be sought" (נִדְרַשְׁתִּי) and "to be found" (נִמְצֵאתִי) in the tolerative sense of the *nif'al*. Isa 65:1a reads:

נִדְרַשְׁתִּי לְלוֹא שָׁאָלוּ נִמְצֵאתִי לְלֹא בִקְשֻׁנִי

For their part, the people did not inquire of God. As in earlier laments (cf. 59:10), they did not seek him. Isa 65:1b concludes that they as a nation did not call on God's name (לֹא קֹרָא בִשְׁמִי cf. 63:18). Isa 65:2 explains the people's conduct; while God extended a hand to the people, they were stubborn (עַם סוֹרֵר cf. 63:10), walked in ways bereft of goodness (הַהֹלְכִים הַדֶּרֶךְ לֹא טוֹב cf. 63:17) and followed their own devices. In this even-handed explanation of an oracle that should have taken place but did not, the final term, "their devices" (מַחְשְׁבֹתֵיהֶם), is peculiar to the later books of the Bible (Est 8:3, 9:25; Dan 11:24; Lam 3:60, 61; arguably Gen 6:5), especially Chronicles (1 Chr 29:18).[36] As well, the parallel vocabulary "seek-find" (דרש-מצא) is a motif of Chronicles.[37] 2 Chr 15:13 makes "seeking the Lord" (דרש) the fundamental requirement of the post-exilic covenant. 2 Chr 7:14, using an alternative root for "seek" (בקש) that is also attested in Isa 65:1, links the "seek-find" motif to repentance and restoration.[38] Chronicles' dynamics of divine retribution[39] are approximated by Isa 65:1–2

---

[36] A discussion of the Chronicler who as both composer and redactor is responsible for Chronicles and portions of Ezra and Nehemiah follows in chapter three. In this chapter all references are limited to the books of Chronicles as a work that postdates the communal lament in Trito-Isaiah by at least one century.

[37] "Seek-find" occurs 32 times in the non-synoptic parts of Chronicles and eight times in the synoptic sections. Althought it is difficult to summarize the significance of this diction, "seeking God" in Chronicles has very important consequences for the individual in question, such as gaining in piety, achieving success and proving oneself to be a "true Israelite." S. Wagner, "דרש," *TDOT* 3:300–301.

[38] On the possibility of the "seek-find" motif carrying a distinctly penitential nuance from 2 Chronicles 6–7 onward, see Brian Kelly, *Retribution and Eschatology in Chronicles* (JSOTSup 211; Sheffield: Sheffield Academic Press, 1996), 53.

[39] The author of Chronicles has been credited with an exacting and highly equitable doctrine of divine retribution, understood as reward as well as punishment. The approach has been described as mechanical, individual and immediate. Among the most influential views have been those of Julius Wellhausen, who speaks of Chronistic retribution as a divine pragmatism in the kingdom of Judah (*Prolegomena to the History of Israel* [Edinburgh: T & T Clark, 1885 (1878)], 49) and von Rad, who understands retribution to be a theoretical exercise in theodicy (*Das Geschichtsbild des chronistischen Werkes* [BWANT, 4.3; Stuttgart: Kohlhammer, 1930], 11). Japhet has attempted to show that Chronicles is a self-contained entity expressing a clear and coherent system of thought, with special emphasis on the writer's system as an understanding of history as a

when the verses are read as a reply to the lament that has preceded them. The reply is careful *not* to condemn the entire nation and it offers, as it turns out, hope to certain people who are indicated obliquely in the following verses.

Isa 65:3–7 identifies more clearly the people who have forfeited hope through their ersatz worship (65:3–4) and distortions of the Yahwistic cult (65:5). These people have provoked God, who promises to repay their iniquities as were repaid the iniquities of old (65:6–7). This section thus differentiates the innocent and the blameworthy, and the exclusive use of cultic criteria recalls how Chronicles stipulates "seeking God" as "the commitment to his worship according to legitimate norms."[40] This differentiation of peoples is elaborated in the subsequent section about good grapes in a cluster that is otherwise rotten (65:8–12). A conclusion to this section is signaled in 65:6–7, when the one to repay iniquity announces that he will not keep silent (לֹא אֶחֱשֶׂה), as was feared in 64:11, nor will he afflict "you" ("us" in 64:11). The word parallels revisit and reevaluate the earlier prayer's conclusion, 64:11, while showing that God will repay proportionally (שִׁלַּמְתִּי) the iniquity of those who have provoked him (65:3).

While the compositional history of Isa 63:7–65:7 is complex, it merits consideration, especially as a window upon the genre of the communal lament. Because it appears that chapter 65 introduces a new mindset that is approximated elsewhere in Chronicles, 63:7–65:7 is in two parts, despite an almost seamless thematic unity about the struggle for collective relationship with God. Cognitive dissonance theory explains the division inasmuch as delay is the issue in 64:11–65:2. A later hand realized the lament was not yet answered and provided a resolution to the original text.[41] But in fact 63:7–65:7 is more like an inner dialogue which eventually arrives at the completion of a deliberation. In Steck's view, such a dialogue took place historically when one group, in the wake of trauma, composed the bleak lament as its signature to the book of Isaiah, and a like-minded group, at most a generation later, wrote chapters 65 and 66 as a corrective addendum to the prayer.[42] Both groups own the prayer and must be credited with its becoming part of the Isaian legacy.

---

continuous expression of the relationship between God and his people. Retribution, Japhet claims, avoids becoming a mechanical concept because it includes repentance, which has "the power to change destiny, personal and national and can counteract the effects of even the worst sin." *The Ideology of the Book of Chronicles*, 116, 190.

[40] Kelly, *Retribution and Eschatology*, 52.

[41] "We do not know how effective such responses may have been but they probably convinced some of Second Isaiah's circle to their own satisfaction sufficiently for them to have preserved the oracle of the prophet along with their own interpretations. They were able to go on working because they had provided sufficient dissonance reduction by these explanatory schemes." Robert Carroll, *When Prophecy Failed: Cognitive Dissonance in the Prophetic Traditions of the Old Testament* (New York: Seabury, 1978), 154–55.

[42] Steck, "Zu jüngsten Untersuchungen von Jes 56:1–8, 63:7–66:24," 241–42.

In view of this general evaluation, one can locate 63:7–65:7 in a time of profound loss that does not lead to final despair. The moment requires a lament that is poignant, especially regarding divine abandonment, but the genre's conventions remain binding. There must be resolution of the sort gained through an oracle of assurance, even if the genre is manipulated. Thus a later hand supplies a *de facto* oracle, 65:1–2. From a literary standpoint, the genre of communal lament sustained the divine-human relationship by transforming its conventions, such as the oracle of assurance. The other form-critical element affected in this manner was the call for vengeance.

In his discussion of the communal laments, Mowinckel devotes a lengthy section to the call for vengeance upon enemies who, typically, are external to Israel; the parties may be named (Ps 83:5–8) or stereotyped as evildoers (רשעים).[43] A parade example of the call for vengeance is Ps 79:10–12, which asks that the enemies' taunts be returned upon them sevenfold. The call is lightly veiled in Ps 74:22–23, which asks God not to forget the foes' clamor and uproar. Mowinckel adds that the enemy's destruction is often called for in the language of curse and blessing, as in Ps 79:10 where the "servants'" outpoured blood becomes a vengeful witness against the scoffing nations.[44] Similarly, Ps 74:20–23 juxtaposes divine favor for the downtrodden with just deserts for the foes and adversaries.

The communal lament Isa 63:7–64:11 calls for no avenging of the enemy, and the lacuna, on the one hand, makes a certain amount of sense. First, as subjects of the Persian king, Jews of this time ran a clear risk when announcing nationalistic initiatives, such as rebuilding the temple, which on separate occasions prompted letters to Susa by hostile neighbors (Ezra 4:4–16, 5:3–17). Second, a subject people is not likely to lash out at enemies; in addition to their loss of sovereignty in 587 B.C.E., the prayer in Trito Isaiah implies a second, more recent setback, perhaps the political demise of the Jewish governor Zerubbabel sometime around 520 B.C.E.[45] Third, the prayer constitutes part of Trito Isaiah, which extends Israel's promise of fulfillment to the nations, who have their place in salvation, albeit in subordinate roles (56:1–8). By not calling vengeance upon foreign peoples, the prayer conforms to Trito Isaiah's universalism, understood as a project of inclusivity.[46] On the other hand, the call for vengeance serves at least two functions. The call effectively redresses the enemies' insult of God. The call also supplies the modicum of collective mettle

---

[43] Mowinckel, *The Psalms in Israel's Worship*, 1:197.

[44] Ibid., 202.

[45] Karl Elliger dates Trito Isaiah to this period of rebuilding the temple. In so doing, he asserts indirectly that the Jews of Judea were wont to do penance for their sins, a claim that he supports with Isa 63:7–64:11. *Die Einheit des Tritojesaia* (BWANT 45; Stuttgart: Kohlhammer, 1928), 99.

[46] Only after the inclusivist project fell from favor, Westermann holds, was it subject to "amendments" such as 60:12 and 63:1–6, both judgments against the nations. *Isaiah 40–66: A Commentary*, 304–05.

that a communal lament requires. Without necessarily stoking the fires of vengeance, a rallying cry goes forth. The literary and historical circumstances notwithstanding, it is conspicuous that the lament does not call for vengeance.

It is worth considering how the call for vengeance, as an element of prayer, becomes subject to modification after the exile. Albertz observes that the accusation against the enemy comes to target those who foment social conflict, whereas earlier its objects were demonic powers.[47] As the call focuses increasingly upon internal rivals, the usual vitriol against enemies without becomes secondary and may be conflated with other elements. Irmtraud Fischer maintains that the call for theophany (Isa 63:19b–64:4a) performs the same function as Ps 79:9b—both are *Rachebitten* or pleas for revenge. Fischer bases her argument on a word parallel between Isa 63:19b–64:4a and Ps 79:9b; furthermore, she claims, 79:13 contains word parallels with several of the prayer's verses, including 63:7 and 64:7.[48] When, however, she asserts that the call for theophany performs another function, that of an entreaty for forgiveness, her argument becomes too diffuse to account for the call for vengeance missing from Isa 63:7–64:11.

The context of Isa 63:1–65:12, however, supports Fischer's premise that the call for vengeance may be realized through another literary element. The key is to be found in the culling of good grapes lest with the bad they be destroyed (65:8). This metaphor portends both blessing for the good, who are accorded the title "servants," (65:9) and destruction for the evildoers (65:12).[49] After the exile occurred, despoiled fruit was a metaphor for retributive destruction. In Jeremiah 24, good figs represent Judah's exiles who have gone to Babylon but are destined to be God's people (24:4–7). On the other hand, bad figs that are no longer edible represent King Zedekiah and those who now live in Judah and face God's vow to destroy them from the land by sword, famine and pestilence (24:8–10). The verses in both Jeremiah and Isaiah typify the shift that Albertz has described; the charge against the nation's foe is redirected at persons within Jewish society. Specifically, Isa 65:8–12 shifts the focus from the community as a whole to two collectivities within it. One, claiming to be the true Israel,[50] issues a call for vengeance upon the other as a postscript to the lament in Isa 63:7–64:11.

One can ask whether those responsible for 65:1–12, which culminates in the image of spoiled grapes destined for destruction, were alluding to 63:1–6, the oracle in which Edom is crushed like grapes in a winepress. In Israel's literature,

---

[47] Albertz, *A History of the Israelite Religion*, 511.

[48] "Die Rachebitte [Psa 79:10b], die dieselbe Funktion innerhalb des Liedes hat wie unsere Theophaniebitte, ist auch mit ähnlichen Worten formuliert." Fischer, *Wo ist Jahwe?*, 215.

[49] The two groups are alluded to in 65:1, an indictment of the evildoers who did not call back to the LORD (65:12) even while the servants were, for their part, seeking the LORD (65:10).

[50] Blenkinsopp, "The Servant and Servants in Isaiah," 168.

the oracle against Edom is a convention which intensified after the fall of Jerusalem as attested in biblical (Obad 1:1–14; Lam 4:22) and epigraphic sources.[51] Because the Edom oracle is representative of the oracles against foreign nations generally,[52] it may supply Isa 63:7–64:11 with a form of *Rachebitte* or call for vengeance. Moreover, the oracle's references to divine anger and wrath (63:3) parallel closely the exilic prophets' pronouncement of God's wrath poured out in a cup. In Second Isaiah (51:17,22) and Jeremiah (25:15), enemies drink from the cup to their own destruction. Similar vengeance is reported in Isa 63:1–6.

Rather than a cup, the oracle focuses upon the instrument of a winepress to describe how God alone has trampled the foe in anger and wrath. Certain details are very similar to those in a passage earlier in Trito Isaiah, Isa 59:15b–21. "Day of vengeance" in 63:4 echoes "garments of vengeance" in 59:17; "there was no one" is attested in 63:5a and 59:16a; and "my own arm brought me victory, and my wrath sustained me" is attested in 63:5b and 59:16b. In light of these parallels, it has been said that this oracle of Edom circulated as an alternative answer to the confession of sin in 59:9–15a, whose answer otherwise appears in 59:15b–21.[53] Also noteworthy, however, is that certain of these lexical correspondences extend to the prayer in 63:7–64:11; "there was no one" occurs in 64:6 and "God's glorious arm" goes forth in 63:12.

The exact relationship between the oracle (63:1–6) and the prayer (63:7–64:11) is elusive, and the redactional coupling of the two texts has been little discussed. Steck proposes that Isaiah's (penultimate) redactors formulated the prayer out of great dismay and reasoned that their appeal for divine intervention would be especially effective as a postscript to the oracle against Edom.[54] If this were so, it would appear that the call for vengeance implicit in the prayer through the Edom oracle was further intensified when a mirror image of the enemy as grapes crushed was supplied in 65:8–12, thus forming a frame for the lament and rectifying any deficit of vengeance in the text itself.

Two contextual developments related to the oracle of assurance and the call for vengeance demonstrate how the composers and redactors responsible for Isa 63:7–64:11 adaptively and creatively displaced elements that would centuries later draw the special attention of form critics. The lament is not independent of its primary context, designated as Isa 65:1–12. The design of Isa 63:7–65:12

---

[51] Arad Letter 24:20; Arad Letter 40:15 refers to "the evil that Edom has done" (הרעה אש[ר] אד[ם] עשתה]). Yohanan Aharoni, *Arad Inscriptions* (Jerusalem: Magnes, 1981), 46, 71.

[52] Joseph Blenkinsopp, *A History of Prophecy in Israel* (Louisville: Westminster John Knox, 1996 [1983]), 179.

[53] Whybray, *Isaiah 40–66*, 226. W. A. M. Beuken has suggested that 63:1–6 has the function of elaborating certain aspects of chapter 59 in light of chapters 60–62 and their depiction of God's righteousness towards the nations. "The Main Theme of Trito-Isaiah: 'The Servants of Yahweh,'" *JSOT* 47 (1990): 74.

[54] Steck, "Zu jüngsten Untersuchungen von Jes 56:1–8, 63:7–66:24," 238.

corresponds well to the type that the earliest composers probably had in mind, the psalm of communal lament. The psalm of communal lament and the prayer in context are compared in table three. The comparison illustrates that in the case of Isa 63:7–65:12, the formulation of prayer has interacted with conventions of genre in a way that is mutually transforming. We next consider how Isa 63:7–64:11 further transforms the communal lament by way of the confession of sins.

TABLE 3

FORM-CRITICAL COMPARISON
OF THE PSALMS OF COMMUNAL LAMENT AND ISA 63:7–65:12

PSALMS OF COMMUNAL LAMENT	ISAIAH 63:7–65:12
	Historical Recital (63:7–14)
Address	Address (63:16)
Lament	Lament (63:15–19a)
Request	Call for an Epiphany (63:19b–64:4a)
Statement of Motive	Confession of Sin (64:4b–6)
Individual's Vow of Confidence	Individual's Vow of Confidence (64:7–8)
	Lament over Jerusalem (64:9–10)
	Conclusion (64:11)
Confidence of Being Heard	Divine Explanation (65:1–2)
Call for Vengeance	Image of the Bad Grapes to be Destroyed (65:8,12)

2.6 The Confession of Sins

At the level of vocabulary there is much in common between the prayer in Trito Isaiah and the psalms of communal lament;[55] the continuity of confessional expression is especially striking and at the same time indicative of a larger phenomenon, genre. Apprehending the continuity requires a direct focus on the confession of sin in the prayer from Trito Isaiah. Appreciating the continuity requires attention to the way in which the prayer distinguishes its confession

---

[55] Isa 63:8 and Pss 44:18, 89:34 (שקר); Isa 63:10 and Ps 78:40, 17 (מרה עצב); Isa 63:11 and Ps 77:20, cf. Gen 46:32 (רעי צאן); Isa 63:12 and Pss 77:17, 78:13 (בקע מים תהמות); Isa 63:15 and Ps 80:15 (הבט משמים וראה); Isa 63:17 and Ps 74:2 (שבטי נחלתך); Isa 64:8 and Ps 79:8 (אל תזכר עון); Isa 64:9 and Ps 79:1 (ערי קדשך). While Isa 63:7–64:11 is quite interdependent with the psalms of communal lament, the prayer to a lesser degree reflects phrasing from Deuteronomy (Isa 64:1 and Deut 32:22) and Lamentations (Isa 64:2 and Lam 1:8,11; Isa 64:11 and Lam 1:10, 2:4).

from similar language in the psalms of communal lament and the Hebrew Bible generally. Three passages in Isa 63:7–64:11 provide this focus and nuance.

Isa 63:7–10. Confessional expression first occurs in Isa 63:7–14, a section about God's saving deeds in the history of Israel. The first half of the unit (vv. 7–10) considers the covenantal rapport that has existed between God and God's people.[56] While God is gracious, merciful and eminently faithful to the covenant, the people are false to the covenant (שקר) and rebellious (מרה) to the point of grieving God (עצב) and turning God against them. At first, (63:8) God claims the people as God's own and declares that they are incapable of deceit (לֹא יְשַׁקֵּרוּ).[57] Here dramatic irony prevails as שקר represents an impossibility to the speaker, but it has a foreboding and quite different meaning to those who understand the situation better. The latter view surfaces in 63:10, which confirms that the people are imbued with שקר. They rebel and grieve God's holy spirit. Thus God turns and fights against them. The operative terms, rebel and grieve (עצב and מרה), although not inherently penitential, may be construed as confessional because they involve a frank admission of guilt on behalf of the people.

Moreover, in this period the term מרה occurs regularly in texts that accuse Israel of rebellion in the face of God's public, historical deeds, especially those in the wilderness.[58] The meaning of מרה as "obstinate" is rooted in Deuteronomic law (Deut 21:18–21); in the Deuteronomistic History, מרה accrues "nomistic nuance" and conforms to one of two stock usages, neither of which is attested in the prayer from Trito Isaiah.[59] In post-exilic literature, מרה appears predominantly (seven times) in Psalms 78 and 106, where מרה denotes

> The rebellious conduct of the patriarchal generation (Ps 78:8) during the wilderness period (78:17,40; 106:7,33) and the occupation (78:56; 106:43). Also, in this time מרה appears with many synonyms; besides those of Deuteronomistic origin we find expressions from the language of wisdom and the general terminology of sin [including] עצב (Ps 78:40).[60]

Like Psalm 78, Isa 63:10 employs מרה in a manner particular to those generations after the exile who shift their Dtr focus from law to historical conceits such as the wilderness. In fact, Isaiah's terms of indictment, עצב and מרה, come, quite possibly, from a psalm, Ps 78:40: "How often they rebelled

---

[56] The covenantal nuances of Isa 63:7–10 are established in 64:7, where we have translated MT's חסדי יהוה as "the LORD's covenant deeds." Although many translators choose not to emphasize the covenantal nature of the divine human relationship, it is very much implicit when this term is used in the context of communal lament, as noted by Mowinckel, *The Psalms in Israel's Worship*, 1:205; cf. Achtemeier, *The Community and Message of Isaiah 56–66*, 113; and Hanson, *The Dawn of Apocalyptic,* 88.

[57] In light of 1 Sam 15:29 and Ps 89:34, it is as if divine steadfastness is being projected onto humanity.

[58] R. Knierim, "מרה," *TLOT* 2:688.

[59] L. Schwienhorst, "מרה," *TDOT* 9:7,9.

[60] Schwienhorst, *TDOT* 9:9.

against him in the wilderness and grieved him in the desert." Nowhere else does the Bible join these two terms of wrongdoing, although a close approximation is found elsewhere in Psalm 78, "Yet they still sinned more against him, rebelling against the most High (לַמְרוֹת עֶלְיוֹן) in the desert." (78:17)

The term שקר (63:8) enjoys a similar affinity with the psalms of communal lament. Its basic meaning, "to behave contrary to a contract, faithlessly, perfidiously,"[61] is consonant with the Old Aramaic Sefire inscriptions.[62] Gen 21:23 and other verses confirm שקר as a biblical term no less rooted in treaty law. Ps 44:18 reads: "We have not forgotten you nor been unfaithful to your covenant (וְלֹא שִׁקַּרְנוּ בִּבְרִיתֶךָ)." Given the covenantal context of 63:7–10, שקר (63:8) finds its parallels in Psalm 44's expression of being untrue to the covenant, from the psalms of communal lament. Yet there is one significant difference. In Ps 44:18, the people assert that despite great calamity they have not forgotten God or been false to the covenant. The psalm affirms their innocence and laments their plight. The prayer in Trito Isaiah, however, depicts a rebel people false to the covenant.

Within the first half of the prayer's historical section (63:7–10), confessional language has the stamp of the psalms and specifically of the psalms of communal lament. By adopting three deliberate expressions of penitence, שקר, מרה, and עצב, the composer is able to underscore both the people as sinners and God as alienated from the covenant by their sins.[63] The prayer's foci are essentially two. The first is the traditional subject of lament, God's distance from the people in travail. The second is the cause of this distance, human faithlessness to the covenant.

Isa 64:4b–6. The verses 64:4b–6 are the prayer's most self-conscious attempt at confession. Similar to 63:8,10, the section correlates references to sin and iniquity with the people's alienation from God. The terms for sin and iniquity are חטא (64:4b) and עון (64:5b,6b); God is described as one who is angry and not apt to save (64:4b), whose name and strength are no longer invoked (64:6), and who has become at best a hidden presence (64:6b). Human sin and God's lamentable remoteness are at the center of a complex, troubled relationship.[64]

Thus, 64:4b keynotes this short confession: "Behold, you grew angry; we have sinned." The statement, on the one hand, is conventional because in psalms

---

[61] M. A. Klopfenstein, "שקר," *TLOT* 3:1399.

[62] Joseph Fitzmyer, *The Aramaic Inscriptions of Sefire* (Rome: Pontifical Biblical Institute, 1995 [1967]), 107.

[63] The terms also echo the book of Isaiah itself, as in 30:9: "For they are a rebellious people, lying sons, who will not hear the instruction of the Lord."

[64] The difficulties are reflected in the pericope itself. Isa 63:7–64:11 is a dense prayer with challenging syntax (64:4bα) and signs of textual corruption (64:4bβ, 64:6bβ). Exegeting the confessional expressions is further complicated by the fact that wrongdoing and its consequences are expressed literally (64:4b), cultically (64:5a) and figuratively (64:5b).

of lament חטא routinely connotes the causal connection between one's ill-chosen action and its consequence.⁶⁵ The syntax, however, is counterintuitive as one expects human sin to spur divine anger, and not vice versa. In light of the conditional construction in Gen 43:9,⁶⁶ Isaiah's verse has been read as legal discourse whereby God's anger stands as the verdict against a sinful people. Only upon conviction is Israel subjected to the full depths of its own sin, in this view first proposed by Franz Delitzsch.⁶⁷ His interpretation is grammatically defensible⁶⁸ and makes the most sense in light of the composer's larger agenda to craft a confession based on God's apparent flight from sinful humanity. It is from this point of view that the verse's final three words, about salvation, can be understood. While some editors would emend the text, it reads rhetorically: "(We are) forever (implicated) in them (our sins), and we shall be saved?" Despite the verse's difficulties, its first-person confession of sin is quite direct and almost formulaic. Among the psalms of lament, such forthright use of חטא is found in 79:9b and in 78:32, also a keynote to a section of confessional material.⁶⁹

The next verse, 64:5, sketches the breadth and depth of the people's defilement in terms that are cultic (64:5a) and figurative (64:5b). Common to both expressions is the self-referential "all of us." The cultic expression, involving the designation "unclean" (טמא), reflects how uncleanness has become

---

⁶⁵ K. Koch, "חטא," *TDOT* 4:313–14.

⁶⁶ Judah says to his father Jacob, "I myself will be surety for him; you can hold me accountable for him. If I do not bring him back to you and set him before you, then let me bear the blame forever." (Gen 43:9). Ps 36:3 holds that the evildoer's self-flattery mitigates against his iniquity being found out and hated, thus providing another instance of this view that public knowledge heightens a misdeed's reprehensibility.

⁶⁷ Delitzsch holds that the *waw* forms the imperfect consecutive, and that ... "'so we have then sinned' ([indicating] the consequent result of sin due to punishment) is [a] better [interpretation] like Gen 43:9. So we stand then as sinners, as the guilty party, the ones responsible. The punishment has placed Israel before the world and before itself as that which it is." "So haben wir denn gesündigt (Folgerung der Sünde aus der Strafe), richtiger aber wie Gen. 43,9: so stehen wir denn als Sünder, als Schuldige da—die Strafe hat Isr. vor der Welt und vor sich selber als das hingestellt was es ist." *Commentar über Das Buch Jesaia* (Leipzig: Dörffling & Franke, 1889), 609. An alternative exegesis considers the second clause to be epexegetical: "You were angry, we having sinned." John Oswalt, *The Book of Isaiah: Chapters 40–66* (Grand Rapids, Mich.: Eerdmans, 1998), 619. Yet a third interpretation takes the first clause to be concessive: You grew angry, "and yet we sinned." Whybray, *Isaiah 40–66,* 264.

⁶⁸ "The imperfect expresses the practical consequences." Edward Young, *The Book of Isaiah* (3 vols.; Grand Rapids, Mich.: Eerdmans, 1965–72), 3.495.

⁶⁹ By indentation, MT indicates Ps 78:32–39 as a distinct unit. Richard Clifford designates vv. 33–40 as meditation or reflection on the miracles and punishments of vv. 12–32. "In Zion and David a New Beginning: An Interpretation of Psalm 78," pp. 121–141 in *Traditions in Transformation: Turning Points in Biblical Faith* (ed. B. Halpern, J. D. Levenson; Winona Lake, Ind.: Eisenbrauns, 1981), 133.

a metaphor for immorality after the exile. Jacob Neusner interprets 64:5a as a commonplace critique of someone who "while ritually pure, does impure deeds."[70] The critique, he notes, is not unique to prophetic literature, and another striking example is found in Hag 2:13–14 (see footnote 114).

The figurative language in 64:5b reads: "And we have fallen like a leaf, all of us," (וַנָּבֶל כֶּעָלֶה כֻּלָּנוּ) a use of the root בלה[71] that is not unknown to the prophets.[72] When the stich concludes: "Like the wind, our iniquities carry us away," the likeliest source is Ps 1:3–4, a distinction between lawful and wicked that mentions the leaf *not* withering and the wind driving away the chaff. Unlike the psalm, Isa 64:5b applies both expressions pejoratively and implies that iniquity determines the direction of people's lives. Wrongdoing's effects or consequences appear to be emphasized when this usage of עון is compared to others.[73] God's help is nowhere to be had. The expression "driving wind" occurs in Ps 78:39, where God stays the divine wrath because mortals are merely a wind that passes and comes not again. Where the psalm notes human foibles, Isa 64:5b laments "our iniquities"; Trito Isaiah has brought wrongdoing more to the fore.

The concluding verse to this section compounds the people's failure with God's abandoning them. In Isa 64:6a lament and confession blend together flawlessly: "There is no one calling upon your name, no one rousing himself to take hold of you." The first idea is a psalmic conceit found in the communal laments (Pss 75:1,79:6,80:18).[74] In the psalms, calling upon God's name is tantamount to revelation in all its mystery and wonder. As calling upon God's name implies that God is immanent, its negation underscores God's absence. The second expression of Isa 64:6a, מִתְעוֹרֵר, about rousing oneself, is both psalmic and Isaian. Typically, it is God who is called to rise up and help the people.[75] That God is not doing so is lamentable; that no mortal rises up to take hold of God is in fact an indictment, possibly against a human leader.[76] In its extent, Isa 64:6a captures a loss of grace and human nerve in the milieu of divine abandonment.

---

[70] Neusner further notes that equating impurity with evil doing is typical of the book of Isaiah as a whole, as witnessed by Isa 6:5. Jacob Neusner, *The Idea of Purity in Ancient Judaism* (Leiden: Brill, 1973), 13.

[71] If the verb is a *hif'il* imperfect, first common plural, MT's form and pointing would indicate the root to be בלל, which *BDB* crosslists. The expected form of the verb is found in 1QIsaᵃ, which thus witnesses to the root בלה. Burrows, *The Dead Sea Scrolls of St. Mark's Monastery,* plate LI (np).

[72] Isa 1:30, 34:4; Jer 8:13; Ezek 47:12.

[73] *BDB* 5771; cf. *KBL* 689. According to these lexica, Isa 64:5 is unique with עון referring to the consequence of or punishment for iniquity. More frequently attested synonyms for the term include offense/transgression and the *guilt* of iniquity.

[74] In the psalter, the expression also occurs in Pss 99:6; 105:1; 116:4, 13, 17.

[75] Pss 44:23, 78:65; Isa 42:13–16, 51:9–11.

[76] Artur Weiser, *The Psalms: A Commentary* (Philadelphia: Westminster, 1962), 73–74.

Fittingly, the confession's crescendo, Isa 64:6b, continues: "For you have hidden your face from us, and made us to melt because of our sins." God hiding God's face is well attested in the prophetic literature[77] and especially the psalms.[78] The psalms also speak of God's face revealed (Ps 17:15), and among the communal laments, Psalm 80 concludes with this image and equates it with salvation: "Restore us, O Lord, God of hosts. Let your face shine, that we may be saved." (80:19) Psalm 44's final section also speaks of God's hidden face, and does so amid repeated calls for God to rise up. Ps 44:24 reads: "Why do you hide your face, why do you forget our oppression and affliction?" While the verse visits the divine and human realms, it nowhere links God's absence to human sin. Not so Isaiah.

Isa 64:6bβ concludes: "You have made us melt by means of our iniquities." Our translation, with the second clause expressing agency, is most probable, over and against a different rendering of ביד based on an appeal to Ugaritic.[79] Another term at issue is MT's וַתְּמוּגֵנוּ, which we read as the contracted *polel* of מוג, the root for "melt."[80] "Melt" connotes moral dissipation elsewhere in the Hebrew Bible (Exod 15:15; Jer 49:23). Certain ancient translators, however, have rendered וַתְּמוּגֵנוּ differently. 1QIsa[a] reads a different root, מגר: "You have cast us into our iniquities."[81] Another ancient variant, "you have delivered us up," is obtained by emending MT and doubling the *nun* to reflect the root מנן. While "delivered us up" is found in the Old Greek translation,[82] "melt" remains superior on two counts. It has the advantage of *lectio difficilior* and makes the best sense contextually. That is, God's absence in 64:6bα is paralleled by the people's diminution, their moral melting away. Human iniquity is the root of this decline and as such provides the signature upon the confession Isa 64:4b–6.

Isa 64:8. In 64:8, the individual's vow of confidence, the theme of confession is sounded in now familiar words: "Be not excessively angry, Lord, and do not remember iniquity forever. Behold, consider, we all are your people." God is not to remember iniquity forever, and while the negative particle normally precedes the verb directly, here the temporal adverb intervenes to emphasize "forever."[83] If punishment must be prolonged, let it not be forever. Unlike 64:4b–6, this capsule confession involves no figures of speech or cultic

---

[77] Isa 8:17, 54:8; Jer 33:5; Ezek 39:23, 24, 29; Mic 3:4.

[78] Pss 13:2; 22:25; 27:9; 69:8; 88:15; 102:3; 143:7.

[79] As Mitchell Dahood has noted, the Ugaritic lexeme ביד can mean "because." He points to Jer 41:9 and Job 8:4 as biblical examples of this usage that he has identified in Ugaritic. "Hebrew-Ugaritic Lexicography I," *Biblica* 44 (1963): 301–02.

[80] *GKC* § 72cc.

[81] ותמגדנו ביד עוונינו While the root in question appears to be מגר, the text from Qumran reflects some confusion of the letters *dâlet* and *rêš*. Burrows, *The Dead Sea Scrolls of St. Mark's Monastery*, plate LI (np).

[82] LXX= παρέδωκας ἡμᾶς (מנן), "you have delivered us up because of our sins."

[83] Paul Joüon, T. Muraoka, *A Grammar of Biblical Hebrew* (Rome: Pontifical Biblical Institute, 1991 [1923]), 604.

jargon; it is a sanguine appeal that God consider God's people and requite iniquity with mercy, not anger.

The verse has been compared to the psalms of communal lament, especially Psalm 79,[84] which reads:

> Do not remember against us the iniquities of our ancestors; let your
>   compassion come speedily to meet us, for we are brought very low.
> Help us, O God of our salvation, for the glory of your name,
>   deliver us, and forgive our sins, for your name's sake. (Ps 79:8–9)

The psalm and the prayer from Isaiah both embellish lament with elements of confession, and this is their greatest similarity. Nonetheless, they have quite different perspectives on wrongdoing and God's redress of the same. The psalm recognizes iniquity but displaces it upon an earlier generation. It speaks of "our sin" but in a context of consolation, i.e. beholding God's face. The psalm invokes divine compassion and supposes that it may come speedily. The prayer, on the other hand, speaks only of God's anger ceasing and presumes no compassion. Moreover, the prayer forebodes an extensive penitence; the request that God not remember forever implies a dispensation that is not anon. In sum, the psalm recognizes sin but is quick to attenuate it while focusing on God's rescue of a people in duress. Isa 64:8 is less confident and situates the psalms' traditional language of lament in a different context. As the prayer takes seriously the penitential phrases that had been grafted onto the likes of Psalm 79, Isa 64:8 turns on the sober hope that God requite iniquity with mercy, not anger.

While Isa 63:7–64:11 exhibits parallels to other Isaian passages and to prophecy, the psalms appear to be of primary influence upon the prayer. Structurally, the prayer aligns with the psalms of communal lament by effecting the oracle of confidence and the call for vengeance, albeit in manners that are indirect, complex and not typical of the psalms. More straightforward is the prayer's replicating the core of the communal lament, which is lament/petition/motivational element. The motivational element in this prayer is the confession of sin, whose language echoes several psalms of communal lament. Study of the prayer's confession of sin (Isa 63:7–10, 64:4b–6, 64:8) has shown at least seven lexical correspondences to the psalms of communal lament.[85] While it is difficult to determine whether the correspondences are due to direct borrowing or the common usage of stock phrases in circulation, the continuity between the lament psalms and Isaiah's prayer remains noteworthy.

---

[84] A. S. Herbert, *The Book of Isaiah Chapters 40–66* (Cambridge: Cambridge University Press, 1975).

[85] The correspondences are based not on words alone but on the patterned associations of words. By contrast, a parallel text of penitence in Trito Isaiah, Isaiah 59:1–15, does not compare as positively with the psalms of communal lament and draws its confessional language primarily from the individual laments' descriptions of oppressors (59:5–8, 13–15a).

AN ANOMALOUS PSALM

By adopting expressions that are typical of psalmic penitence, the prayer underscores both the people as sinners and God as having departed their sinful realm.[86] Indeed, the larger prayer's two foci converge in its confessions of sin. God's distance from the people in travail is rendered an effect of human faithlessness to God's ways. It is in focused passages that this confluence is expressed.

No less important, however, are discontinuities that tend to be theological. In Isa 63:7–64:11 confession of sin is no token expression of emotional distress, as in several of the psalms of communal lament. Rather, this confession is seminal data whose importance is on a level with God's seeming to take leave of human history. As the exile has given fresh impetus to retribution theology generally, so this prayer has reconsidered sin and made it an illuminating dimension of human history; any given verse may be cast in light of what sin has wrought. Because this development involves contrast and nuance, it is not enough simply to designate the prayer as Deuteronomistic. As a development of the lament genre, the text demonstrates a distinct appropriation of Dtr theology in the milieu of the exile and its wake.

2.7 Deuteronomistic Theology

The study to follow prescinds from the thorny issues of who wrote the Deuteronomistic History, when the history was composed, and what significant redactions it underwent. The focus is upon developments in the theology of retribution at the time of the exile and thereafter. There is a systematic quality to these developments, as scholars have begun to show. Werline discusses how the Deuteronomic idea of repentance first enters prayer discourse at the time of the exile,[87] and Albertz interprets Exodus 32–34 as the work of Dtr "lay theologians" documenting how apostasy, as a metaphor for the exile, has made Israel's relationship with God newly problematic.[88] Certain post-exilic redactions of the prophets are both Deuteronomistic and indicative of Asaphite

---

[86] As both the prayer and the psalms are exploring the intersection of lament and confession, both situate confession in a context of the covenantal God no longer present to the human realm. God's presence and, especially, absence are stated in terms of the covenant (Isa 63:7,10; Pss 44:18, 89:34), the divine name (Isa 64:6a; Ps 79:9,6) and the divine countenance (Isa 64:6b; Pss 44:24, 80:19). Concomitant with this divine dispatch is human deceit (Isa 63:8; Ps 44:18), sin (Isa 64:4b; Pss 78:32, 79:9) and iniquity (Isa 64:5b,6b,8; Ps 79:8).

[87] Although Werline's study of the penitential terminology from Deuteronomy is helpful, he overreads this evidence and concludes that during and after the exile Deuteronomy was the only influence upon penitential prayer, to the exclusion of the psalms. *Penitential Prayer In Second Temple Judaism*, 25.

[88] Albertz, *A History of the Israelite Religion*, 475–76.

psalmody, as shown by Stephen Cook.[89] R. F. Person focuses on how Deuteronomic scribes may have supported the Persian policy regarding local cults in sixth- and fifth-century Judaea.[90] Finally, the books of Chronicles demonstrate a distinct shift in Deuteronomistic thinking on retribution that occurs later than the composition of Isa 63:7–64:11 but may have influenced the inclusion of "seek-find" language in the redactional Isa 65:1–2, as noted above (see footnote 37).

Studying Dtr influence in Isaiah involves an analysis of the terminology representative of this tradition. The analysis considers each of the prayer's sections individually and is keyed to terms having to do with wrongdoing and retribution while including all terms that in any way support Dtr thinking. To anticipate one conclusion, the terminological expressions will differentiate themselves in strata that correspond roughly to the pre-exilic, exilic and post-exilic periods. Establishing these strata is one goal of this chapter. The major goal is to read such historical designations back into the seven sections of Isa 63:7–64:11 and thereby add a temporal distinction to important theological developments observed with the confession of sin. Occasionally, the analysis will employ data other than terminology, such as the sequence of historical events and the comparative use of history.

63:7–14. Historical Recital Focused on God's Benevolence and Guidance: It was noted that unlike those psalms which recite large spans of history (Pss 68, 105, 106, 135, 136), the prayer in Trito Isaiah selects two events, crossing the Reed Sea and wandering in the wilderness, to embellish with commentary. It is significant that the prayer includes nothing of biblical history prior to the patriarchs (cf. Pss 29:3–10, 135:7, 136:1–9) or after the death of Moses (cf. Pss 68:11–31, 78:56–72, 89:3, 132:1–18).[91] To begin Israelite history with the patriarchs presupposes a redaction of pentateuchal material that predates P's final form of the five books, as it is keynoted by the creation theology in Genesis 1–11.[92] To conclude with Moses' death suppresses the conquest and signals to the Persian overlords that Jews have no designs on sovereignty.[93] Thus Isa 63:7–14 may be post-exilic and prior to P. Moreover, it appears Deuteronomistic in its choice of historical coordinates. Generalized evidence for this view includes the

---

[89] Cook has posited a connection between Dtr thought and the Asaphite psalms as part of his explanation of Mic 7:14–20, the book's epilogue, as a post-exilic composition. "Micah's Deuteronomistic Redaction and the Deuteronomists' Identity," pp. 216–231 in *Those Elusive Deuteronomists: the Phenomenon of Pan-Deuteronomism* (JSOTSup 268; ed. L. Schearing and S. McKenzie; Sheffield: Sheffield Academic Press, 1999); see also Cook's *Prophecy and Apocalypticism* (Minneapolis: Fortress, 1995).

[90] R. F. Person, *Second Zechariah and the Deuteronomic School* (JSOTSup 167; Sheffield: JSOT Press, 1993), 147–75.

[91] These historical parameters also affect Pss 44, 66, 74, 77, 78 (the first of two historical cycles, vv. 13–24), 105, 106 and 114.

[92] Albertz, *A History of the Israelite Religion*, 472.

[93] Ibid., 473.

sequence where God delivers the chosen people (vv. 7b–9), Israel turns against God (v. 10a), and God responds in kind (v. 10b).[94] The sequence pivots on retribution theology as derived from the type of Dtr thought that is typified in Judg 2:11–23. More exact evidence is to be derived from the terminology in Isa 63:7–14.

The prayer begins by recalling God's praises (תְּהִלֹּת יְהוָה), a Deuteronomic term (Deut 26:19) that typically appears in the phrase "a name, a praise and a glory."[95] The phrase recurs twice in the Dtr level of Jeremiah (13:11, 33:9), and in both cases תהלה becomes associated with sin and rebellion, either directly (13:11) or indirectly (33:8–9). In this vein, Isa 63:7 proceeds to evoke a covenantal context in which God's faithfulness contrasts with the people's deceit.[96] To magnify the contrast, there follow allusions to other Dtr passages that highlight the root גמל, to be translated "requite." Thus, God's requiting Israel with great goodness runs counter to Israel's dealing corruptly with God, as in the Song of Moses, where a faithful God is requited (גמל) with corruption (Deut 32:5–6). Moreover, Deut 32:6 extols God as "your father who created, made and established you," much like the paternal references to God in Isa 63:16 and 64:7. The recurrence of these paternal references and of גמל in both Isa 63:7–64:11 and the Song of Moses (Deut 32:6) reflects a vein of (Judahite) family piety that was integrated into Yahwistic piety during and after the exile by the Dtr movement.[97]

Further proof of the familial pattern is found in "He lifted them up and carried them" (Isa 63:9), a phrase using the very connotations of the root נשא that are employed in the Song of Moses (Deut 32:11) and two other Dtr passages that rehearse God's providential care (Exod 19:4, Deut 1:31).[98] One of the two, Deut 1:31, compares God's bearing the people in the wilderness to a man bearing his son, intimating family piety and providing a parallel to Isa 63:9b, about God's lifting up and carrying the people. Although the connection between this section and the ethos of family piety fostered by the Deuteronomic movement is not necessarily exclusive, no other discernible context – including the psalms of communal lament – accounts for so much of the theological

---

[94] The same type of sequence occurs twice in Psalm 78; vv. 12–32 and 44–55 employ a sequence of miracle, sin, divine anger, and punishment. See Clifford, "In Zion and David a New Beginning: An Interpretation of Psalm 78," 129.

[95] The phrase appears in Moshe Weinfeld's catalog of Deuteronomic and Dtr terminology. See his *Deuteronomy and the Deuteronomic School* (Oxford: Oxford University Press, 1972), 328.

[96] Regarding the covenantal nuances of Isa 63:7, see n. 56.

[97] Previously, Yahwistic piety had revolved around the temple, monarchy and land, all of which were greatly compromised with the fall of Judah in 587 B.C.E. R. Albertz, *A History of the Israelite Religion,* 400.

[98] The Dtr character of Exod 19:4–6a is demonstrated by Joseph Blenkinsopp, "The Narrative in Genesis-Numbers: A Test Case," pp. 84–115 in *Those Elusive Deuteronomists,* 87–89.

terminology found here. This section was either composed or significantly reworked along the lines of Dtr familial piety some time after the exile at a point contemporary with the initial stages of pentateuchal redaction.

63:15–19a. Lament: Abandoned and dispossessed of their sanctuary (63:18), the people join in lament. They consider their wrongdoing (63:17a) and ask God to relate to them as redeemer (גְּאָלֵנוּ) and, especially, father (אָבִינוּ). The appellations imply the familial piety promoted in Dtr circles after the exile and discussed above. The people's self-identification, however, points to an earlier period. They are "servants" (עֲבָדֶיךָ: 63:17b) understood as those who serve the LORD by diurnal devotions. Moshe Weinfeld notes that in the Deuteronomic literature, this sense of the root עבד is always accompanied by other devotional expressions, such as "fearing the Lord."[99] Thus, in Isa 63:17, the reference to servants is preceded directly by a reference to "fear of you" (i.e. the LORD). Of itself, "fearing the LORD" has a generic, Deuteronomic resonance (Deut 4:10; 5:26; 6:2,13,24; 8:6; 10:12,20; 13:5; 14:23; 17:19; 28:58; 31:12,13), as is does its parallel in 63:17, "(erring from) your ways" (Deut 9:12,16; 11:28; 31:29).

More precisely, the verb in Isa 63:17a, "to cause to err," תעה in *hif'il*, is typical of the classical prophets (Isa 3:12, 9:15; Hos 4:12; Amos 2:4; Mic 3:5) and does not imply an exilic or post-exilic context. Similarly, God's zeal (קִנְאָה: 63:15) is a theologoumenon of the (pre-exilic) "Yahweh-alone prophets," whose use of the term connoted divine love, jealousy, power and determination to reward and punish (cf. Deut 4:26, 5:9, 6:15).[100] Because the term passed on to the Deuteronomic school and anchored its theological system during and after the exile (Deut 32:16, 21b; Exod 34:14), the situation is a bit unclear. It is possible but not necessary to relate 63:15 to the pre-exilic prophets. A pre-exilic setting might further explain the perplexing 63:18a, "For a short while your holy people had possession [of your sanctuary]." Inasmuch as the Josianic reform flourished for a relatively brief period of time,[101] 620–609 B.C.E., its oversight of the temple was short-lived and may be the basis behind this expression, although the evidence for this is largely circumstantial. One may conclude that the lament's predominant echoes are to those prophets who represent an early stratum of Deuteronomic theology,[102] whereas Isa 63:16,17b indicate a selective hand which has brought the lament up to date with its contemporary, post-exilic milieu.

---

[99] Weinfeld, *Deuteronomy and the Deuteronomic School*, 332.

[100] Morton Smith, *Palestinian Parties and Politics that Shaped the Old Testament* (London: SCM, 1987 [1981]), 39.

[101] Ibid.

[102] Yaira Amit provides a discussion of Deuteronomic discourse in the early part of the seventh century. Her point of reference is the Book of Judges, whose Deuteronomic phrasing is not, in her opinion, secondary. Amit holds that Deuteronomic phrasing originated in Judges and subsequently influenced the Deuteronomic movement. *The Book of Judges: The Art of Editing* (Leiden/Boston/Cologne: Brill, 1999), 364–75.

63:19b–64:4a. Call for an Epiphany: As this section is based upon the Sinai theophany (Exod 19:16–25), a general sense of when the Sinai traditions became included in accounts of God's acts on behalf of Israel helps to set the *terminus a quo* of the section. A key to this task will be the section's one Deuteronomic expression, "terrible things" (נוֹרָאוֹת) in 64:2 (cf. Deut 10:21; 2 Sam 7:23). In von Rad's view, Sinai traditions became a part of Israel's historical accounts sometime after the scripture's pre-literary phase, and the blending won popular approval only at the time of the exile or later.[103] Indicative of this development is that as often as נוֹרָאוֹת is associated with significant historical events such as the Exodus (Deut 10:21; 2 Sam 7:23) or the Taking of the Land (Ps 106:22), it is never descriptive of God's actions upon Sinai. Isa 64:2 departs from this pattern: "When you do awesome deeds that we do not expect, you come down, the mountains tremble before you." This verse and probably this section thus postdate the inclusion of the Sinai traditions among Israel's historical traditions and appear to be post-exilic. Theologically, there are no significant Dtr influences upon this section.

64:4b–6. Confession of Sin: An admission of sin (64:4b) keynotes this section, and the context is that of God's anger, קצף. Albertz highlights the term's Dtr parallel in Deut 1:34–35, part of the same stratum used above to interpret Isa 63:9.[104] In fact, the root studied earlier, נשא, recurs later in this confession of sins (64:5). The common vocabulary indicates a basis of comparison to be probed further. This portion of Deuteronomy (1:19–40) recounts the people's refusing to enter and possess the land of the Anakim, as told earlier in Num 14:11–25b. Both pentateuchal accounts, according to Albertz, are Deuteronomistic from the tradition's post-exilic lay theologians.[105] Are these tradents also responsible for Isa 64:4b–6?

The evidence does not support such a finding. The Isaian confession never extols God's mercy or asks for forgiveness (cf. Num 14:17–19); it ruminates on the multiple effects of sin. Whereas Moses' confession elicits from God an immediate assurance of forgiveness (Num 14:19), the prayer in Trito-Isaiah lacks such assurance. The prayer has no oracle of salvation, and the confession 64:4b–6 concludes with God hiding God's face. While God's hiding/revealing

---

[103] Cf. Gerhard von Rad, "The Form-Critical Problem of the Hexateuch," pp. 1–78 in *The Problem of the Hexateuch and Other Essays* (New York: McGraw-Hill, 1966), 53–54. Von Rad's position presupposed the now outdated view that the Bible's first six books form a Hexateuch whose structure corresponds to that of short, credal speeches found in the context of worship. A lasting contribution of hexateuchal scholarship has been the discovery that the Sinai traditions were originally discrete from the credal traditions. This fact has led scholars in recent years to speculate about the type of theme or tradition that the Sinai narratives represented in antiquity. See G. W. Coats, "Hexateuch," *The HarperCollins Bible Dictionary* (San Francisco: HarperSanFrancisco, 1996), 420.

[104] Albertz, *A History of the Israelite Religion*, 627.

[105] Ibid.

God's face typically relates to one's prospects for salvation, here as in the later portions of Deuteronomy it carries retributive force as a concomitant of God's anger (Deut 31:17,18; 32:20). Thus, while this confession's language is comparable to Dtr material redacted into the Pentateuch, its penitential theology is less didactic and probably predates that of Albertz's post-exilic, lay theologians. It would be wrong, however, to characterize this section as theologically immature in light of the extensive material that it has culled and transformed from the psalms of communal lament (Pss 44:24; 78:32, 39; 79:9b; 80:19).

64:7–8. The Individual's Vow of Confidence: It was noted above that the paternal reference in 64:7 reflects a vein of (Judahite) family piety which the Dtr movement integrated into Yahwistic piety during and after the exile. In 64:8, the penitential expression קצף is merely a catchword from the previous section (cf. 64:5), and the petition "remember not our iniquities" has been adopted from Ps 79:8, as discussed above. Nothing in this section otherwise distinguishes its Dtr character.

64:9–10. A Distinct Lament over Jerusalem: The destruction of the holy city, Zion/Jerusalem, corresponds well with a dating of the prayer to 587 B.C.E. or sometime thereafter. The description, as noted above, is similar to that of Isa 1:7. It is furthermore important that the Temple is characterized not as a sacrificial cult but as the locus of general worship used by the ancestors (אֲשֶׁר הִלְלוּךָ אֲבֹתֵינוּ). The perspective may be characterized as Deuteronomistic,[106] and it suggests that this section predates the Pentateuch's priestly redaction in the post-exilic era.

64:11. Conclusion: Asking whether the LORD will keep absent and silent so as further to oppress the people, this signature to the prayer echoes 63:15, 62:2 and 65:6. The one expression not internal to Trito Isaiah, "will you afflict us?" (וּתְעַנֵּנוּ) involves a use of language typified in Deuteronomic (Deut 8:2–3,16) and Dtr (1 Kgs 11:39) contexts. There, God tests the people for two reasons, to prove their faith and to purify them so that in the end God might "do them good" (Deut 8:16). The second, didactic function is lacking, however, in Isa 64:11. In this verse the testing is received as affliction with no didactic dimension. It carries the sense of "batter": "Your anger is heavy upon me, and all your waves batter me" (Ps 88:8). In this case, the prayer's Dtr language sloughs off any positive connotation in order to emphasize the divine-human rupture at the center of the lament.

Analysis indicates three strata of Dtr terminology correlating roughly to the pre-exilic, exilic and post-exilic periods. First, a Deuteronomic stratum not later than the seventh century is found in the first lament, Isa 63:15–19a. A later mode of familial piety in 63:16,17b suggests these verses are secondary. The other lament, Isa 64:9–10, corresponds to the second stratum, from the sixth century,

---

[106] Ibid., 476. Weinfeld notes that with the shift from pre-deuteronomic literature to Deuteronomic literature, expressions of cultic worship were transformed for devotional worship not dependent on a cult. *Deuteronomy and the Deuteronomic School,* 332.

which is Deuteronomistic. This stratum reflects the trauma of the exile and it is typified by the confession of sin (64:4b–6). Also in this stratum is the individual's vow of confidence (64:7–8) as marked by the increasingly pronounced (familial) piety of the time. As well, the prayer's conclusion (64:11) corresponds to this stratum. Third, a Dtr stratum that is clearly post-exilic lies behind the historical section (63:7–14) and the call for an epiphany (63:19b–64:4a). While the former continues to reflect familial piety, both sections include language otherwise conspicuous of pentateuchal formation.

One may conjecture that the prayer is composed around a lament from the seventh century or earlier (63:15–19a); the composition, dating from the mid to late sixth century, is extant in the form of a confession, an individual's vow of confidence, a contemporary lament and conclusion (64:4b–11). Not long thereafter, a historical section (63:7–14) and a call for epiphany (63:19b–64:4a) were either added or substantially revised from the prayer's initial form. Analysis supports dating the prayer to the sixth century with select parts more representative of the centuries prior and subsequent.

2.8 Conclusion: *Sitz im Leben*

The foregoing analysis confirms the prayer's post-exilic character and undermines the view that it is pre-exilic. Although it is a minority position, at least one scholar has dated the entire lament to the eighth century B.C.E. Supposing that the primary context of Trito Isaiah is theological rather than historical, John Oswalt holds that "the prophet himself" is responsible for Isa 56–66, which describe the marks of divine grace that come upon those who internalize the law and enter into intimate relationship with God.[107] Oswalt's concern for theological unity in the Book of Isaiah leads him to dismiss as inchoate the historical evidence in Isa 56–66. The problem, he claims, is that one finds evidence of pre-exilic, exilic and post-exilic composition.[108] Such diversity, it has been shown, is reflected especially in 63:7–64:11. With this lament, a complex history of composition does not compromise its theological integrity. The prayer's theological core reflects a critical appropriation of the psalms of communal lament by pious Jews in Israel's homeland shortly after the exile.

The analysis here also challenges the position that the lament is a sectarian work. Paul Hanson has interpreted the positive references to Moses (Isa 63:11–12) as the attempt to champion a group of Levites over a certain group of Zadokites, who have assumed the monikers "Abraham" and "Israel" (63:16) and expelled their rivals from the temple (63:18).[109] The critique of Hanson[110] must now include two additional points. Beyond the Levites, Moses is a key figure for

---

[107] Oswalt, *The Book of Isaiah Chapters 40–66*, 452–53.
[108] Ibid., n. 24.
[109] *The Dawn of Apocalyptic*, 98.
[110] While Hanson has made an important contribution to the study of post-exilic Judah, his position has been disputed by H. G. M. Williamson and others (see n. 17).

the Dtr writers whose partiality to Sinai as a *topos* has influenced the lament (63:19b–64:4a). Also, it is simpler to argue that dismay over the patriarchs reflects discontinuity with the past. That is, after the promises of the monarchy, temple and land have failed, any sort of religion *cum traditione* involving the patriarchs has become dubious[111] while the religion of the day is oriented toward a personal relationship with God.

Moreover, the prayer's language is mainstream, not marginal. It has been seen that each of the prayer's theologically significant statements is representative of prevailing currents in Dtr thought, and the most notable literary influence upon the prayer is the psalms of communal lament, hardly sectarian literature. Indeed, as has been maintained from the outset, the prayer is for and by "all of us," the host of Jews in the homeland during and after the exile. This determination also mitigates against the view that prayer comes from Samarians polemicizing against the Jerusalemites who have barred the northerners from the temple project (Ezra 4:1–2).[112]

If one is to describe the "group" behind this prayer, the outstanding trait is that they are theologically resourceful in combining piety with rigorous theological reflection. That is, the prayer adopts the desire for direct relationship with God (63:16, 64:7) as a concomitant to its investigation of sin and sin's effects, namely God's perceived absence. The prayer allows no cheap grace, but its elements of popular piety serve as blind hope in a God who is otherwise remote. The clearest example of this is the juxtaposition of the individual's vow of confidence and the confession of sins. The vow's paternal language attenuates the theological pessimism of the confession.

The changes in tone (64:6 to 64:7, also 63:19a to 63:19b) and in grammar (specifically, shifts in person in 63:7)[113] further indicate that at least this section of the composition may have been subject to antiphonal recitation by a group in cultic worship (63:18,64:5,11). It is not implausible that sections of Isa 63:7–64:11 were used in cult as a communal lament by Judeans who thought themselves to be post-exilic Israel. Elliger locates just such a group of penitent sinners at the time of the prophets Haggai and Zechariah, when the Second Temple was built (see footnote 45). He credits the group with Isa 63:7–64:11,

---

[111] The phenomenon is reflected in *b. Šabb.* 89b, where God tells Abraham and Jacob that the people have sinned against him. While God is hoping the patriarchs will seek mercy on the people's behalf, they propose that God wipe out the population. Eventually Isaac argues that God spare the people whom God has called his "children."

[112] In the view of Achtemeier, the authors are disenfranchised Levites with northern roots such that "this prayer fairly reeks with northern, Mushite, Deuteronomic-Levitic-Jeremianic tradition." *The Community and Message of Isaiah 56–66,* 118. Her position draws on that of Hanson and an earlier line of scholarship attributing Isa 63:7–64:11 to a sixth-century Samarian prophet, as in Laurence E. Brown, *Early Judaism* (Cambridge: Cambridge University Press, 1929) 70–112.

[113] Tone and grammar are among the criteria for judging the liturgical quality of texts in Trito-Isaiah. See Blenkinsopp, *A History of Prophecy in Israel,* 218.

and there is at least one striking parallel between the lament and the prophecy of Haggai.[114] It is difficult to say more about this group, save that its profile coincides with the pre-priestly lay theologians whom Albertz associates with the Dtr school during and after the exile. At least during the sixth century, there is no reason this group could not comprise returnees *and* families not deported (cf. Ezra 6:21). In this view, not all those who had remained in the land were syncretists and some based their belief squarely upon "the earlier prophets and the other ancient Israelite traditions."[115]

---

[114] Hag 2:10–19, the third of the prophet's messages, is dated 18 December 520. An exchange between the prophet and priests in 2:13–14 focuses on uncleanness. After the priests rule that uncleanness is more contagious than holiness and may be passed on to the third degree (2:13), Haggai responds, "So is this people, and so is this nation before me, declares Yahweh, and so is every work of their hands, and what they offer *there* is unclean." (2:14) Cultic ritual has been used figuratively to bring into focus the people's sinfulness, in the view of David Hildebrand, who argues that the fundamental issue of the passage is repentance ("Temple Ritual: Paradigm for Moral Holiness in Haggai 2:10–19," *VT* 34 [1989]: 165, 168). In just this manner, the confession of sins in the Isaian lament uses the terminology of ritual holiness to address ethical holiness: "We have all become like the unclean person, and all our righteous deeds like a soiled garment." The idea central to both texts is טמא, "unclean." A single milieu has shaped both the confession of sins and Haggai's third message. Hag 2:13–14 illuminates Isa 64:5b inasmuch as both come from non-priests who use cultic terminology to counsel ethical holiness. This exact an explanation of Isa 64:5b has been heretofore unavailable.

[115] Berquist, *Judaism in Persia's Shadow*, 74.

3

EZRA 9:6–15—LAW AND LITURGY

3.1 Text

9:6 I said, "Oh my God, I am too ashamed and disgraced to lift my face to you, my God, for our iniquities have risen over our heads and our guilt is great unto the heavens. 9:7 From the days of our ancestors unto this day, we are in great guilt, and on account of our iniquities we, our kings, and our priests have been given over to the kings of the lands, over to the sword, to captivity, plunder and shamefacedness, as is the case today. 9:8 But now, for a little moment, favor has been shown by the LORD our God, leaving us a remnant and giving us a stake in his holy place, in order for God to brighten our eyes and give us a little respite in our subjugation. 9:9 For we are subjects, but our God has not forsaken us in our subjugation; (God) has extended to us his steadfast love before the kings of Persia, to give us a respite for rebuilding the house of our God, for repairing its ruins and for giving us a fence in Judah and Jerusalem. 9:10 And now, our God, what shall we say after this, for we have forsaken your commandments 9:11 which you commanded by your servants the prophets saying, "The land which you are entering to possess is a land unclean from the contaminations of the land's peoples and from their abominations, (it is a land) which they have filled from one end to the other with their impurity. 9:12 Therefore, do not give your daughters to their sons in marriage, nor take their daughters for your sons, and you should never seek their peace and prosperity, in order that you may be strong and eat the good things of the land and leave it as an inheritance to your children forever." 9:13 And after all that has come upon us for our evil deeds and our great guilt—although you our God have punished us less than our iniquities deserve and have given us a remnant such as this— 9:14 shall we again break your commandments and intermarry with the peoples who practice these abominations? Would you not be angry with us to the point of denying any survivor or remnant?

9:15 O LORD, God of Israel, you are just, for we remain a remnant today. We now are before you in our guilt, for it is impossible to stand before you on account of this.

3.2 Text-Critical Issues and Notes

Our translation takes into account the three principal texts extant from antiquity; there are two Greek versions (Esdras A, B) as well as the Hebrew and Aramaic text of Ezra (MT). MT has been fairly well transmitted, especially the prayer of Ezra 9:6–15. Apparently the Masoretes went so far as to anticipate text-critical problems and indicated solutions, as with the difficult adverbial phrase of 9:6, "have risen *over our heads*."[1] The fragments from Qumran (4QEzra) verify that MT "has been very faithfully preserved from one of the plural forms of the text which circulated in the Second Temple period."[2] The high text-critical quality of MT commends it as the basis of the present study, and the textual tradition that it represents may through 4QEzra be dated to the first century B.C.E. Esdras B or 2 Esdras is a literal translation of the Hebrew and Aramaic text of Ezra.[3] Differences between the two texts are minimal, and Wilhelm Rudolph cites 25 variants in which Esdras B is preferable to MT; none of these occurs in Ezra 9:6–15.[4] The other Greek version, Esdras A, includes the material in Ezra as well as parts of 2 Chronicles (chapters 35–36) and Nehemiah (7:72–8:12).[5] Because Esdras A is the basis for *Jewish Antiquities* XI.1.1–5.5, which Josephus wrote late in the first century C.E., its *terminus ad quem* is secure. Its *terminus a quo* is less certain, and thus its precise relationship to MT has been debated with regard to dating and other issues.

---

[1] Because of haplography, MT reads: "have become many over a head." Rather than למעלה ראש, it should read למעלה מעל הראש (cf. 2 Chr 34:4). Perhaps to indicate the latter reading, the Masoretes have put an anomalous *dagesh* in the *resh*. H. G. M. Williamson, *Ezra, Nehemiah* (WBC 16; Waco: Word Books, 1985), 126.

[2] Eugene Ulrich, "Ezra and Qoheleth in Manuscripts from Qumran," pp. 139–57 in *Priests, Prophets and Scribes: Essays on the Formation and Heritage of Second Temple Judaism in Honour of Joseph Blenkinsopp* (ed. E. Ulrich et al.; JSOTSup 149; Sheffield: Sheffield Academic Press, 1992), 153. This article contains a preliminary edition of 4QEzra, which is available in *Discoveries in the Judaean Desert* 16 (ed. E. Ulrich et al.; Oxford: Clarendon Press, 2000), 291–93. The MS contains a small portion of the biblical book (4:2–6, 9–11; 5:17–6:5) excluding the prayer 9:6–15.

[3] Within the text of Esdras B, important variations between the codices Vaticanus (LXX^B) and Alexandrinus (LXX^A) are to be noted. *Esdrae liber II* (ed. R. Hanhart; Göttingen: Vandenhoeck & Ruprecht, 1993).

[4] Rudolph, *Esra und Nehemia samt 3 Esra*, xx.

[5] 1 Esdras also contains narrative material (3:1–5:6) not found in MT. *Esdrae liber I* (ed. R. Hanhart; Göttingen: Vandenhoeck & Ruprecht, 1974).

It has been argued that Esdras A represents a text type earlier than that of MT,[6] and that in certain cases Esdras A provides a superior reading (although this claim does not extend to Ezra 9:6–15).[7] On the other hand, a case has been made that Esdras A derives from MT because, among other things, MT's chronology of events is reflected in the Greek version with signs that the latter's author "tried to correct the chronology of the canonical Ezra" when he perceived flaws in its ordering of events.[8] A mediating position is that of Eugene Ulrich, who speculates that 1 Esdras may be a variant edition of MT Ezra in this sense: It is "a new version altogether, though dependent on its predecessor."[9] On the authority of the views and evidence presented, we assume the priority of the Hebrew and Aramaic Ezra, and we employ it as the basis of translating and discussing Ezra 9:6–15. At the same time, we note well the discrepancies among the three texts and those attested in other ancient versions.[10]

When Esdras B is compared to MT, there is one omission and six one-to-one variants; Esdras A shows four omissions, three additions and seven variants. Certain of these variants may be highlighted for their theological significance. "Remnant" (פְּלֵיטָה MT 9:8,13,14) occurs in Greek as "root" (ἡ ῥίζα, 1 Esdr 8:75,84,85,86) and "salvation" (ἡ σωτηρία, Esdras B 9:8,13). The temple's "ruins" (חָרְבֹתָיו MT 9:9) appear as "desert" (τὴν ἔρημον 1 Esdr 8:78, τὰ ἔρημα Esdras B 9:9), and "just" (צַדִּיק MT 9:15) appears as "true" (ἀληθινὸς, 1 Esdr 8:86). The implications of these and other variants are incorporated in this chapter's discussions. The following chart reproduces the text-critical data in full.

---

[6] Frank Moore Cross, "A Reconstruction of the Judean Restoration," *JBL* 94 (1975): 7–8.

[7] Rudolph, *Esra und Nehemia,* xvi.

[8] Blenkinsopp observes the misguided attempt in Esdras A to impose a linear chronology on events in Ezra 4 (MT). He further argues that Esdras A is not excerpted from a version of Chronicles-Ezra-Nehemiah earlier than MT on two points: Esdras A's narrative is clear and complete, while Nehemiah's absence at the public reading of the law (1 Esd 9:49; Neh 8:9) is due to internal reasons. *Ezra-Nehemiah: A Commentary,* 71.

[9] Ulrich, "Ezra and Qoheleth in Manuscripts from Qumran," 156.

[10] Although the Vulgate follows MT, it often diverges from both it and the Greek versions. The Syriac follows the Hebrew and Aramaic text closely while providing a number of variants that result from interpretation rather than the presence of another text tradition. See Myers, *Ezra, Nehemiah,* lxvi–ii.

TABLE 4

OMISSIONS (>), ADDITIONS (+) AND VARIANTS (=) OF EZRA 9:6–15 IN THE PRINCIPAL ANCIENT TEXTS

(No symbol preceding an entry indicates agreement with MT)

V.	MT	Esdras A	Esdras B	Vulgate
9:6	להרים	>	τοῦ ὑψῶσαι	
9:7	ובעונתינו	+ καὶ τῶν πατέρων	ἐν ταῖς ἀνομίαις ἡμῶν	
9:7	אנחנו	+ σὺν τοῖς ἀδελφοῖς ἡμῶν	ἡμεῖς	
9:7	כהנינו	ἱερεῦσιν	= οἱ υἱοὶ ἡμῶν	
9:8	להשאיר לנו פליטה	= καταλειφθῆναι ἡμῖν ῥίζαν καὶ ὄνομα	= τοῦ καταλιπεῖν ἡμῖν εἰς σωτηρίαν	= dimitterentur nobis reliquiae
9:8	ולתת לנו יתד	>	καὶ δοῦναι ἡμῖν στήριγμα	
9:9	את חרבתיו	= τὴν ἔρημον Σιων	= τὰ ἔρημα αὐτῆς	= solitudines eius
9:10	ועתה	καὶ νῦν	>	
9:11	עבדיך	= τῶν παίδων	δούλων σου	
9:11	בטמאתם	>	ἐν ἀκαθαρσίαις αὐτῶν	
9:12	וטובתם	>	καὶ ἀγαθὸν αὐτῶν	
9:13	פליטה	= ῥίζαν	= σωτηρίαν	= salutem
9:14	ולהתחתן	= τὸ ἐπιμιγῆναι	ἐπιγαμβρεῦσαι	
9:14	שארית ופליטה	= ῥίζαν καὶ σπέρμα καὶ ὄνομα	= ἐγκατάλειμμα καὶ διασῳζόμενον	
9:15	צדיק	= ἀληθινὸς	δίκαιος	iustus
9:15	פליטה	= ῥίζαν	= διασῳζόμενοι	= salvaremur

3.3 The Context of Ezra 9–10

For reasons discussed in chapter one, Ezra's mission is dated to 458 B.C.E., and it is four months after his arrival in Jerusalem that he becomes involved in a conflict over intermarriage. The conflict is described in Ezra 9–10. Certain officials (הַשָּׂרִים) among the returned exiles (hereafter, the golah community[11]) are chagrined that in Judah there are Jews married to non-Jews. The intermarriage is described in Deuteronomic terms as a transgression of the law and as disobedience to the prophets (9:10–11). Moreover, the foreign women are said to practice abominations (הַתּוֹעֵבוֹת—9:1,14), a term that is drawn from the Levitical codes against impurity.[12] Thus, the ensuing move to exclude foreign spouses is essentially an attempt to purify and safeguard the entire golah community from a religious standpoint, and to do so on legal grounds.[13]

The "people of Israel and the priests and the Levites" (9:1) constitute the accused, who later are listed individually in Ezra 10:18–44.[14] The gravest offenders are officials and prefects (9:2), elites who would be most likely to contract cross cultural marriages.[15] The officials bringing the charges find sympathizers in an obscure group known as "those who tremble at the word of God" (כֹּל חָרֵד בְּדִבְרֵי אֱלֹהֵי יִשְׂרָאֵל 9:4,10:3; cf. Isa 66:2,5). Also prominent in the campaign are Ezra along with Shecaniah (10:2–4) and others (10:15). Ezra's group prevails inasmuch as a procedure for sending away foreign wives and their

---

[11] Returnees from the exile fell in league with certain Judeans who had remained in the land. Together they formed a temple-based polity, the so-called golah (גולה) community under Persian auspices. See Joseph Blenkinsopp, "Temple and Society in Achaemenid Judah," pp. 22–53 in *Second Temple Studies 1 Persian Period* (ed. D. J. A. Clines; Sheffield: JSOT Press, 1991), 53.

[12] On the Levitical code, see Lev 18:24–30. To comprehend better the foreign wives' impurity, see the biblical accounts of Solomon's wives (1 Kgs 11:1–8) and Jezebel (1 Kgs 16:31–32). In both cases, the foreign wives' impurity is taken to be the cause of syncretistic phenomena entering into Yahwism.

[13] Such policy was not unprecedented in the provinces of the Achaemenid Empire. The Udjahorresnet inscription, an Egyptian text from the early years of the reign of Darius I, describes the expulsion of all foreigners from the sanctuary of Neith in order that it be restored to its former splendor. Specifically, the foreigners and their unclean things were removed so that the sanctuary could be cleansed and sacrifice be resumed. The text has been published by A. Tulli, "Il Naoforo Vaticano," *Miscellanea Gregoriana* (Rome: Tipografia Poliglotta Vaticana, 1941), 211–80.

[14] Lester Grabbe suggests that friction between a priestly bloc and "Ezra's faction" may underlie the campaign against intermarriage in Ezra 9–10. Ezra 9:1, however, indicates that the campaign targets clerics and non-clerics alike. See his *Judaism from Cyrus to Hadrian* (Minneapolis: Fortress, 1992), 137.

[15] This view is asserted by E. Lipinski: "The privileged Jewish classes in Jerusalem ... contracted exogamous marriages not only with the so-called 'foreign women' issued from the 'people of the land,' but also with the women from Ashdod, Ammon and Moab (Neh 13:23)." "Marriage and Divorce in the Judaism of the Persian Period," *Transeu* 4 (1991): 64.

children is set in motion. In most cases, however, divorce would have involved financial disruptions, and one is rightly dubious of the campaign's ultimate success.[16] It is especially difficult to reconcile greater insularity with Judaism's subsequent expansion, which would require a burgeoning population base.[17]

So as better to understand what Ezra confronted, it is helpful to review the contemporary *realia* of marriage and marriage preferences. From Elephantine come Jewish marriage contracts dating to the fifth century. They indicate that the ritual involved the bridegroom requesting that the bride be given to him, declaring solemnly that the woman is his wife, paying a brideprice or *mohar* to the head of the bride's family, and drawing up a marriage contract.[18] The golah community may well have had similar practices, especially with regard to the marriage contract. Malachi, written in fifth century Palestine, refers to "the wife of the contract,"[19] identified earlier in the verse (Mal 2:14) as "the wife of your youth." She represents a first wife whom a husband would need to divorce before marrying a "daughter of a foreign god (Mal 2:11)." Such divorce is a faithless act (Mal 2:15–16). While marriage at the time was not considered indissoluble, Mal 2:10–16 condemns capriciously divorcing the wife of one's youth to pursue a foreign marriage. As Malachi defends the Jewish wife's well-being, it warns against a foreign wife bringing the husband to compromise his worship of Yahweh (2:11). This decidedly religious warning from Malachi is echoed in various texts, including Ezra.[20] Ezra 9–10 opposes the intrusion of

---

[16] According to two contemporary Jewish marriage contracts from Elephantine, the wife has a right of immediate return of her considerable dowry in the case of divorce. The citations, B2.6:26 and B3.8:24, are contained in Bezalel Porten and Ada Yardeni, *Textbook of Aramaic Documents from Ancient Egypt, 2. Contracts* (Jerusalem: Hebrew University, 1989), 30, 78.

[17] A. Lemaire, "Populations et territoires de Palestine à l'époque perse," *Transeu* 3 (1990): 43–45.

[18] Lipinski, "Marriage and Divorce," 65–68.

[19] Many commentators hold that the Hebrew ברית refers exclusively to the covenant indicated in Mal 2:10, which is not a marriage contract but the agreement by which the fathers, acting on behalf of their ancestors, agree not to intermarry. Our view, that Mal 2:14 refers to the marriage contract with the wife of one's youth, has support in Roland de Vaux, *Ancient Israel* (2 vols.; New York: McGraw Hill, 1965), 1:33. Moreover, the pact in Mal 2:14 parallels the marriage contract (ברית) between Laban and Jacob, that the latter be married only to Leah and Rachel and see to their well-being (Gen 31:43–50). In the texts from Malachi and Genesis, God is witness (עד) to the covenant and is invoked to safeguard the marriage.

[20] George Nickelsburg has identified a literary tradition critical of the Jerusalem temple and/or priesthood and stretching "from at least the time of Malachi until the turn of the era." The tradition, he argues, is discernible in the books of Malachi, Ezra, and the pseudepigraphic 1 Enoch. Nickelsburg establishes marked comparisons between the guilty watchers in 1 Enoch and the priestly officials introduced in Ezra 9:1,2: both parties defile themselves through relations with women not of their group, both parties ask a "scribe" (cf. 1 Enoch 12:3–4 and Ezra 9:6) to intercede for them, and both of these intercessions evoke the prayer of confession (1 Enoch 13:4–5 and Ezra 9:6). *1 Enoch 1:*

foreign wives promoting cultic abominations. In light of the foreign wives' religious proclivities, Ezra 10:3 calls for their expulsion through channels of divorce.

In advocating divorce from foreign spouses, however, the author of Ezra 9:1–10:19 faces a challenge. There is no clear precedent in the Torah for the expulsion of foreign wives and their children, the action proposed and ratified in 10:3–5. The Torah and indeed the Hebrew Bible appear both to tolerate intermarriage (Gen 41:45; Num 12:1–8; Ruth 1:4; 2 Sam 3:3) and to sanction its termination (Gen 21:10–14; Num 25:1–18); there is no unambiguous warrant for what occurs in Ezra 9–10. To resolve the problem, the author turns to Deut 7:1–3 and exegetes the verses so as to generate a legal argument. The verses state that with the taking of the land, the Israelites are not to intermarry or otherwise make covenant with the seven nations whom God has dispossessed on their behalf. The prohibition of intermarriage is itself no warrant for the forced divorce of foreign spouses, but it may become so through exegesis.

The instruction of Deut 7:1–3 is recalled several times in Ezra and Nehemiah (Ezra 9:1,11–12; Neh 13:25). One of these cases is critical to our study. In Ezra 9:1, four of the groups with whom Israelites may not marry (Deut 7:1–3) are listed with two foreign nations barred from entering the assembly of the LORD (Deut 23:3–6). Thus, the later sanction, exclusion, is applied to the earlier offence, intermarrying with people of the land. So that Ezra's community may fully accept the new formulation, additional support is adduced when the collective of foreign peoples (Ezra 9:1) is accused of "abominations" (Ezra 9:11,14). The term refers to the Levitical codes against impurity and abominations, which are to be punished by cutting off from the community anyone whom the land has not first vomited out (Lev 18:26–29). In short, Ezra addresses the problem of precedent with "an intentional exegetical attempt to extend older pentateuchal provisions to new times."[21]

As events unfold, the author's exegetical achievement is enhanced through its articulation. Using ritual and rhetoric, Ezra rails against intermarriage while making a confession of sin that is public and communal (9:6–15). In praying on behalf of the golah community, Ezra functions as the spiritual leader of all those who fear God, in contrast to Nehemiah, who later addresses an intermarriage

---

A Commentary on the Book of 1 Enoch, Chapters 1–36;81–108 (Hermeneia; Minneapolis: Fortress, 2001), 230. Roughly contemporary with 1 Enoch, Ben Sira (LXX 44:16) refers to Enoch as a model of repentance to all generations (ὑπόδειγμα μετανοίας ταῖς γενεαῖς).

[21] Fishbane, *Biblical Interpretation in Ancient Israel*, 116. Fishbane is correct in that this exegetical sequence is not attested before Ezra; however, the uniqueness of the exegesis in Ezra 9 need not be overstated. Later, the author of Jubilees will combine legislation against consuming blood with the penalty of being uprooted from the land (*Jub.* 6:12, 14). Betsy Halpern-Amaru observes: "Thus, we have concepts and commandments associated with the particular Israelite land covenant inserted into the context of the cosmic Noah covenant ...." *Rewriting the Bible,* 28.

situation on his own.[22] Ezra's penitential prayer shows a clear structure with sections marked by expressions such as "and now" (ועתה—9:8,10,12). This chapter's goals are to study the prayer as the golah community's spiritual response to the historical situation, and to articulate the relationship of the prayer to its legal and literary context, Ezra 9–10. This will be done through investigations of the prayer's form, content and authorship.

3.4 Form-Critical Inventory of Ezra 9:6–15

Although Ezra 9:6–15 is clearly a written work that is cast in prose, it has a degree of oral character by virtue of its social setting. The social setting is very public and suggests that orality along with literacy form a complex background to the text, whose composition occurs at a decisive moment in Jewish history toward a more literate society. Along the continuum between orality and literacy in post-exilic Judah, the prayer remains at least partially in what Susan Niditch calls "the world of orality."[23] When the prayer begins, the speaker is Ezra, but after one verse there is a change from first-person singular to plural. The change, in Ezra 9:7, is intended to show that a solidarity of guilt binds together the speaker and all of his contemporaries while it reaches back to their ancestors.[24] Under judgment for their sins, the people as a whole remain in exilic-like conditions and offer a prayer in five parts.

The first part, an invocation (9:6), is penitential in tone; there follows a somber illustration from history (9:7–9); a citation from scripture constitutes the third part (9:10–12); a petition or plea is then directed toward the hearers (9:13–14); and a final statement is designed to motivate God to respond to the prayer. There is scant resemblance between the prayer's form and that of the psalms of communal lament, whose form-critical core comprises lament/petition to God/statement of motive (see table 2 in chapter 2). Nor is there strong correspondence with any of scripture's traditional *Gattungen*, and this is not surprising. Because the *Gattungen* are delineated rather precisely according to one or two primary features, texts lacking these features are said not to conform to the type.[25] Moreover, as genres the *Gattungen* tend to disintegrate with the

---

[22] This observation is elaborated by Antonius H. J. Gunneweg, *Esra* (KAT 19.1; Stuttgart: Gerd Mohn, 1985), 163.

[23] Niditch consistently locates Israel on the oral end of the continuum between orality and literacy. The sense in which Niditch uses the term "world of orality" in reference to Ezra's public oration in Nehemiah 8 seems also to apply to Ezra 9. See her *Oral World and Written Word* (Louisville: Westminster John Knox Press, 1996), 104–5.

[24] It is self-evident that the shift to second-person intends to establish solidarity; that it is a solidarity based upon common guilt is the view of Williamson, *Ezra, Nehemiah*, 134.

[25] In his critique of Gunkel, Andreas Szörényi implies that psalms said to belong to a given *Gattung* are more dissimilar than Gunkel would have one believe: "Die einzelnen Psalmen zeigen dann die Eigentümlichkeiten ihrer literarischen Gattung; darum ist es auch nicht zu wundern, wenn sie einander ähnlich sind." *Psalmen und Kult im Alten*

passage of time, which means that form-critical procedures do not work in the same way. The challenge remains, however, to explain how the text of Ezra 9:6–15 is internally organized.

After outlining the prayer's structure in a manner similar to that above, F. C. Fensham concludes, "Confession of sin stands in the center of the whole prayer."[26] His view is shared by H. G. M. Williamson, who adds that the prayer's confessions of sin contain hortatory elements, "as though Ezra were very conscious of the audience who surrounded him."[27] The language of sin is highlighted at the prayer's beginning and end (9:6–7,15) and is in fact distributed copiously throughout the prayer. Ezra 9:6a is an individual confession of sins, followed by 9:6b–7 as a communal confession of sins. Both confess iniquities (עֲוֹנֹתֵינוּ) and guilt (וְאַשְׁמָתֵנוּ). Ezra 9:10–12 is a specific confession of sins with reference to intermarriage, by which the people have forsaken God's commandments (עָזַבְנוּ מִצְוֹתֶיךָ). In 9:13 they refer to their evil deeds (בְּמַעֲשֵׂינוּ הָרָעִים) and great guilt (וּבְאַשְׁמָתֵנוּ הַגְּדֹלָה). Ezra 9:15 provides a concluding admission of guilt. Indeed, the confession of sin is a hallmark of this prayer and serviceable grounds for comparison with the psalms of communal lament, whose language of sin and wrongdoing raises the question of the divine-human relationship.

3.5 Form-Critical Inquiry I: Ezra 9:6–15 and the Communal Laments

We have observed that the form-critical likeness between Ezra 9:6–15 and the psalms of communal lament is less than striking. The latter's form-critical repertoire includes only two elements that are also attested in Ezra 9:6–15.[28] One observes an address (9:6) and, arguably, a statement of motive (either in 9:8–9 or 9:15). Significantly, the central element of a lament, the petition to God, is lacking in Ezra 9:6–15, which instead issues its hearers a plea not to intermarry (9:14). As the prayer incorporates a relatively small proportion of communal laments' form-critical repertoire, the commentaries differentiate the prayer from the psalms, if they link the two at all.[29] Rather, the prayer in Ezra, especially 9:10–14, is said to be oriented to Torah and its exegesis.[30] The prayer's

---

Testament: Zur Formgeschichte der Psalmen (Budapest: Sankt Stefans Gesellschaft, 1961), 111.

[26] Fensham, *The Books of Ezra and Nehemiah*, 128.

[27] Williamson, *Ezra, Nehemiah*, 128.

[28] To recall the form-critical pattern identified by Mowinckel: address, lament, request, statement of motive, vow, and confidence of being heard. *The Psalms in Israel's Worship*, 1:193–219.

[29] Blenkinsopp, *Ezra-Nehemiah: A Commentary*, 181; Williamson, *Ezra, Nehemiah*, 129.

[30] Indicating a historical dimension, Fishbane holds that Ezra's prayer reflects the worship of Israel during its exile in Babylonia, when the basis of worship became the reading and studying of Torah under Levitical guidance. See his *Biblical Interpretation in Ancient Israel*, 113. While the evidence for this conclusion is only circumstantial, a

relationship to Torah, however, does not rule out *a priori* significant points of contact with the communal and individual psalms of lament. In fact there are six lexical parallels to consider.

(1) *Ezra 9:6a.* "I am ashamed and disgraced" (וְנִכְלַמְתִּי , בֹּשְׁתִּי). The translation reflects the most typical meaning of each word,[31] although it is important to note that by the time of Ezra the root כלם has gained a specific meaning in cultic penitential rites. 2 Chr 30:15 reports that when the Passover lamb was sacrificed, the priests and Levites *were ashamed*, sanctified themselves and brought burnt offerings to the temple. The two verbs coupled in Ezra 9:6 are said to be a cultic formula, but it is uncertain whether the language is historical and represents an actual liturgy.[32] When the compound expression is applied in more general contexts, the one speaking is typically in lament (Jer 14:4; 31:19; Pss 35:4, 26; 71:13; 109:29). The most exact parallel is between Ezra 9:6a and Ps 44:16:

כָּל הַיּוֹם כְּלִמָּתִי נֶגְדִּי
וּבֹשֶׁת פָּנַי כִּסָּתְנִי׃

Translation: "All day my disgrace is before me, and shamefacedness has covered me." The psalm employs the roots' nominal forms rather than finite verbs, but otherwise the expressions are grammatically parallel (first person singular) and both speak of shamefacedness. Ps 44:16 is unmatched as a parallel to Ezra 9:6a.

It is important to note not simply that Psalm 44 is a communal lament, but, as noted in the previous chapter, that echoes of 44:10–20 are found in another post-exilic confession of sins, Isa 63:7–10. Ps 44:18, which insists the people have not been false to the covenant, is echoed in Isa 63:8 only to be contradicted two verses later, when the people are said to rebel and grieve God's holy spirit. In Isaiah the psalm's protestation of innocence is inverted and recast as a confession of sin. Echoing the same psalm, Ezra 9:6 likewise takes an expression of lament and reverses its theology. While the psalm attempts to trace the people's travail back to God (44:23), Ezra, in solidarity with the people, *is* guilty and acknowledges his shame and disgrace. Furthermore, Ezra's prayer exonerates and indeed glorifies God as just in the events God oversees (9:15).

---

newfound emphasis on the study of Torah can be observed more generally in scripture contemporary with the book of Ezra, such as the post-exilic redactions of Josh 1:8, Ps 1:2 and Isa 59:21. All three texts refer to Torah study and reflect "a later Jewish ideal incorporated ... in the Hebrew Bible ... at one of the final stages of the compilation of the Canon." Alexander Rofé, "The Piety of the Torah-Disciples at the Winding-Up of the Hebrew Bible: Josh 1:8; Ps 1:2; Isa 59:21," pp. 78–85 in *Bibel in jüdischer und christlicher Tradition: Festschrift für Johann Maier* (ed. H. Merklein et al.; Athenüms Monografien Theologie 88; Frankfurt: Hain, 1993), 80–81.

[31] *BDB* 954, 3637.
[32] S. Wagner, "כלם," *TDOT* 7:194.

Because Ezra's prayer compounds the people's guilt with God's righteousness, its reversal of lament theology is more thoroughgoing than that of Isa 63:7–10.

(2) *Ezra 9:6b*. "Our iniquities have risen over our heads, and our guilt is great unto the heavens" (עֲוֹנֹתֵינוּ , וְאַשְׁמָתֵנוּ). As with the previous expression, two words form a *zeugma* to attain a particular meaning. Iniquity coupled with guilt leaves a person overwhelmed by iniquity's "oppressive burden," i.e. what actually transpires within iniquity.[33] This is seen in the daunting portrayal of sin's height and breadth found in Ezra 9:6b–7.[34] The core of the sinner's experience is the sense of "being confronted by God."[35]

At this point in time the term עָוֺן or "iniquity" is being newly attested in genres such as the confession of sins. An example of this phenomenon is Ezra 9:6b, which mentions both iniquity and guilt. Conversely, Ps 69:6 mentions only guilt yet provides a parallel to Ezra 9:6b:

אֱלֹהִים אַתָּה יָדַעְתָּ לְאִוַּלְתִּי
וְאַשְׁמוֹתַי מִמְּךָ לֹא נִכְחָדוּ׃

Translation: "O God, you know my folly, and my guilt is not hidden from you." The guilt of which Ezra speaks in 9:6b in connection with the golah community's mixed marriages is incurred principally through evil deeds (Ezra 9:13) and through folly, as this source text indicates.[36] Psalm 69, a lament of the individual, thus offers commentary on the verbs in Ezra 9:6b.

The strongest correspondence to iniquity-and-guilt is found in the law of trespass against *sancta* (Lev 22:14–16). Lev 22:16a speaks of the "iniquity of guilt":

וְהִשִּׂיאוּ אוֹתָם עֲוֺן אַשְׁמָה בְּאָכְלָם אֶת־קָדְשֵׁיהֶם

Translation: "They cause them to bear the iniquity of guilt by eating their sacred offerings." The iniquity of guilt is what a person must bear if another person defiles the sanctified gifts that the first has brought to God. This particular sanction enjoys some creative application within the Hebrew Bible. For example, Jer 2:3 explains that because Israel was holy to the Lord as is a first harvest, its

---

[33] R. Knierim, "עָוֺן," *TLOT* 2:865–66.

[34] Gunneweg proposes that the combination of two motifs, solidarity in sin and sin as something with almost objective dimensions, is fundamental to the entire prayer. "Das Motiv der Solidarität in der Schuld und das Verständnis der Schuld als einer fast objektiven Größe, die über den Kopf hinauswachsen kann und den Himmel um Rache schreit, gehören zusammen und sind überhaupt eine der Grundvoraussetzungen der ganzen Konzeption." *Esra*, 165.

[35] Knierim, *TLOT* 2:865–66. The phenomenon of being confronted by God in one's guilt is similarly important to the Isaian psalm of lament discussed in the previous chapter (cf. n. 67 of chapter 2).

[36] D. Kellerman, "אשם," *TDOT* 1:437.

destruction by foreign enemies was punished, with the guilty suffering evil.[37] How might Lev 22:16a be applied to the golah community? Consider that a Jew marrying a foreigner so compromises the community that it is as if one person had defiled another's sacred offering. The transgression results in iniquity and guilt upon the party making the offering, which in this case is the entire golah community whose solidarity in guilt extends even to Ezra. A means of expiation appears in Ezra 10:19, the instruction that violators bring a guilt offering, אשם, to atone for their intermarriage, a veritable desecration of the holy seed of Israel.[38] A second corrective, forcible divorce, is exegetically derived from a separate portion of the Pentateuch, the Deuteronomic law code.

(3) *Ezra 9:8.* "To brighten our eyes" (לְהָאִיר עֵינֵינוּ). The verse describes God's favor in four parallel infinitives, the third being "to brighten" our eyes. In the Hebrew Bible, this is not a common way to describe God's favor, and there are only two possible parallels. It is unlikely that the prayer alludes to the brightened eyes of Jonathan after Saul's son has eaten honey and unwittingly contradicted his father's oath that no soldier take food before battle (1 Sam 14:27,29). A more likely parallel occurs in Psalm 13, a lament of the individual. While making petition, the subject asks God to brighten his eyes lest he sleep unto death (13:4b):

הָאִירָה עֵינַי פֶּן אִישַׁן הַמָּוֶת:

A response to the plea comes shortly in 13:5–6, where God's steadfast love and salvation are extended to the subject as a recompense. If this lament has influenced Ezra 9:8, there has been little if any theological adaptation. Rather, it is a matter of transferring an expression from a psalm of lament to the prayer.

(4) *Ezra 9:9.* "Our God has not forsaken us" (לֹא עֲזָבָנוּ אֱלֹהֵינוּ). When Ezra claims that despite the community's subjugation, God has not abandoned the

---

[37] According to Fishbane, Jer 2:3 "reassembles all the technical terms [of Lev 22:14–16] but reuses them in an idiosyncratic, exegetical manner. Indeed, in Jeremiah's rhetoric the various terms take on a figurative, even metaphorical, aspect." *Biblical Interpretation in Ancient Israel,* 302.

[38] The interpretation involves two matters that are not explicit in the Bible but clearly important to Ezra's understanding. First, nowhere is Israel said to be a thing holy in the cultic sense, a sacred seed whose admixture with foreigners is מעל (Ezra 9:2). Rather, Ezra makes this association by extending Deuteronomy's view of Israel as a holy people (7:6; 14:2, 21; 26:19; 28:9) to a new sphere of reference. In doing this he is probably aware of Jer 2:3. Second, the Bible does not teach that all intermarriage is a serious violation such that blood is adulterated and atonement required, including that guilty spouses be sent away. Again, Ezra has drawn upon Deuteronomic and related concepts in order to interpret and forge policy for the complex question of intermarriage. Ezra's process, in the view of Jacob Milgrom, is not especially original and follows the "aggadic midrash" of Jer 2:3. "Ezra's innovation consists in taking a theological concept and a prophetic image and weaving them into a midrash." Jacob Milgrom, *Leviticus 1–16* (AB 3; New York: Doubleday, 1991), 359.

community, it brings to mind two biblical points of view. The psalms affirm that God does not forsake the righteous (Ps 37:25), and this view is typically expressed in psalms of trust (Pss 9:11; 16:10) that may also involve lament. An example is Ps 22:2, "My God, my God, why have you forsaken me?" On the other hand, 1 and 2 Chronicles indicate that God *does* forsake those who forsake God (1 Chr 28:9; 2 Chr 12:5, 15:2, 24:20). That Israel has not been forsaken is understood by the prayer's author as an example of God's freedom to bypass the law of retribution and to favor those who do not deserve it. In effect, the prayer employs a viewpoint from the psalms of trust to nuance the type of retribution theology found in Chronicles. In turn, the prayer amends psalmic thinking such that sometimes even the less than righteous are not abandoned by God. In this case, Ezra's words have no clear dependence upon a lament such as Ps 22:2, but it is quite possible that the composer considered the psalms' view of forsakenness.

(5) *Ezra 9:9.* "Giving us a fence in Judah and Jerusalem" (גָּדֵר). Most scholars read the reference to a boundary metaphorically since nowhere in the scriptures does this word refer to an actual city wall, with the possible exception of Mic 7:11. The word, rather, suggests the protective boundary erected around a vineyard, as in Num 22:24, Isa 5:5, Ps 80:13, and Prov 24:31. This view finds support from jar handles from Gibeon stamped with גדר.[39] In Ezra's context, the reference is to action by the Persian authorities to protect Judah from its surrounding enemies.

The historical context emphasizes that agents of God protect the province against threat from without. The most proximate biblical references are Isa 5:5 and Ps 80:13, where God or God's agent removes a wall that had been protecting a vineyard, and the vineyard is destroyed.[40] The action is undertaken for no apparent reason save God's capriciousness. When Ezra's God supplies rather than removes the wall for protection, it emphasizes that the people's distress is due not to God's whim, but to something else—their own wrongdoing. The scenario in Ezra 9:7–9 is the negative image of Ps 80:8–16. In that psalm of communal lament, God's people, in the image of a vine, flourish for a time but suffer as if its wall were breached (80:8–16). Later, Ps 80:17–19 resumes a positive tone and closes, "Restore us, let your face shine, that we may be saved." The psalm's guardedly optimistic tone parallels that of Ezra 9:6–15 while the dark interlude about the vine (80:8–16) recalls the prayer's several confessions of sin.

(6) *Ezra 9:13.* "You our God have punished us less than our iniquity deserves" (חָשַׂכְתָּ לְמַטָּה מֵעֲוֹנֵנוּ). Although somewhat opaque, this phrase asserts that in the economy of retribution, God has devalued the people's iniquity. As in

---

[39] James B. Pritchard, *Hebrew Inscriptions and Stamps from Gibeon* (Philadelphia: University of Pennsylvania, 1959), 9–10.

[40] While Isa 5:5 indicates a structure of grassy briar or of rocks, the reference in Ps 80:13 is purely metaphorical and thus more germane to Ezra 9:9. Andrés Fernández, "La Voz גדר en Esd. 9:9," *Biblica* 16 (1935): 82–83.

9:9, the prayer bases divine retribution on something other than the principles operative in Chronicles. The prayer's view of the matter is that the suffering of the exile was considerably less than what Israel's sins deserved. The formulation is like that of Ps 78:50: "God did not spare them [the Egyptians] from death." The verb (חשׂך) is identical in both texts, but the usages are different in that God attenuates none of the Egyptians' guilt and spares them no punishment.

In conclusion, Ezra 9:6–15 shows six points of contact with the lament psalms, communal and individual. When one considers the psalms of lament most generally, there is lexical convergence distributed evenly in the prayer, except for 9:10–13, a legal section. This evidence challenges the views of the commentaries, which tend to distance the prayer from the psalms, if they link the two at all. Like many of the commentators, Samuel Balentine dissociates Ezra 9:6–15 from the communal laments because, in his view, its focus on God effaces the community and its situation.[41] He adds that because the prayer contains no protestation of innocence but instead emphasizes confession of sin, it is a transformation of lament.[42] Balentine is correct that the prayer is a transformation of lament, but because he does not study Ezra 9:6–15 in detail, he does not articulate the exact relationship between the prayer and the communal laments.

The prayer appropriates lament in two ways. Sometimes an expression is transferred directly, without exegetical modification, as with "our God has brightened our eyes," Ezra 9:8 from Ps 13:4b. More often Ezra's prayer employs an expression and recalibrates the implicit levels of guilt. In a departure from Ps 44:16, Ezra, in solidarity with the people, *is* guilty and acknowledges his shame and disgrace (Ezra 9:6a). Later in the prayer Ezra alludes to Psalm 80 but focuses on the pessimistic interlude about the vine (80:8–16), so as to reinforce the prayer's various confessions of sin. On the other hand, when the image of a wall appears in Ezra's prayer (9:9), it is a vehicle for Ezra to exonerate God, who rather than exposing the golah community continues its protection through Persian oversight. God treats the people well despite their great guilt, a paradigm opposite that of the psalms of communal lament, where an ostensibly blameless people are nonetheless abandoned by their God.[43]

To achieve the change in paradigms, Ezra's prayer focuses blame away from God, onto the people. The specific means to this end is the repeated confession of sin, which occurs four times in the course of the prayer. Ezra 9:6a is an

---

[41] Samuel Balentine, *Prayer in the Hebrew Bible: The Drama of Divine-Human Dialogue* (OBT; Minneapolis: Augsburg Fortress, 1993), 90–91.

[42] Ibid., 117.

[43] In their differing views of God, both the lament psalms and the prayer entertain a certain indeterminacy about God. The psalms presume a remote God but, paradoxically, often conclude with the assurance of being heard. On the other hand, Ezra 9:6–15 appears to present an immanent God who devalues the people's iniquity while protecting them from foreign threat (9:9,13), but in fact these favors serve only to magnify the community's ingratitude should it continue to intermarry against God's law.

individual confession of sins, followed by 9:6b–7 as a communal confession of sins. Ezra 9:10–12 is a specific confession of sins with reference to intermarriage, and 9:15 provides a concluding admission of guilt. This predominance is not accidental, as David J. A. Clines observes:

> This prayer [is] simply a confession of sin and not a prayer of forgiveness; the gravity of Israel's sin, which has called into question its whole existence as the people of God, must not be minimized by too ready an appeal to the divine mercy (cf. Neh 9:32–37).[44]

Suppressing all petition for forgiveness, the prayer revolves around the confession of sin. The several admissions of guilt support the text's larger strategy, which is to take leave of the psalms of lament while retaining and reversing their basic categories: sin, guilt and divine response. It is a case of "counterstatement" understood as "antithetic relations within a genre."[45]

Although the prayer of Ezra 9:6–15 has six lexical parallels to the lament psalms, it is not patterning itself upon this genre univocally or exclusively. Indeed there is at least one other genre to consider before achieving an adequate form-critical inventory of Ezra 9:6–15. The Levitical sermon has been treated by Gerhard von Rad and, more recently, Rex Mason, who has designated a corpus of 32 such addresses in the books of Chronicles.[46] Three speeches in particular, by kings David, Jehoshaphat and Hezekiah (1 Chr 28:2–10; 2 Chr 19:6–7,9–11; 29:5–11), parallel Ezra 9:6–15 thematically[47] while corresponding to the prayer form-critically. The similarities, discernible with a cursory reading of the texts, warrant a thorough form-critical study of the relationship between Ezra 9:6–15 and the Levitical sermon.

---

[44] Clines, *Ezra, Nehemiah, Esther*, 122. Fensham similarly observes that confession of sin "stands in the center of the whole prayer." *The Books of Ezra and Nehemiah,* 128.

[45] Fowler, *Kinds of Literature,* 174–75.

[46] Before von Rad, numerous scholars contributed to the hypothesis that before the exile there arose a form of Deuteronomic preaching that subsequently extended to the post-exilic period, when it served as a model for speeches in 1 and 2 Chronicles. This scholarship is reviewed by Dietmar Mathias in his "'Levitische Predigt' und Deuteronomismus," *ZAW* 96 (1984) 23–24. The most often cited treatment of the matter has been von Rad's essay "The Levitical Sermon in I and II Chronicles." Von Rad's essay does not delineate the sermon's formal structure, which is provided by Rex Mason, who identifies eight elements and indicates their relative importance. See his *Preaching the Tradition: Homily and Hermeneutics after the Exile Based on 'Addresses' in Chronicles, the 'Speeches' in the Books of Ezra and Nehemiah and the Post-Exilic Prophetic Books* (Cambridge: Cambridge University Press, 1990), 137–42.

[47] For example, 2 Chr 19:7 asserts the justice of God (cf. Ezra 9:15) and 2 Chr 29:6–9 is a historical recital of the fathers' unfaithfulness (cf. Ezra 9:7).

3.6 Form-Critical Inquiry II: Ezra 9:6–15 and the Levitical Sermon

Von Rad observes four features of the Levitical sermon: (1) its form-critical pattern is roughly that of doctrine-application-exhortation; (2) it justifies its demands by invoking Deuteronomy and a number of other "ancient scriptural texts of acknowledged authority"; (3) the sermon carries "immediate relevance to the contemporary situation"; and (4) after the exile the Levitical sermon falls into desuetude, especially in terms of points two and three.[48] In the post-exilic phase, von Rad maintains, citing authoritative sources merely compensates for the preacher's diminished authority, and the content of the sermon is "less relevant to the historical setting than one might have wished."[49] In our study, the fourth point will not have bearing because it is historically suspect, arising as it does from the opinion that Israelite religion declined after the exile with its emphasis shifting from prophecy to law.[50]

In many respects Ezra 9:6–15 fits von Rad's profile of the Levitical sermon. First, it contains the three elements of doctrine (9:11–12), application (9:6b–7) and exhortation (9:13–14). Second, the doctrine involves the exegesis of ancient legal precedents. The most prominent of these are Deut 7:1–3 and 23:3–6, but also included are Lev 18:24–30 and 22:16a (cf. above). On the third point, however, scholars have questioned the historicity of von Rad's *Sitz im Leben*, as based on a putative Levitical preacher.[51] Thus, the prayer's actual correspondence to a historical setting must be argued rather than asserted. The work of Otto Plöger[52] speaks to this issue by showing how the prayer in Ezra

---

[48] "The Levitical Sermon," 271–74.

[49] Ibid., 278.

[50] In his conclusion, von Rad's bias comes forth as he damns with faint praise. He states that post-exilic, cultic Judaism was not wholly decadent inasmuch as these sermons could have acquiesced into moral legalism but instead attempted to retrieve strains of classical prophecy. Ibid., 280.

[51] Von Rad's work on the Levitical sermon has led John Van Seters to question this and other "oral" forms such as etiologies, cult legends, anecdotes, and novellas. He is especially dubious of texts dependent upon a set motif such as C's preaching Levite. Van Seters notes that writers such as Herodotus at times used such forms and motifs to fabricate material that served their own literary purposes, and he presumes that biblical writers may have done the same. As a result, he holds that "identifying a genre does not tell us anything about its 'original' *Sitz im Leben* or the process of transmission of a particular story or narrative unit. In spite of its form, it may have existed only in literature." Van Seters does not cite Ezra 9:6–15, but his criticism is directed at this sort of text. See his *In Search of History: Historiography in the Ancient World and the Origins of Biblical History* (New Haven/London: Yale University Press, 1983), 48–49.

[52] Plöger holds that the author of Chronicles composed Ezra 9:6–15. In the article cited here, Plöger's thesis is that C is influenced by Deuteronomic discourse more than by the Priestly writings, despite C's liturgical affinities with the latter. Thus Plöger's orientation to Ezra 9:6–15 is essentially that which von Rad took vis-à-vis the Levitical

9:6–15 may reflect the golah community's vicissitudes and hopes.[53] Furthermore, Plöger offers insight into the prayer's composition with respect to the contemporary milieu of prayer.[54] In the end, however, Plöger overstates the prayer's level of hope, which is undercut by *four* confessions of sin, and thus his attempt to locate the prayer historically begs the question of its own accuracy. Indeed *Sitz im Leben* and historical context remain the achilles heel of claims for the Levitical sermon.[55]

The lacuna in von Rad's work, a form-critical inventory of the Levitical sermon, is remedied by Mason, who in identifying eight elements indicates the prevalence of each: specific address, call for attention, prophetic formula, appeal to or citation of scripture/illustration from history, encouragement formula, inversion or word-play, closing rhetorical question.[56] Six of these eight elements may be identified in Ezra 9:6–15.

(1) *Ezra 9:6a. Specific Address:* "Oh my God" (אֱלֹהַי). To begin the prayer, God is twice addressed in the vocative as "my God." The phrasing is typical of this prayer (9:6,8,9,10), in contrast to the address "God of Israel" elsewhere in the book of Ezra (9:4,15; also 1:3; 3:2; 4:1,3,6,21; 5:1; 6:14,22; 7:6,15; 8:25).

(2) *Ezra 9:6b. Call for Attention:* "I am too ashamed and disgraced to lift my face to you, my God" (בֹּשְׁתִּי וְנִכְלַמְתִּי לְהָרִים אֱלֹהַי פָּנַי אֵלֶיךָ). The prayer in fact subverts the convention by presenting reasons for God *not* to pay attention to Ezra. The protestation is merely an effect, however, as Ezra presumes that he has God's attention in the verses that follow.

---

sermon. *Reden und Gebet im deuteronomistischen und chronistischen Geschichtswerk*, 35–49.

[53] Plöger focuses on 9:15 as the prayer's signature verse: "O LORD, God of Israel, you are just, for we remain a remnant today. We are now before you in our guilt, for it is impossible to stand before you on account of this." Plöger asserts that the verse is a clear reference to mixed marriages as a practice which could violate the integrity of the remnant that is the true Israel. Plöger allusively links 9:15 to Ezra 10:2, which addresses mixed marriages explicitly. Both verses yoke a frank admission of guilt or faithlessness to a declaration of hope. Optimism and hope (*Hoffnung*), Plöger adds, remain available to the community throughout the dark events precisely because the community has availed itself of sincere prayer and the honorable confession of its sin. Because of the community's prayer, Plöger holds, God causes it to succeed. Ibid., 48.

[54] Plöger proposes that as speech material (*Reden*) became available to the author, he would frame it with material drawn from the milieu of prayer (*Gebet*). For Plöger, the prayer in Ezra 9:6–15 is a window on post-exilic Jewish theology. Ibid., 45.

[55] Mason's proposal that the Levitical sermon reflects a *Sitz im Leben* of the early Second Temple sermon has met with skepticism. Marc Z. Brettler critiques the proposal as conjectural and rather circular while concluding, "[The Second Temple sermon's] existence is quite tenuous indeed." "A 'Literary Sermon' in Deuteronomy 4," pp. 33–50 in *A Wise and Discerning Mind: Essays in Honor of Burke O. Long* (BJS 325; ed. R. Culley and S. Olyan; Providence, R.I.: Brown Judaic Studies, 2000), 40.

[56] *Preaching the Tradition*, 137–42.

(3) *Ezra 9:7. Illustration from History:* "From the days of our ancestors unto this day, we are in great guilt, and on account of our iniquities we, our kings, and our priests have been given over to the kings of the lands" (מִימֵי אֲבֹתֵינוּ אֲנַחְנוּ בְּאַשְׁמָה גְדֹלָה עַד הַיּוֹם הַזֶּה וּבַעֲוֹנֹתֵינוּ נִתַּנּוּ אֲנַחְנוּ מְלָכֵינוּ כֹהֲנֵינוּ בְּיַד מַלְכֵי הָאֲרָצוֹת). In 9:6b, Ezra's shame and disgrace are attributed to "*our* iniquities and great guilt." That is, a sense of communal guilt is introduced so that Ezra may fully identify with the golah community. In the complementary v. 7, guilt and iniquity constitute the horizontal sweep of Israelite history, beginning with the patriarchs. Thus Ezra identifies with the first people under God and the golah community, sinners all.

(4) *Ezra 9:12. Encouragement Formula:* "Be strong and eat the good things of the land" (תֶּחֶזְקוּ וַאֲכַלְתֶּם אֶת טוּב הָאָרֶץ). In Fishbane's analysis, "be strong" is an old military exhortation formula that was subject to innovation in the exilic and post-exilic writings.[57] For example, the expression becomes synonymous with observing Torah through Josh 1:5–9. The meaning of "be strong" in Ezra 9:12 will be elaborated below in our section on authorship.

(5) *Ezra 9:9–11. Play on Words:* "subjugation-forsake // forsake-servants" (וּבְעַבְדֻתֵנוּ לֹא עֲזָבָנוּ אֱלֹהֵינוּ // כִּי עָזַבְנוּ מִצְוֹתֶיךָ אֲשֶׁר צִוִּיתָ בְּיַד עֲבָדֶיךָ). The prayer quips that while God has not forsaken "us" in our subjugation, "we" have forsaken God's commandments given through the prophets, who are God's subjects or servants. The contrast is reinforced through word play with the roots עבד and עזב, as they are ordered chiastically. The word pair also enjoys the sort of sound similarity that can support thematic motifs.

(6) *Ezra 9:14. Closing Rhetorical Question:* "Shall we again break your commandments and intermarry?" (הֲנָשׁוּב לְהָפֵר מִצְוֹתֶיךָ וּלְהִתְחַתֵּן). To the rhetorical question, "Shall we again break your commandments and intermarry with the peoples who practice these abominations?" the answer clearly is to be "no," based on God's devaluing or making "less" the people's iniquity and leaving them a remnant (9:13). Anything short of full compliance, however, portends God's anger (cf. Ezra 5:12) leading to the destruction of even the remnant.

The six formal correspondences between Ezra 9:6–15 and the Levitical sermon strongly suggest that the prayer has a relationship to the genre. The relationship is integral inasmuch as the six correspondences are distributed evenly across the prayer. Furthermore, a sophistication evident in the call for attention (9:6a) and the play on words (9:9,11) indicates that the author had facility in the use of conventions related to the form. Nonetheless, the mere presence of a large percentage of form-critical features does not translate into a generic determination. In the case of Ezra 9:6–15, if the Levitical sermon is the intended form or genre, its conventions should be means to realizing the prayer's *raison d'être*, penitential piety expressed primarily through the confession of

---

[57] Fishbane discusses "be strong" and other exhortations in "'The Sign' in the Hebrew Bible," *Shenaton* 1 (1975): 217–19.

sin.[58] However, the confession of sin is prominent in the prayer (9:6a,6b–7,10–12,15) but nowhere accounted for in the sermon's generic schema. Form and function are ill matched. Thus it would be skewed to list Ezra 9:6–15 among the Levitical sermons or at least to do so unconditionally.

3.7 Form-Critical Determination: Ezra 9:6–15 a Mixed Genre

The prayer in Ezra 9:6–15 has form-critical relationships to the psalms of communal lament and the Levitical sermon. It is a faithful approximation of the Levitical sermon inasmuch as it satisfies von Rad's three criteria of the genre while displaying six of the eight generic features that Mason posits. The prayer's relationship to the lament psalms is more complex with a recurrent confession of sin laying new emphasis on the issue of human guilt. The prayer may thus be described as a transformation of the lament genre that is based on the formal elements of the Levitical sermon. In formal terms, the prayer approximates the mixed genre as defined by Gunkel.[59]

Specifically, Gunkel describes compositions that arise from the complaint songs but also express thoughts not associated with the genre.[60] His primary example is Lamentations 3, which begins with a broad complaint (3:1–18) but follows with comforting ideas in the form of petitions (3:19–20) or assertions of confidence (3:21–24). The composition also includes concepts from wisdom poetry (3:26–41). In its final 20 verses, Lamentations 3 revisits the communal and individual complaint songs as they express elements such as the confession of sin (3:42).

In a similar manner, the prayer in Ezra 9:6–15 is oriented to the laments but has included elements from a secondary genre, the Levitical sermon. It is moot to attempt to prove that Ezra 9:6–15 is a mixed genre in the exact manner of Lamentations 3. While the latter text sheds light on the former, we are dealing with two generic recombinations that do not fall easily into fixed patterns and are essentially *sui generis*. On the other hand, literary theory may help us to describe the intersection of lament and sermon in Ezra 9:6–15. Fowler's discussion of the "generic mixture" is here relevant, as are the remarks of Rolf Knierim on mixed genres as a window on history.

Knierim maintains that in the historical process of a society, "There is an inherent dialectic between the communication of the typical and communication of the changing expectations of society."[61] In tracing the critical debate on generic mixtures from Renaissance to contemporary times, Fowler arrives at a

---

[58] Dubrow observes: "However detailed the conventions associated with a literary form may be, they represent not merely an injunction to adopt certain topoi but to adapt those topoi to the aesthetic and social conditions of one's age and to the predispositions of one's own temperament." *Genre*, 14.

[59] On mixed genre, see Gunkel, *Einleitung in die Psalmen*, 397–415.

[60] Ibid., 400–402.

[61] Knierim, "Old Testament Form Criticism Reconsidered," 60.

similar conclusion: "Classical and neo-classical theorists have preferred pure, unmixed genres, whereas in periods 'inimical to tradition' their fusion has been exalted." [62] The post-exilic Judeans responsible for Ezra 9:6–15, we have suggested, were a community divided over the issue of intermarriage, and their dispute could not be resolved through an appeal to existing law, the functional equivalent of "classical theory." One group's recourse to an exegetical interpretation of law served as the impetus to the non-traditional fusion of genres resulting in Ezra 9:6–15.

The result is not surprising in light of the dialectic identified by Knierim: "The force of the dialectic away from conventional expectations may be more of a factor in communication than fixed, conventional schemes."[63] A case in point, he holds, is the mixed genre, which is in no way the deterioration of "pure" genres. Rather, a text representing a mixed genre, such as Ezra 9:6–15, reflects its "sociohistorical conditions more typically than any pure genre could," and its identity is "constituted by their socio-historical context ... not by the lack of conventional pattern."[64] Of mixed genres, Knierim concludes, "They exist in their own right."[65]

3.8 *Sitz im Leben* of Ezra 9:6–15

Oriented to the laments, the prayer in Ezra 9:6–15 is in fact a sermon, a rhetorical device addressed to whoever is represented as being present. Ezra's role is that of preacher in a specific sense that harks back to the classical prophets. In Amos, Micah and Ezekiel the prophet announces Israel's impending misfortune by way of a "preaching" that parallels his "prophesying" (Amos 7:16, Mic 2:6, Ezek 21:2,7). In these cases such preaching is designated by the root נטף in *hif'il*, which literally means "to drip." The preaching's content and context, moreover, are what truly distinguish it as a discourse, as we will demonstrate presently. Discernible in Ezra's penitential preaching are content and contextual features that point back to prophecies of misfortune in Amos, Micah and Ezekiel.

First, a prophet's preaching of misfortune could involve "disgrace," as in Micah 2. The chapter includes a scenario in which the wealthy are enslaving people for their debts and requiring payment in the form of ancestral inheritances (2:2). The same fate is to be visited upon the wealthy, according to a prophecy (2:4b–5) that they roundly dispute. Their challenge not to preach, Mic 2:6, is in vain, however, and their shame does not subside:

אַל תַּטִּפוּ יַטִּיפוּן לֹא יַטִּפוּ לָאֵלֶּה לֹא יִסַּג כְּלִמּוֹת

---

[62] Fowler, *Kinds of Literature*, 181–83.
[63] Knierim, "Old Testament Form Criticism Reconsidered," 60.
[64] Ibid.
[65] Ibid.

The preaching of Mic 2:6 warns that wrongdoing's concomitant is shame (כלמה), and both effects are part of a future scenario presented by the prophet. Such content is also found in Ezra 9:6, where iniquities and guilt leave the speaker disgraced (וְנִכְלַמְתִּי) such that he cannot lift his face to God. It is difficult to determine if the reference to disgrace (כלם) derives directly from Mic 2:6 or the psalms of communal lament (44:10), and perhaps both have affected the content of Ezra's preaching.

Second, a prophet's preaching of misfortune often provided graphic examples of destruction, typically by the sword (חרב). When Amos is warned not to preach (7:16), he responds by warning that his adversary's land will be parceled out and his children killed by the sword (7:17). Similarly, when Ezekiel is told to preach against the sanctuaries in Jerusalem (21:7), he announces that God will put down wicked and righteous alike with a sword (21:8). Indeed the sword will slay all peoples from south to north (21:9). Later, when Ezra 9:8 speaks of the misfortune suffered on account of guilt and iniquity, the litany begins with the destruction of the sword and proceeds to mention captivity, plunder and shame. The term חרב is widespread in the scriptures such that we should not presume direct influence from Amos 7:17 or Ezek 21:8–9 to Ezra 9:8. Rather, the preaching of the three verses provides correlation in content based on the term sword, חרב.

Third, the context of prophetic preaching is often polemical, with an authority admonishing the speaker to silence, as in Mic 2:6. Likewise in Amos 7:16 the priest Amaziah contests the prophet's oracles against the king. It is likely that the directives offered in Ezra 9 were also subject to dispute, based on the "tremblers at the word of God," Ezra's lay support group (כֹּל חָרֵד בְּדִבְרֵי אֱלֹהֵי יִשְׂרָאֵל—Ezra 9:4,10:3). While the identity of this group is not transparent, the references in Isaiah (Isa 66:2,5) and Ezra indicate a group involved in religious conflict with a sharply defined identity over and against their fellow Jews. Joseph Blenkinsopp notes three points of comparison between the tremblers in Isaiah and Ezra: both would be expected to espouse a rigorist interpretation of the law, both would charge their opponents with syncretism, and both would emphasize mourning and fasting.[66] Thus, there is a likelihood that Ezra's preaching arose in a polemical context and won support from a certain faction.

In the post-exilic period, preaching (נטף in *hif'il*) as a specific function of prophecy is attested in a new way. The preaching of misfortune is no longer directed toward the future, as in Amos, Micah and Ezekiel. Rather, it recounts the past as a time of suffering in retribution for sins. If the preacher's audience is attuned to the recounting, they become disposed to repent and confess their sins,

---

[66] Blenkinsopp concludes: "In view of the common evaluation of Ezra and his work the conclusion suggested is surprising, even disconcerting: he appears to have found his principal support among a prophetic-eschatological group which espoused a rigorist interpretation of the law and which was out of favor with the religious leadership of the province." *Ezra-Nehemiah: A Commentary,* 178–79.

as in Ezra 9:6–15. Ezra's sermon is never identified as preaching in that it nowhere contains נטף in *hif'il*. However, it employs the preaching of misfortune to facilitate repentance and the confession of sins, a function that may be observed in other post-exilic prophecies such as Zech 1:1–6.

Finally, Amos's confrontation with the priest Amaziah at the Bethel sanctuary (Amos 7) establishes that prophetic activity could come under the oversight of cultic authorities. From this point forward, there existed in Israel dissident prophecy: "We hear of frequent attempts to silence prophets or to bring them into line with state policies and the expectations associated with official prophetic role performance."[67] There is no explicit evidence that Ezra 9 is reacting to coercion from a cult official, and there are issued no prohibitions on "preaching." Nonetheless, Ezra 9:6–15 may represent the continuation of dissident prophecy into the post-exilic period. To the chagrin of certain officials, prophets still might "preach" incisively on the day's issues in the spirit of their forebears. Furthermore, the preaching, at least in the case of Ezra 9:6–15, could forge penitential expressions from the language of the laments to hark back intentionally to a milieu of communal worship.

3.9 Ezra 9:6–15 and Deuteronomic Law

The communal laments along with the Levitical sermon are defining influences on the prayer in Ezra 9. Another such influence is that school of thought which has drawn directly on Deuteronomic language and law to generate much of the history writing in the Hebrew Bible. The school is responsible for the books of Joshua, Judges, Samuel and Kings as we now have them, a collection referred to as Dtr. Along with this school, most survivors of the exile at the time of Ezra's mission interpreted history thus: The disasters that have beset Israel are divine punishment for faithlessness to God since "the days of our fathers" (Ezra 9:7, cf. Judg 2:11–23). A whole pattern of history is thus portrayed in rebellion and forgiveness, with the law standing as the fundamental test of Israel's obedience and at the same time a sign of divine promise and instruction.[68] In Dtr, history and law are preeminent. Both emphases have influenced the author of Ezra 9:6–15. As a historian, he does not trace the cycles of human sin and divine retribution; the historical review of Ezra 9:7 is highly elliptical. His focus is law, and he touches on related matters such as prophecy. With the law as his goal and guide, the author works interpretively and exegetically with the Deuteronomic tradition, as is indicated by the following verses.

(1) *Ezra 9:7.* "We have been given over to the sword, to captivity, plunder and shamefacedness" (בָּחֶרֶב בַּשְּׁבִי וּבַבִּזָּה וּבְבֹשֶׁת פָּנִים). To describe Israel's misfortune and subjection to foreign rule, the prayer employs terms commonly used in combination by the exilic and post-exilic writers. Using two or more of

---

[67] Blenkinsopp, *A History of Prophecy in Israel*, 157.
[68] Ackroyd, *Exile and Restoration*, 75–76.

the above terms, Jer 20:4, Dan 11:3, Ps 78:61–62 and 2 Chr 29:9 describe Israel's defeats at the hands of the Babylonians, the Seleucids, the Philistines and the Assyrians, respectively. In Ezra's prayer, the terse recital of history with the four terms is no less impressive in its span. Religious infidelity begins in the days of our ancestors (Ezra 9:7), i.e. the patriarchs, and extends to the contemporary time.[69] While the four terms collectively are not attested in Dtr per se, they are Deuteronomic in that they define Israel's disasters as the result of Israel's having sinned and angered God. The specific sins, such as idol worship (Ps 78:61–62, 2 Chr 29:9) and rejecting the prophet (Jer 20:4), are serious concerns of the Deuteronomists.

(2) *Ezra 9:8.* "Favor has been shown" (הָיְתָה תְחִנָּה). Dtr uses this root meaning "favor" or "mercy" only three times. On two of those occasions, God does *not* grant favor (תְחִנָּה) to the inhabitants of Canaan (Deut 7:2, Josh 11:20), in keeping with God's *not* sparing the Egyptians from death (Ps 78:50). Ezra 9:8 articulates the corollary to the Deuteronomic view, namely that God *does* show favor to the remnant of Israel, the golah community. The Deuteronomic influence is indirect but still discernible.

(3) *Ezra 9:8.* "A stake in his holy place" (יָתֵד בִּמְקוֹם קָדְשׁוֹ). This verse further elaborates God's favors to the remnant, whose "stake" in the rebuilt temple is described metaphorically as the claim to a tract of land. With said claim a family or clan may dwell on the land in pitched tents (Isa 54:2).[70] Ezra's expression shows the influence of Deuteronomy 12, where the temple is described as the place which the Lord will choose to place his name and make his home (Deut 12:5,11,14). Reading synchronically, one may align the place for God's divine name to dwell, the family's place to dwell in pitched tents, and the tent sanctuary staked in the wilderness with bronze pegs (Exod 27:19; 35:18; Num 3:37).

(4) *Ezra 9:10.* "We have forsaken your commandments" (עָזַבְנוּ מִצְוֹתֶיךָ). In Dtr, Elijah accuses King Ahab of forsaking the commandments of the Lord and following the Baals (1 Kgs 18:18). Elsewhere (2 Kgs 17:16), the historian lists causes for the fall of the Northern Kingdom, including the people's forsaking God's commandments and worshipping idols (calves, a pole and Baal). When Ezra 9:9 speaks of forsaking commandments, it refers to intermarriage by the golah community. By equating intermarriage with idol worship, which is strictly prohibited in the Deuteronomic code, the prayer's author gains considerable support for his case against Judeans marrying foreigners.

(5) *Ezra 9:11.* "Your servants the prophets" (עֲבָדֶיךָ הַנְּבִיאִים). This expression is the standard Deuteronomic designation for the prophetic

---

[69] In contrast, Hosea locates Israel's fall from grace in the wilderness (Hos 9:10), and Ezekiel traces it back further to Egypt (Ezek 20:7–8).

[70] Favored by Blenkinsopp (*Ezra-Nehemiah: A Commentary*, 183–84) and Williamson (*Ezra, Nehemiah*, 135), this interpretation allows for alternatives. Isa 22:3 compares Eliakim to a stake fastened to a secure place, and thus the community may depend on him.

succession, beginning with Moses, the model prophet.[71] In a Deuteronomic theology of history, Yahweh testifies by the prophets in order to call the nation back to himself and to observing the commandments. This theology is reflective of the early prophets, whose oracles are invariably fulfilled and thus define the course of history.[72] Ezra 9:11 clearly corresponds to the Deuteronomic investiture of the prophet as law's spokesperson. The verse implies that prophecy has mediated and extended the Deuteronomic legal tradition across Israelite history.

(6) *Ezra 9:11.* "The land which you are entering to possess" (הָאָרֶץ אֲשֶׁר אַתֶּם בָּאִים לְרִשְׁתָּהּ). Possessing the land is a common term of fulfillment in the book of Deuteronomy and in Dtr.[73] When the expression occurs in Deut 7:1, it is followed by the prohibition against Israelites marrying with the seven ancient peoples who ruled over Canaan. The blending of ideas regarding land and marriage is consistent with the "vision of dispossession" that informs Moses' final discourses in the book of Deuteronomy (Deut 29:25–27; 30:17–18).[74] In Ezra 9:11–12, the prayer exegetes and harmonizes Deut 7:1; 23:3–7 and other laws as a means of adopting the Deuteronomic "vision of dispossession" in fifth century Judah.

(7) *Ezra 9:11.* "And from their abominations"[75] (בְּתוֹעֲבֹתֵיהֶם). The term "abominations" is attested in Dtr with reference to child sacrifice (Deut 18:9; 2 Kgs 16:3) and Manasseh's ersatz worship (2 Kgs 21:2). The term is *not* found in those marriage laws (Deut 7:1–3, 23:3–7) that underlie Ezra's prayer. The prayer takes up abominations, therefore, in order to establish an exegetical bridge between the Deuteronomic code and Leviticus 18, an instruction on purity and defilement. Lev 18:26–30 describes the peoples whom God has cast out of the land as abominators who must be cut off from among God's people. Thus the teaching in Leviticus is advantageous to the prayer's author on two counts. First, it authorizes the punishment (exclusion) which Ezra's group proposes despite its absence from the Deuteronomic code. Also, it establishes linkage between the

---

[71] Blenkinsopp, *Ezra-Nehemiah: A Commentary*, 184.

[72] Gerhard von Rad, "The Deuteronomic Theology of History in I and II Kings," pp. 205–21 in *The Form-Critical Problem of the Hexateuch and Other Essays* (New York: McGraw-Hill, 1966), 213.

[73] The root ירש appears 204 times in the Hebrew Bible, including 63 times in Deuteronomy, 24 in Joshua, 21 in Judges, 10 in 1 and 2 Kings. Thus 118 of the root's 204 occurrences are found in Dtr.

[74] Halpern-Amaru claims that legislation linked to Israel's tenure in the land implies "a vision of dispossession" as well as another key Dtr theme, the conditional covenant between God and God's people. *Rewriting the Bible*, 20.

[75] It would be possible to read with the Vulgate and translate: "like their abominations." We have chosen to emphasize the parallelism of the preposition *bet* with the preceding "from the contaminations of the people of the land." MT need not be emended because its use of the *bet instrumentum* is well established (Exod 5:3, 16:3; Mic 4:14).

punishment and the punished, by way of the misdeeds ("abominations") that mark the offenders in both Leviticus 18 and Ezra 9.

(8) *Ezra 9:12.* "Do not give your daughters to their sons" (בְּנוֹתֵיכֶם אַל תִּתְּנוּ לִבְנֵיהֶם). Ezra 9:12 begins with this paraphrase of Deut 7:3, a law that prohibits arranging intermarriages. Ezra 9:12 continues: "You should never seek their peace and prosperity" (וְלֹא תִדְרְשׁוּ שְׁלֹמָם וְטוֹבָתָם עַד עוֹלָם). The second injunction quotes Deut 23:6, with reference to the Ammonites and Moabites. There follows in Ezra 9:12 a result clause: "In order that you may be strong and eat the good things of the land" (לְמַעַן תֶּחֶזְקוּ וַאֲכַלְתֶּם אֶת טוּב הָאָרֶץ). This result clause draws on Deut 11:8 and 6:11. A final result clause concludes the instruction thus: "And leave it as an inheritance to your children forever" (וְהוֹרַשְׁתֶּם לִבְנֵיכֶם עַד עוֹלָם). We have noted that this verb, whose root ירשׁ indicates possessing the land, is typical of Deuteronomy (see footnote 73); the reference may be to Deut 1:38–39, which promises possession of the land to the descendants of the exodus generation. In sum, Ezra 9:12 employs four phrases from Deuteronomic discourse to renew the prohibition against intermarriage and apply it to non-Judahites. In its breadth, the Deuteronomic law proves a highly serviceable resource for standardizing post-exilic customs.

(9) *Ezra 9:14.* "Shall we again break your commandments?" (הֲנָשׁוּב לְהָפֵר מִצְוֹתֶיךָ). With its legal exposition complete, the prayer assumes a more rhetorical tone but continues to draw on Deuteronomic language. For example, the term "break" (פרר) is attested in Dtr always with regard to the covenant (Judg 2:1, 1 Kgs 15:19), a usage that is established in the Pentateuch. Ezra 9:14 maintains this association and may refer to Deut 31:16,20, verses which predict that by idol worship in the promised land the people will break God's covenant and in fact abandon God (עזב—31:16; cf. Ezra 9:9). It is noteworthy that much post-exilic writing, with the exception of Zech 11:10–14, applies this term for "break" to human plans or plots that are frustrated. The prayer in Ezra 9:6–15, however, plays on the term's covenantal connotations as established in the Pentateuch and extended into Dtr.

There are nine lexical points of contact between Ezra 9:6–15 and Deuteronomic discourse. While these points are concentrated in 9:11–12, they are attested throughout the text. In introducing the prayer, we emphasized the author's orientations to history and especially to law. Subsequently, we have noted the prayer's preference for Deuteronomic language in treating both history (9:7,11) and law (9:10–12). Deuteronomic language is a vehicle for the prayer's other *topoi*, God as merciful and just (9:8–9, 15) and God's people as imperfect covenant partners (9:6–7, 10, 13, 15). This constellation of *topoi* imparts to the prayer a Deuteronomic character, yet the prayer is not a Deuteronomic "liturgical oration" in the standard sense of the term.[76] Specifically, the prayer does not express the uniqueness of God and his exclusive sovereignty as

---

[76] The Deuteronomic "liturgical oration" is described by Weinfeld in *Deuteronomy and the Deuteronomic School*, 32–45.

evidenced through the theme of world creation.[77] In Ezra 9:6–15, God's salient attribute is justice.[78] To describe better the prayer in its Deuteronomic aspect, we need recall our earlier findings with regard to the lament psalms and the Levitical sermon.

Earlier in this chapter we saw that lament language from the psalms, like the Deuteronomic discourse just examined, is distributed rather evenly in the prayer, and that the form-critical elements of the Levitical sermon are also well represented. All three influences must be duly recognized. Thus, it would be mistaken to describe Ezra 9:11–12 as distinctively legal exegesis that has been set in a liturgical framework, i.e. 9:6,7,15. The prayer resists atomization, and its two primary influences, law and liturgy, are equally significant throughout. These values are established in the prayer's keynote, "I am disgraced," (נִכְלַמְתִּי—9:6), which points source-critically to both the scriptural confession of sins (Jer 3:25, 31:19) and Deuteronomic parenesis.[79]

In summation, we may say that the author of Ezra 9:6–15 is exegeting with precision and specificity the law understood primarily as the Deuteronomic code but including other works such as the Levitical code of purity. His command of legal codes is on a par with his masterful use of literary forms, such as the Levitical sermon, which structures the prayer. In addition, his original appropriation of the lament psalms shows even further literary acumen in adapting creatively the prayer of prior generations.

Despite its exegetical orientation to the Deuteronomic code, any sense of the prayer as interpretive literature should not be overstated. Grabbe has pointed out that the interpretive approach to the Torah did not develop rapidly, and that through the fifth century B.C.E. the codified Torah was still in the charge of priests, who were responsible for interpretation.[80] Thus Ezra 9:6–15 is different in kind from the *pesharim* and other biblical *relecture* of the second and first centuries B.C.E. With this in mind, it can be said that Fishbane overstates the evidence when arguing for intertextuality in Ezra 9:6–15. For example, Fishbane identifies within the prayer an indirect allusion to incest by the daughters of Lot, who thus conceived and bore Ammon and Moab. He bases the claim on

---

[77] Ibid., 42–43.

[78] Although emphasis on God's justice is not a part of the liturgical oration, neither is it inconsistent with Deuteronomic thinking. Von Rad credits the Deuteronomists with retrieving from the ancient cult the *Gerichtsdoxologie* proclaiming that God's role in Israel's sinful history has been just. See his *Theologie des Alten Testaments* (Munich: Chr. Kaiser Verlag, 1969), 1:354–55.

[79] Wagner, *TDOT* 7:190.

[80] In Grabbe's view, "there is little evidence that Jewish religious writings now [fifth century B.C.E.] became interpretive literature, as so often claimed." Grabbe holds that biblical interpretation and commentary became very important, but did so later and less pervasively than is conventionally thought. *Ezra-Nehemiah,* 195. As a later development, biblical interpretation is not to be conflated with the accomplishments of Ezra's time, namely putting the traditional law into a fixed written text of service to the golah community.

exegetical connections between Ezra 9:11, Lev 18:26–30 and, finally, Gen 19:31–38.[81] It is unlikely that the prayer's legal exegesis is so Byzantine. Clearly the composer harmonizes legal matter from Deuteronomic and Levitical codes in order to address a crisis regarding intermarriage. Less plausible is the putative biblical allusion to Gen 19:31–38 that would explain why Ammonites and Moabites are forbidden as marriage partners. In Ezra 9:6–15, animus for the Ammonites and Moabites is one of several issues to be traced back rather to the author of the prayer.[82]

3.10 Excursus: The Authorship of Ezra 9:6–15

The authorship of Ezra has been much debated in the past three decades, and the issue continues to generate fruitful inquiry.[83] A case in point is Ezra 9–

---

[81] Fishbane, *Biblical Interpretation in Ancient Israel*, 119.

[82] The author of this prayer would be especially attracted to Deuteronomy 23 because it sanctions exclusion, which is analogous to the banishment of foreign spouses urged in Ezra 9. Deut 23:4a reads: "The Ammonite and the Moabite shall not come into the assembly of the LORD." In composing Ezra 9:1, the author selected and exegeted this statement both for the sanction it contains and for an additional reason. Deut 23:4a holds up to ridicule the Ammonites and the Moabites, two people who are routinely denigrated in Chronicles. For example, before it is said that Rehoboam did what was evil and did not seek the LORD, 2 Chr 12:13b discloses that Rehoboam is the son of Naamah the Ammonite. Not found in the source text (1 Kgs 14:28–29), the gratuitous remark implies a cause-and-effect relationship between the king's mother and her son's evildoing. Also, only Chronicles relates that the conspirators against King Joash were Zabad, the son of Shimeath the Ammonite woman, and Jehozabad, the son of Shimrith the Moabite woman (2 Chr 24:26; cf. 2 Kgs 12:22). These passages effectively discredit Ammonite and Moabite women, who are the target of the divorce legislation devised in Ezra 9–10. The common authorship of Ezra 9–10 and Chronicles is demonstrated in the excursus to follow.

[83] The pivotal question is whether the Chronicler, understood as the author of 1–2 Chronicles and hereafter referred to as C, had a decisive role in the production of the book of Ezra. The common authorship of Chronicles and Ezra-Nehemiah had been the critical consensus since the first half of the nineteenth century. Sara Japhet ("The Supposed Common Authorship of Chronicles and Ezra-Nehemiah Investigated Anew," *VT* 18 [1968]: 330–71), H. G. M. Williamson (*Israel in the Book of Chronicles* [Cambridge: Cambridge University Press, 1977]) and others have begun to challenge the consensus. They aim to prove the completely separate origin of Chronicles and Ezra-Nehemiah based on phenomena such as Chronicles and Ezra-Nehemiah using different expressions to refer to the same entity. While this challenge has made it impossible simply to reassert the classical arguments for the unity of Chronicles and Ezra-Nehemiah, it fails to recognize factors that explain why C would use a diverse but not inconsistent range of expression across Chronicles and Ezra-Nehemiah. These factors include C's extensive use of sources and his sensitivity to differences between a pre-exilic context and a post-exilic context. Responding to this challenge, recent arguments for C's authorship of Ezra-Nehemiah (cf. Blenkinsopp, *Ezra-Nehemiah: A Commentary*, 47–54)

10, which comprises a narrative and a prayer; it is important to ask whether the two forms have come together as the result of one seamless composition, or whether the prayer was composed separately and joined to the narrative by a second hand. Scholars commonly note that the prayer coheres well with its setting, and some press further to understand the prayer and narrative as parts of a single composition by the same person or school. For example, James VanderKam has suggested that the book of Ezra was composed as an independent work with a distinctive vocabulary and the particular themes of restoration and divine mercy.[84] He views Ezra 9:6–15 as a part of this composition, and holds that the author is someone other than the C.[85] Among those scholars who identify C as the author of Ezra, Otto Plöger[86] and Ulrich Kellermann[87] expressly hold that C composed the prayer in Ezra 9:6–15 as well as Ezra-Nehemiah. VanderKam, Plöger and Kellermann all take the position that a seamless composition extends across Ezra 9–10, accounting for both the narrative and the prayer.

The investigation here, however, will indicate something slightly different than the above positions, namely that C is the author of 9–10 but probably not of the prayer in 9:6–15. C's relationship to the prayer may be stated thus: C did not write Ezra 9:6–15 but availed himself of these verses when composing Ezra 9–10. In the most likely scenario, C had the prayer available to him as he was writing the final portion of Ezra and, despite certain discrepancies between the prayer and C's theology, he wove the prayer into his own composition. These determinations require piecemeal argumentation, none of which is overwhelmingly conclusive on its own. Taken together, however, the pieces allow us to draw conclusions. The first conclusion, that C is in all likelihood the author of Ezra 9–10, can be adduced on the basis of three points.

The first of these points concerns sources. It appears that Ezra 9–10 is a conflation that draws upon two versions of an episode about intermarriage in the golah community. The two versions are discernible in Ezra 9:1–5 and 10:1–8. Blenkinsopp identifies five verbal redundancies between the first five verses of chapter nine and the first eight verses of chapter ten; the redundancies suggest

---

are especially persuasive and stand behind our hypothesizing that C is responsible for the composition of Ezra 9–10.

[84] James VanderKam, "Ezra-Nehemiah or Ezra and Nehemiah?" pp. 55–75 in *Priests, Prophets and Scribes: Essays on the Formation and Heritage of Second Temple Judaism in Honour of Joseph Blenkinsopp* (ed. E. Ulrich et al.; JSOTSup 149; Sheffield: Sheffield Academic Press, 1992), 75.

[85] Ibid., 60, 65–66.

[86] Plöger speculates that C formulated the prayer of Ezra (9:6–15), and that he got the idea for doing so from Neh 1:5–11, a short penitential prayer that originally belonged to the memoir of Nehemiah. *Reden und Gebet im deuteronomistischen und chronistischen Geschichtswerk,* 46–47.

[87] Kellermann, after noting that Ezra 9 begins with "chronistic" conventions, asserts: "Das Gebet 9:6–15 erscheint dabei so gut im Kontext verklammert, daß es von Anfang an dazu gehört haben muß." *Nehemia: Quellen Überlieferung und Geschichte,* 65.

that two distinct versions have informed the telling of events.[88] The result is what Blenkinsopp calls a "consecutive account."[89] To confirm the plausibility of such an editorial move by C, we may present external evidence from C's genealogies. Within the genealogy of Judah, which is found in 1 Chr 2:3–4:23, the treatment of Jerahmeel's line is bipartite and differentiated. That is to say, in listing Jerahmeel's descendants, C uses two different sources that are not wholly compatible and appear juxtaposed. The first source is represented in 1 Chr 2:25–33, the second in 2:34–41. The former passage is a segmented genealogy while the latter is a linear genealogy. Moreover, Williamson notes, the second block of material (2:34–41) "introduces a tension between vv. 31 and 34 concerning whether Sheshan had sons or not."[90] Between the two sources there are discrepancies, but the discrepancies are minor enough that C allows them to stand. Moreover, C continues to construct composite genealogies after that of Jerahmeel.[91] Were C's compositional judgment applied to the sources behind Ezra 9–10, it would result in the text as we now have it, a conflation of two prior accounts.

The second point of contact between the Chronicler and Ezra chapters 9–10 has to do with the manner of expiating guilt once mixed marriages have been consummated. In Ezra 10:11, Ezra tells the people that because they have increased the guilt of all Israel by marrying foreign women, they must make confession before the Lord, do God's will, and separate themselves from the people of the land and from (their) foreign wives. The key expression is the imperative "make confession before the Lord" (וְעַתָּה תְּנוּ תוֹדָה לַיהוָה), which may also be translated "Give praise now to YHWH."[92] In fact, in a context such as this, the senses of "confess" and "praise" are not mutually exclusive as the

---

[88] Blenkinsopp, *Ezra-Nehemiah: A Commentary*, 187.

[89] Ibid.

[90] H. G. M. Williamson, "Sources and Redaction in the Chronicler's Genealogy of Judah," *JBL* 98 (1979): 358.

[91] E.g. The descendants of Levi are treated in consecutive accounts (1 Chr 5:27–41 and 6:1–15) reflecting two different sources, Genesis 46 and Numbers 3, respectively. The second listing embellishes the line of Gershom's descendants (6:5–11 has no precedent in Numbers) while the first functions as a schematic listing of Jerusalem's chief priests up to the exile (information which is also available in 1 Chr 6:34–38, 9:10–11; Ezra 7:1–5; Neh 11:10–11 and 2 Esd 1:1–3). Between the two accounts of Levi's genealogy there are parallels and outright redundancies, yet C's method is not confused, and his motive may be to insinuate parity between the long established (Zadokite) and relatively recent (Aaronide) claimants to liturgical prerogative in post-exilic Judah. There are at least two other instances of redundant genealogies that have resulted from C drawing upon multiple sources. The descendants of Benjamin are enumerated in 1 Chr 7:6–12//Gen 46:21 and 1 Chr 8:1–28//Num 26:38–41. The descendants of Saul occur in 1 Chr 8:29–40//1 Sam 9:1–2 and 1 Chr 9:35–44//1 Sam 14:49.

[92] Blenkinsopp, *Ezra-Nehemiah: A Commentary*, 193.

root ידה indicates in Hubert Grimme's words *ein doppeltes Bekennen*.[93] The construction recalls another transgressor who is admonished to confess and praise. In Josh 7:18–19, Achan receives the following command: give glory to the Lord and confess to the Lord the sin of appropriating devoted goods (שִׂים־נָא כָבוֹד לַיהוָה אֱלֹהֵי יִשְׂרָאֵל וְתֶן לוֹ תוֹדָה). A sin against God, Achan's misdeed jeopardizes Israel's otherwise successful occupation of the land. Achan has brought misfortune upon his people, as do the mixed marriages in Ezra 9–10. Moreover, the imperative to confess/praise (Josh 7:19) clearly parallels Ezra 10:11.[94] In fact, between the two texts there is an intermediary link.

Achan's transgression is mentioned elsewhere in the Bible only once. An allusion to the incident appears in the Chronicler's genealogy of Judah. 1 Chr 2:7 reads: "And the children of Carmi: Trouble, troubler of Israel who acted faithlessly over the ban" (וּבְנֵי כַרְמִי עָכָר עוֹכֵר יִשְׂרָאֵל אֲשֶׁר מָעַל בַּחֵרֶם). This allusive note assumes that the reader knows the story of Achan and could on his or her own recall its details. The same recall is likely presupposed in the composition of Ezra 10:11, the admonition to give praise/confess to God for acting faithlessly and marrying foreign women. The allusion in C's genealogy demonstrates his familiarity with Achan of Joshua 7 and suggests the suitability of Achan as a point of reference if C has composed Ezra 10:9. While the literary relationship between Josh 7:18–19 and 1 Chr 2:7 is debatable,[95] it is plausible that C knew the story of Achan, presumed his readers knew it, and may well have alluded to it Ezra 10:9.

The third point indicating C's authorship of Ezra 9–10 relates to "covenant," the means by which the people, under Ezra, are to extricate themselves from mixed marriages. In Ezra 10:3–5, Shecaniah addresses the people thus:

> "So now let us make a covenant with our God to send away all these wives and their children, according to the counsel of my lord and of those who tremble at the commandment of our God; and let it be done according to the law. Take action, for it is your duty, and we are with you; be strong, and do it." Then Ezra stood up and made the leading priests, the Levites,

---

[93] Hubert Grimme cites both Josh 7:19 and Ezra 10:9 as examples of the "double confession." The confession establishes the speaker both as one who has sinned against the Lord and who approximates God's likeness. "Der Begriff von hebräischen הודה und תודה," *ZAW* 58 (1940–41): 236–37.

[94] Comparisons of Ezra 10:11 and Josh 7:18–19 may be found in Blenkinsopp, *Ezra-Nehemiah: A Commentary*, 193, and Williamson, *Ezra, Nehemiah*, 155.

[95] Japhet understands 1 Chr 2:7 as an "allusion" to Josh 7:1ff, with the latter text serving as the source for the former. Her view is supported by the standard dating of the biblical texts in question. *I & II Chronicles* (Louisville: Westminster/John Knox Press, 1993), 14–23. Dating Joshua to the exilic or post-exilic periods, A. Graeme Auld holds that in the Achan episode there could be "mutual influence between Joshua and Chronicles." *Joshua Retold* (Edinburgh: T&T Clark, 1998), 113–14.

and all Israel swear that they would do as had been said. So they swore. (Ezra 10:3–5)

How is this particular covenant to be characterized? In these verses, there are three operative terms that are interrelated and, to an extent, synonymous: covenant (בְּרִית), the law as a legal precedent (תּוֹרָה), and oath-making (שָׁבַע). A covenant is established on the basis of a legal precedent, and the pact is sealed by oaths. Establishing a covenant by this process is consistent with C.[96] Moreover, the lexical configuration of "covenant/law/oath-making" is indicative of C's writing. For example, a tripartite expression of covenant appears in portion of a hymn, 1 Chr 16:15–18:

> Remember his covenant (בְּרִיתוֹ) forever, the word that he commanded, for a thousand generations, the covenant that he made with Abraham, his sworn promise (שְׁבוּעָתוֹ) to Isaac, which he confirmed to Jacob as a statute (חֹק), to Israel as an everlasting covenant,...

The crux of this injunction is that Israel is to remember God's covenant, which is tantamount to a sworn promise and which can function as a legal precedent. As in Ezra 10:3–5, the hymn indicates covenant through three distinct expressions: God's covenant with Abraham (בְּרִיתוֹ), God's sworn promise to Isaac (שְׁבוּעָתוֹ), and the statute (חֹק) to Jacob. The ultimate source of these terms is Psalm 105 (105:8–11), which C has adopted nearly verbatim.[97] The psalm's three essential points on covenant align with those of 1 Chr 16:15–18 and Ezra 10:3–5, and in two cases the vocabulary is the same (בְּרִית, שְׁבוּעָה). The confluence of conceptual terminology among Ps 105:8–11, 1 Chr 16:15–18 and Ezra 10:3–5 indicates that C knew this psalmic description of covenant and valued it such that he would readily adopt it, as in 1 Chronicles 16, or paraphrase it, as in Ezra 10.

To summarize thus far, a presumption that the Chronicler has written Ezra 9–10 gains cogency in light of the three points presented. Two broad portions of the section, the beginnings of chapters 9 and 10, represent the original outlines of two separate stories that C has conflated, as is his wont. The section's crux, remitting the sin of intermarriage (10:9), invokes a formula of confession/praise from Judges that C alludes to elsewhere, in his genealogy of Judah (1 Chr 2:7). Finally, the community is reconstituted in covenantal terms (10:3–5) that C has employed as part of the hymn found in 1 Chronicles 16. There is a preponderance of evidence that Ezra 9–10 is the work of the Chronicler.

---

[96] Dennis McCarthy, "Covenant and Law in Chronicles-Nehemiah," *CBQ* 44 (1982): 35.

[97] Even though the citation in 1 Chr 16:15–18 is nearly verbatim from Psalm 105, Bernard Gosse concludes that a minor textual modification in fact suggests that C is rewriting ("*relecture*") his source rather than copying it. "Les citations de Psaumes en 1 Ch 16,8–36 et la conception des relations entre Yahvé et son peuple dans la rédaction des livres des Chroniques," *Église et Théologie* 27 (1996): 318, n. 10.

Thus we turn to the sermon in Ezra 9:6–15, which has not been a part of our discussion of C to this point. What is the evidence that C has or has not composed this sermon? There are, on the one hand, similarities between Ezra 9:6–15 and 1–2 Chronicles. C. C. Torrey established that the sermon's language and style are at times quite characteristic of C.[98] Moreover, the sermon, like C, draws attention to themes such as communal guilt (Ezra 9:6; 1 Chr 21:3; 2 Chr 24:18; 28:10,13; 33:23) and God's faithfulness to an unworthy people (Ezra 9:8–9; 1 Chr 28:9; 2 Chr 12:5; 15:2; 24:2). Our goal, however, is to determine a specific relationship between the books of Chronicles and the text in question, and to state the plausibility of common authorship as exactly as possible. The evidence breaks down into three points, all of which undermine the likelihood that C has written Ezra 9:6–15. We will see that the author, unlike C, adheres rather strictly to received, Deuteronomic traditions and is faithful as well to a pentateuchal history of Israel that allows the nation's autonomy to be compromised.

The first point revolves around the idealization of Israel's sovereignty routinely found in Chronicles. A prime example is 1 Chronicles 16, the hymn referred to earlier. This composition adopts verses from Psalms 105, 96 and 106, respectively. The hymn follows Psalm 105 from the psalm's beginning to its fifteenth verse. At this point, Psalm 105 is abandoned as the source text in favor of Psalm 96. The move is calculated to avoid all mention of Israel's captivity in Egypt, which Psalm 105 elaborates in its verses 16 and following. This section of the psalm contradicts C's view that from patriarchal times Israel has dwelled in its land continuously. In fact, C routinely suppresses references to a subordinate Israel, and thus many of the historical traditions of the Pentateuch and Former Prophets are displaced with genealogies in 1 Chronicles 2–9. Japhet notes that the Chronicler's concept of the early history of Israel is "distinctive and revolutionary... a concept of people and land which is autochthonic in its basic features."[99]

The Chronicler's innovative concept of Israelite history finds no support in the sermon of Ezra 9:6–15. Rather, the sermon dwells upon Israel's loss of autonomy: "On account of our iniquities we, our kings, and our priests have been given over to the kings of the lands, over to the sword, to captivity, to plunder and shamefacedness, as is the case today." (9:7b) It is difficult to imagine C composing this recital of Israelite history, which begins with the patriarchs and subsequently refers to the captivity in Egypt. With enslavement to Egypt suppressed in Chronicles, its assertion here suggests a different author. The terms for Israel's misfortune, especially חֶרֶב (sword) and שְׁבִי (captivity), are

---

[98] C. C. Torrey lists common vocabulary and shared constructions to conclude that the passage, Ezra 9:1–15, contains "a very large proportion of words and expressions found elsewhere only (or in a few cases chiefly) in the writings of the Chronicler." *The Compositional and Historical Value of Ezra-Nehemiah* (Giessen: Riokersche Buchhandlungen, 1896), 20.

[99] Sara Japhet, "Conquest and Settlement in Chronicles," *JBL* 98 (1979): 218.

Deuteronomic,[100] a fact that helps to account for the sermon's composition. The author invoked Deuteronomic and other established traditions in recounting Israel's misfortune since ancient times.

The second point against C's authorship of Ezra 9:6–15 focuses upon the precise injunction against intermarriage in Ezra 9:12:

> Therefore, do not give your daughters to their sons in marriage, nor take their daughters for your sons, and you should never seek their peace and prosperity, in order that you may be strong and eat the good things of the land (אֶת טוּב הָאָרֶץ) and leave it as an inheritance (וְהוֹרַשְׁתֶּם) to your children forever (לִבְנֵיכֶם עַד עוֹלָם).

In order to ban intermarriage in post-exilic Judah, the author employs various Deuteronomic expressions. These expressions form the first half of the verse. The second half contains motive clauses also bearing a Deuteronomic stamp. The motive clauses include "eat the good things of the land," "leave it as an inheritance," and "to your children forever." With these motive clauses highlighted, Ezra 9:12 parallels a passage in Chronicles.

In 1 Chr 28:8–10, David orders the people to observe the commandments so that they might "possess the good land" (תִּירְשׁוּ אֶת הָאָרֶץ הַטּוֹבָה) and "leave (it) to their descendants as an eternal inheritance" (וְהִנְחַלְתֶּם לִבְנֵיכֶם אַחֲרֵיכֶם עַד עוֹלָם) In 1 Chr 28:10, there follows an admonition for Solomon to "be strong" (חֲזַק), as in Ezra 9:12. Thus, there exist several lexical parallels between Ezra 9:12 and 1 Chr 28:8–10. The two texts, however, are *faux amis* because of the exhortation at the center of Ezra 9:12, "be strong."

The expression "be strong" is an old military "exhortation formulary" that C adapts to the post-exilic milieu.[101] C typically issues this exhortation as "act strongly" (חֲזַק וַעֲשֵׂה) or as "be strong and of good courage" (חֲזַק וֶאֱמָץ). The former is attested in 1 Chr 28:10 and 2 Chr 19:11, and the latter in 1 Chr 22:13, 28:20, and 2 Chr 32:7. C uses a compound construction twice in David's exhortation to Solomon (1 Chr 28:10, 20), and virtually everywhere else in Chronicles that חֲזַק is attested in a motive clause or as an imperative. The

---

[100] To describe Israel's misfortune and subjection to foreign rule, the sermon employs terms commonly used in combination by the exilic and post-exilic writers: פָּנִים בַּחֶרֶב בַּשְּׁבִי וּבַבִּזָּה וּבְבֹשֶׁת. In Ezra's sermon, the terse recital of history with the four terms is no less impressive in its span. Religious infidelity begins in the days of our ancestors (Ezra 9:7), i.e. the patriarchs, and extends to the contemporary time. While the four terms collectively are not attested in Dtr per se, they are Deuteronomic in that they define Israel's disasters as the result of Israel's having sinned and angered God. The specific sins, such as idol worship (Ps 78:61–62, 2 Chr 29:9) and rejecting the prophets (Jer 20:4), are serious concerns of the Deuteronomists.

[101] As noted above (n. 57), "be strong" is an old military exhortation formula that was subject to innovation in the exilic and post-exilic writings, according to Fishbane's analysis. His treatment of "be strong" and other exhortations is found in "'The Sign' in the Hebrew Bible," 217–19.

expression חֲזַק וַעֲשֵׂה is exclusive to Chronicles with one exception, Ezra 10:4. In this verse, which we have linked to C on other grounds, Shecaniah concludes his short speech thus, "Be strong and do it." (חֲזַק וַעֲשֵׂה)

If C has composed Ezra's prayer in the preceding chapter 9, one would anticipate the old military formula re-cast as חֲזַק וַעֲשֵׂה or חֲזַק וֶאֱמָץ, and not simply חֲזַק or some form thereof. Ezra 9:12, however, reads לְמַעַן תֶּחֶזְקוּ, "in order that you may be strong." The expression suggests an author other than C.

The third point regarding the authorship of Ezra 9:6–15 stems from C's adaptation of a central Deuteronomic topos, retribution. In the books of Chronicles, retribution becomes subject to a rather precise economy whereby God deals with each generation as its deeds deserve.[102] This phenomenon is operative in the exhortation to Solomon cited above. 1 Chr 28:9b reads: "If you seek him, he will be found by you, but if you forsake him, he will reject you forever." Some of the most exacting uses of recompense in C's history concern the kings of the divided monarchy, whose deeds and misdeeds become the rationale for significant historical events. A commonly cited example is 2 Chronicles 12, which attributes the Egyptian Shishak's successful campaign against Jerusalem to King Rehoboam's abandoning God's law.[103] Rehoboam and all Israel suffer the invasion in the king's *fifth* year as a direct response to their waywardness, which ostensibly began in the king's *fourth* year (2 Chr 12:1–2). We know this because another verse (2 Chr 11:17) reports that for *three* years Rehoboam and his supporters walked in the way of David and Solomon.

The sermon of Ezra 9:6–15 does not calibrate chronology thus. The prayer depicts wrongdoing and punishment as global phenomena that have beset generations of Israelites and again threaten the Jews of post-exilic Judah. On this point, Antonius Gunneweg rightly describes the prayer's "retribution theology" as projecting the calamities of the past onto the present day.[104] One verse especially, Ezra 9:13, runs counter to C's strict economy of retribution:

---

[102] Elias Bickerman notes parallels to this phenomenon in Hellenistic literature and Ancient Near East texts; he adds that as this phenomenon evolves, C typifies the movement from collective responsibility for crimes to an idea of personal responsibility. *From Ezra to the Last of the Maccabees; Foundations of Post-biblical Judaism* (New York: Schocken Books, 1962), 24–27. For a systematic description of how C portrays historical events to establish causal connections between transgressions and retributions as well as righteousness and reward, see Japhet, *The Ideology of the Book of Chronicles and Its Place in Biblical Thought*, 166–67.

[103] See Raymond Dillard, "Reward and Punishment in Chronicles: The Theology of Immediate Retribution," *WTJ* 46 (1984): 168; and Japhet, *The Ideology of the Book of Chronicles and Its Place in Biblical Thought*, 168–69.

[104] Here and elsewhere, Gunneweg's analysis of the sermon is insightful, although one must question his identification of the author as C. Assuming that C is the author, Gunneweg and others read the sermon closely but fail to note and address discrepancies between this text and Chronicles. *Esra,* 166.

LAW AND LITURGY

> And after all that has come upon us for our evil deeds and our great guilt—you, our God, have punished us less than our iniquities deserved...

The key phrase, "punished us less than our iniquities deserved," is the standard translation of חָשַׂכְתָּ לְמַטָּה מֵעֲוֺנֵנוּ, which literally means, "You have kept back, downward, part of our iniquity."[105] It is difficult to envision C composing a verse such as Ezra 9:13, even if we take into consideration the more merciful portrait of God that has recently been attributed to C by Brian Kelly.[106] That is to say, an earlier verse, Ezra 9:11, asserts that "We have forsaken your commandments which you commanded by your servants the prophets." In C's system, rejecting the prophetic word would compound the people's guilt and confirm the grounds for retribution.[107] The sermon, however, does not understand God's punishment and pity according to a system. Pity and punishment, rather, seem to be a reflection of God, who is said to be just (9:15) and gracious (9:8).

In summary, the sermon in Ezra 9:6–15 reflects an author who, unlike C, has a conventional adherence to Deuteronomic traditions and a forthright view of Israel's history. He is frank about past compromises in Israel's autonomy, and he attributes these to the people's iniquities and guilt. Divine mercy mitigates sin and its consequences in such a manner that retribution is an approximate rather than exacting exchange between God and humans.

The author of Chronicles is clearly a different person, and his relationship to the sermon is somewhat complex. We have demonstrated that C would not have written Ezra 9:7b,12b and 13, which are inconsistent with basic presuppositions in C's worldview. That is to say, strong differences emerge between C's views and those of the sermon on matters such as Israel's autonomy, Solomon's marriages and God's manner of retribution. However, in turning to Ezra chapters 9–10, another of C's compositions, we do not find that Israel's autonomy or God's retribution are particularly at issue. Thus the inclusion of the sermon here creates no immediate contradictions, and verses such as 9:7, 12 and 13 rest somewhat easily in their immediate context of Ezra 9–10. Moreover, incorporating the sermon into the narrative has certain advantages.[108]

To conclude, C's relationship to the sermon may be explained thus: C did not write Ezra 9:6–15 but availed himself of the sermon when composing Ezra 9–10. In the most likely scenario, C had the sermon available to him as he was

---

[105] *BDB*, 362.

[106] Focusing on passages such as 2 Chr 7:12–22, Kelly argues that the language of C indicates a primary concern for repentance and restoration "rather than strict retribution as such." He maintains that in C's system of divine justice, the determining factors are often repentance and mercy, not merit. *Retribution and Eschatology*, 62, 108.

[107] Ibid., 243.

[108] Bickerman notes that with ancient historiography, the narrative typically becomes fuller when the compiler approaches his own time; hence the events of 458 are embellished by a sermon of communal confession attributed to the historical Ezra. *From Ezra to the Last of the Maccabees*, 27–28.

writing the final portion of Ezra and, despite certain discrepancies between the prayer and C's viewpoints, he wove the text into his own composition. Thus we note that the contiguous verses (9:3–5, 10:1) are consistent enough with the prayer to require its conclusion. The weaving of Ezra 9:6–15 into Ezra 9–10 is impressive and has led some to assume that C wrote the sermon. But in dealing with Chronicles, it is wise to recall that: "A reworked text need not have explicit signs that it is a revision of an earlier source. We therefore cannot tell, simply by looking at a text, how removed it might be from the event that it is narrating."[109] Nor, regarding the conclusion to the book of Ezra, can we establish exactly the difference and differentiation between C's recounting the campaign against Judahite intermarriage (Ezra 9–10) and another author's sermon (9:6–15) based upon those same events.[110]

---

[109] Marc Z. Brettler, *The Creation of History in Ancient Israel* (London/New York: Routledge, 1998 [1995]), 45.

[110] To reconstruct more fully C's role vis-à-vis Ezra 9:6–15, it is helpful to appeal to theory. Jonathan Dyck distinguishes between C's "intentions," which express theological commitment to his central idea or ideas, and "textual meanings and contextual functions," which are elements not "intended" by C and thus not central to a reconstruction of his theology. (*The Theocratic Ideology of the Chronicler* [Leiden/Boston/Cologne: Brill, 1998], 38). Thus, certain of the prayer's key ideas, such as communal guilt and God's great mercy, resonate with C's "intentions" or core theological principles. Most importantly, if C understood the prayer's views on autonomy and retribution as "contextual functions" that need not align exactly with his own views, he could easily incorporate the prayer into Ezra 9–10 In this scenario, C would be tolerating counter data on autonomy and retribution because the sermon in which they are found otherwise supports his historiographical agenda.

4

NEH 9:6–37—A TRANSFORMATION OF THE COMMUNAL LAMENT

4.1 Text

9:6 You alone are LORD;
You have made the heavens, the heaven of heavens, and all their host,
The earth and all that is on it,
The seas and all that is in them.
You give them all life, and the host of heaven worships you.
9:7 You are the LORD, the God who chose Abram
And brought him out of Ur of the Chaldeans
And gave him the name Abraham;
9:8 And you found his heart faithful before you,
And made with him a covenant to give the land of the Canaanites, the Hittites, the Amorites,
The Perizzites, the Jebusites, and the Girgashites to his descendants;
And you have fulfilled your promise, for you are just.
9:9 And you saw the affliction of our ancestors in Egypt
And heard their cry at the Reed Sea.
9:10 You performed signs and wonders against Pharaoh,
And all his servants and all the people of his land,
For you knew that they acted insolently against them [our ancestors],
You made for yourself a name, which remains to this day.
9:11 You divided the sea before them,
So that they passed through the sea on dry land,
But their pursuers you threw into the depths,
Like a stone into mighty waters.
9:12 With a column of cloud you led them by day,
And with a column of fire by night,
To light for them the way in which they should proceed.
9:13 You came down upon Mount Sinai, and spoke with them from heaven,

And gave them just ordinances and true laws, good statutes and
   commandments,
9:14 And you declared your holy sabbath to them
And gave them commandments and statutes and a law through Moses
   your servant.
9:15 You gave them bread from heaven for their hunger,
And you brought water out of the rock for their thirst,
And you told them to come and to possess the land that you had sworn to
   give them.
9:16 But they and our ancestors acted insolently and stiffened their necks
And did not obey your commandments.
9:17 They refused to obey, and they did not remember the wonders that
   you performed among them;
They stiffened their necks and appointed a leader to return to their
   subjugation in Egypt.
But you are a forgiving God, gracious and merciful, long-suffering and
   great in steadfast love;
So you did not forsake them.
9:18 Even when they had made a molten calf for themselves
And said, "This is your god who brought you up from Egypt,"
And had carried out great blasphemies,
9:19 You, by your great mercies, did not forsake them in the wilderness;
The column of cloud did not fail to lead them in the way by day,
Nor the column of fire by night to light for them the way they should go.
9:20 You gave your good Spirit to instruct them,
And you did not withhold your manna from their mouths,
And you gave them water for their thirst.
9:21 Forty years you sustained them in the wilderness [and] they lacked
   nothing;
Their clothes did not wear out and their feet did not swell.
9:22 And you gave them kingdoms and peoples, and apportioned them by
   head count,
Thus they took possession of the land of Sihon the king of Heshbon and
   the land of Og the king of Bashan.
9:23 Their descendants you multiplied like the stars of heaven,
And brought them into the land that you had told their ancestors to enter
   and possess.
9:24 So the descendants entered and possessed the land,
And you subdued before them those dwelling in the land, the Canaanites,
And gave them into their hands, with their kings and the peoples of the
   land,
To do with them as they pleased.
9:25 And they captured fortified cities and a bountiful land,
And took possession of houses filled with goods, hewn cisterns, vineyards
   and olive orchards, and fruit trees in abundance;
Thus they ate, and were sated and grew fat, and indulged themselves in
   your great goodness.
9:26 Nevertheless they were rebellious and revolted against you
And cast your law behind their backs;

They killed your prophets, who had warned them to turn back to you,
And they committed acts of great contempt.
9:27 Thus you gave them into the hands of their enemies who oppressed them.
But in the time of their suffering they cried out to you
And you heard from heaven, and according to your great mercies you gave them saviors
Who delivered them from the hands of their enemies.
9:28 But they no sooner rested than they again did evil before you,
So you abandoned them to the hands of their enemies, who had dominion over them, such that they turned and cried to you,
And you heard from heaven, and many times you delivered them according to your mercies.
9:29 You warned them so that they would turn back to your law.
Yet they acted insolently and did not obey your commandments,
But sinned against your ordinances, by the observance of which one will live.
They turned a stubborn shoulder and stiffened their neck and would not obey.
9:30 Many years you were patient with them,
And warned them by your spirit through your prophets.
Yet they would not heed; therefore you delivered them
Over to the peoples of the lands.
9:31 Yet in your great mercies you did not make a full end of them,
You did not abandon them, for you are a gracious and merciful God.
9:32 And now, our God—the great and mighty and fearsome God, keeping covenant and steadfast love—
Do not make light of all the hardship that has beset us,
Our kings, our leaders, our priests, our prophets, our ancestors, and all your people,
Since the days of the kings of Assyria until today.
9:33 You have been just in all that has come upon us,
For you have acted faithfully yet we have acted wickedly.
9:34 Our kings, our leaders, our priests, and our ancestors have not observed your law
Or hearkened to the commandments and warnings that you gave them.
9:35 Even when in their own kingdom amid the great goodness you bestowed on them
In the wide and rich land that you gave them,
They did not serve you nor did they turn from their evil pursuits.
9:36 And so today we are slaves,
Slaves in the land that you gave to our ancestors to eat of its fruit and enjoy its bounty.
9:37 But its abundant yield goes to the kings whom you have put over us because of our sins;
They have power also over our bodies and our livestock according to their pleasure,
And we are in great distress.

4.2 Text-Critical Issues and Notes

Our translation reflects both the Hebrew text of Nehemiah (MT) as well as the Greek version known as Esdras B. The previous chapter noted that the MT of Ezra-Nehemiah has been fairly well transmitted, and that the fragments from Qumran (4QEzra) allow this textual tradition to be dated to the first century B.C.E. The high text-critical quality of MT commends it as the basis for a study of Neh 9:6–37. Esdras B or 2 Esdras is a literal translation of the Hebrew and Aramaic text of Ezra-Nehemiah.[1] Generally, textual variants between MT and Esdras B result from the latter's more economical expression and do not involve substantive differences in meaning. When Esdras B is compared to MT with regard to Neh 9:6–37, there are two additions, 10 omissions and 12 one-for-one variants. According to Rudolph, in two of these cases Esdras B is preferable to MT,[2] including 9:17, which we have translated with the Greek (ἐν Αἰγύπτῳ "in Egypt" over MT's unintelligible בְּמִרְיָם). The Greek variant that attributes the prayer to Ezra (9:6) is an emendation and has not been adopted.

One interesting pattern suggests that variants in Esdras B tend to coincide with the citing of phrases from elsewhere in scripture. For example, Neh 9:21 "and their feet" (MT וְרַגְלֵיהֶם) differs from "their sandals" (Esdras B τὰ ὑποδήματα). Both, however, are scripturally based; the former quotes Deut 8:4, the latter Deut 29:4. Also, in 9:26 "back" (MT גֵּו) differs from "body" (Esdras B σώματος). The former quotes exactly 1 Kgs 14:9 and Ezek 23:35, while the latter quotes the verses more freely. A third variant related to scriptural citation occurs in 9:31, regarding the attributes of God;[3] the Greek version's adverb of time differs from that of the Hebrew. In sum, it appears that the citation of scripture had something other than a stabilizing effect on the text of Neh 9:6–37.

When there are variants between MT and Esdras B, the Vulgate sometimes reads with the former and sometimes the latter. On occasion it provides a separate variant, as in Neh 9:17 (*quasi per contentionem* "as through exertion"). In certain cases, the Arabic, Ethiopic or Syriac versions invite comparison. A complete list of versions and variants follows.

---

[1] Within the text of Esdras B, important differences between the codices Alexandrinus (LXX^A), Vaticanus (LXX^B) and Sinaiticus (LXX^s) are noted in the table of variants below. See Hanhart, *Esdrae liber II*.

[2] Rudolph, *Esra und Nehemia*, xx.

[3] In this verse Newman identifies a "divine attribute formula" that also occurs in Exod 34:6–7 and Num 14:13–19. She maintains that "slight modifications" in the quotation indicate a "conscious rhetorical strategy" that, among other things, stresses the merciful aspects of God. See her *Praying By the Book*, 88–91.

A TRANSFORMATION OF THE LAMENT

TABLE 5

OMISSIONS (>), ADDITIONS (+) AND VARIANTS (=) OF NEH 9:6–37 IN THE PRINCIPAL ANCIENT TEXTS

(No symbol preceding an entry indicates agreement with MT)

V.	MT	Esdras B	Vulgate	Arabic (A) or Ethiopic (E)
9:6	אתה הוא	+ καὶ εἶπεν Εσδρας	tu ipse	+ dixerunt (E)
9:7	מאור כשדים	= ἐκ τῆς χώρας τῶν Χαλδαίων	= de igne	
9:8	לתת 1°	+ αὐτῷ	+ ei	
9:8	לתת לזרעו	= καὶ τῷ σπέρματι αὐτοῦ	= ut dares semini eius	
9:17	במרים	= ἐν Αἰγύπτῳ	= quasi per contentionem	
9:17	סליחות	> (LXX^B)	= propitius	
9:18	אשר העלך	= οἱ ἐξαγαγόντες ἡμᾶς	qui eduxit te	
9:18	ויעשו נאצות גדלות	καὶ ἐποίησαν παροργισμοὺς μεγάλους	feceruntque blasphemias magnas	> (A)
9:19	ואת הדרך	= τὴν ὁδόν	= iter	
9:21	ורגליהם	= τὰ ὑποδήματα (LXX^{A,S})	pedes eorum	
9:22	ותחלקם לפאה	= καὶ διεμέρισας αὐτοῖς	= et partitus es eis sortes	> (A)
9:22	ואת ארץ 2°	>	et terram	
9:23	לרשת	= καὶ ἐκληρονόμησαν αὐτήν	= et possiderent	
9:24	ויבאו...הארץ	>	et venerunt filii et possederunt terram	
9:25	ואדמה שמנה	>	et humum pinguem	
9:26	וימרו	= ἤλλαξαν	provocaverunt	

9:26	גום	= σώματος	terga	
9:28	כרחמיך רבות עתים	= ἐν οἰκτιρμοῖς σου πολλοῖς	in misericordiis tuis multis temporibus	
9:29	והמה הזידו	>	egerunt	
9:31	וברחמיך הרבים	= καὶ σὺ ἐν οἰκτιρμοῖς σου τοῖςπολλοῖς	in misericordiis autem tuis plurimis	
9:31	כי אל	= ὅτι ἰσχυρὸς εἶ	quoniam Deus	
9:33	ואנחנו הרשענו	= καὶ ἡμεῖς ἐξημάρτομεν	autem impie egimus	
9:35	במלכותם	= ἐν βασιλείᾳ σου	= in regnis suis bonis	
9:36	ואת...עליה	>	et quae bona sunt eius et nos ipsi servi sumus in ea	
9:37	ותבואתה מרבה	>	et fruges eius multiplicantur	

4.3 Context: Neh 7:5–10:40

The Nehemiah memoir, a first-hand account of the historical Nehemiah's achievements, provides the schema for the larger narrative now extant as the Book of Nehemiah.[4] The book also contains blocks of material not derived from the memoir, such as 7:5–10:40, an editorial construct of diverse materials. Evidently this block or construct has been spliced into the memoir. Although there is debate as to where the construct begins and ends,[5] it comprises topics such as the completion of the Jerusalem wall, the list of returnees from exile, the

---

[4] Among scholars there is consensus as to the existence of a Nehemiah memoir. Opinions vary as to the type of composition that the memoir represented. For a survey of these views, see Kellermann, *Nehemia: Quellen, Überlieferung und Geschichte*, 4–8, 76–84.

[5] E.g., Williamson argues that the list of returnees from Babylon (7:5b–72a) belongs to the Nehemiah memoir and that the interpolated material begins at 7:72b. *Ezra, Nehemiah*, 268–69. Kellermann maintains that the Nehemiah memoir does not resume until 12:27a and 12:31, the latter of which returns to first-person narration. *Nehemia: Quellen, Überlieferung und Geschichte*, 74–75. Following Blenkinsopp, we understand the interpolated material to comprise 7:5–10:40, such that the theme of repopulating Jerusalem is raised in 7:4 and resumed at 11:1. Within the construct, a "semblance of unity" results from the link between the penitential prayer and the covenantal agreement that follows it. *Ezra-Nehemiah: A Commentary*, 46–47.

reading of the law with celebration of *Sukkoth*, the dismissal of foreigners from the community, and the functioning of the cult. In all likelihood, the incorporation of these topics into the construct proceeded in stages. For example, in its first stage Nehemiah 9–10 was arguably a ceremony of penitential prayer (9:1–37) followed by a covenantal agreement to observe God's law with regard to intermarriage (9:38, 10:28–30); subsequently were added the list of priests, Levites and laity (10:1–27) and additional stipulations of cultic law (10:31–39).[6] In its final form, Nehemiah 9–10 summarizes the reforms described in Nehemiah 13, which stands as the conclusion of the Nehemiah memoir.[7] Nehemiah 13 was perhaps a point of reference when Nehemiah 9–10 was given its final form. The core of Nehemiah 9–10, however, is a penitential prayer linked to a covenantal agreement. In this Nehemiah 9–10 parallels Ezra 9–10, which also frames a penitential oration (Ezra 9:6–15) with a resolution solemnized as a covenant (Ezra 10:3).[8]

As frameworks for prayer, Ezra 9–10 and Nehemiah 9–10 display similarities and differences. In terms of content, both texts refer to Deut 7:3 as the warrant against intermarriage with non-Israelites. Ezra 9 addresses intermarriage in the penitential prayer itself (Ezra 9:12) and interprets the warrant in light of another text, Deut 23:3 (Ezra 9:1–2, 12). In Nehemiah, however, the warrant is cited outside the prayer (10:29–30) and is never subject to exegesis.

As for structure, in chapter three we noted that the verses contiguous to the prayer in Ezra (9:3–5, 10:1) are sufficiently consistent with the prayer to require its inclusion. Were the prayer not in place, the text would "bleed" as if ruptured. Similarly, in Nehemiah attention is paid to the seams joining the prayer to the narrative. To segue into the prayer, the author places in the mouths of the Levites a blessing upon God and God's name from everlasting to everlasting (9:4–5). Because the blessing typically concludes a psalm, Neh 9:4–5 anticipates a new prayer beginning in 9:6.[9] Following the prayer, a transition (וּבְכָל זֹאת

---

[6] A primary indication that 10:1–27 and 10:31–39 are secondary is that the direct speech beginning in 9:5 continues at 9:38 and 10:28, as noted by Rudolph, *Esra und Nehemia*, 172–73. For further indications, see Blenkinsopp, *Ezra-Nehemiah: A Commentary*, 311.

[7] To wit, Neh 10:30 re. intermarriage // Neh 13:23–29; Neh 10:31 re. sabbath // Neh 13:15–22; Neh 10:39 re. temple tithes of grain, wine and oil // Neh 13:12.

[8] Boda provides a detailed comparison of Ezra 9–10 and Nehemiah 9–10 as "covenant ceremonies" that are uniquely post-exilic and different in kind from those that appear in a Dtr context. Boda's comparison is accurate and comprehensive, and his suggestion that the "covenant ceremony" is a *Sitz im Leben* of these penitential prayers would be most convincing were his supporting data relating to "common activities" and "common perspectives" further integrated into his argument. See his *Praying the Tradition*, 32–41.

[9] In citing the cases where this blessing concludes a psalm, Blenkinsopp stipulates the one case when the blessing begins a prayer, 1 Chr 29:10. For Blenkinsopp, the fact

10:1) points toward the community's resolve to adhere to the law. The transition, whether translated concessively as "despite all this" or more broadly as "because of all this," implies one common voice extending from the prayer (9:6–37) to the covenant (10:1), thus linking the two core elements of Nehemiah 9–10.

In terms of vocabulary, there is a degree of overlap between Ezra 9–10 and Nehemiah 9–10. For example, both characterize the people's resolve as a "covenant," but each uses a different Hebrew expression.[10] Both associate oaths with the covenant, but it appears that different formulas are invoked.[11] Both exhort the people to confession (ידה in *hitpaʻel*), but again the connotations are not identical.[12]

Inasmuch as we have established C as the author of Ezra 9–10 and observe similarities between it and Nehemiah 9–10, the question of authorship arises. Both texts are conspicuous in their using ידה in *hitpaʻel* and Deut 7:3 as a legal precedent. Other comparative data may readily be adduced.[13] Although we

---

that the Chronicler alone begins prayer thus is counted as evidence for C's composing Nehemiah 9. *Ezra-Nehemiah: A Commentary*, 296–97.

[10] Ezra 10:3 uses the traditional term בְּרִית while Neh 10:1 uses אֲמָנָה, a term connoting resolve without implying that God is direct partner to the covenant. In its nominal form, the term is unique to Nehemiah (11:23), but as an adverb the term occurs in the story of Achan (Josh 7:20), which was known to C (see 1 Chr 2:7).

[11] In the previous chapter we noted that the author of Ezra 9–10 shows interest in Psalm 105's treatment of covenant; the psalm's three essential points on covenant align with those of Ezra 10:3–5, and in reference to "covenant" and "oath" the terms are the same (שְׁבוּעָה, בְּרִית). In Neh 10:1, 29, however, people partake of the covenant by pronouncing a curse and an oath, a novel course of action that anticipates the ceremony of covenant renewal later attested at Qumran (see 1QS I–II).

[12] In the case of Ezra 10:11, תְּנוּ תוֹדָה לַיהוָה parallels the imperative to confess/praise in Josh 7:18–19. In Ezra 10:1, however, the expression וּכְהִתְפַּלֵּל עֶזְרָא וּכְהִתְוַדֹּתוֹ ("Ezra prayed and made confession") is a short, post-biblical confession that may be traced back to a priestly context in which the confession of sins constituted a part of the sacrificial ritual (Lev 5:1–6, Num 5:5–10). Such a context obtains as well in Neh 9:2,3, where the Israelites "confess their sins and the iniquities of their ancestors" (וַיִּתְוַדּוּ עַל חַטֹּאתֵיהֶם וַעֲוֹנוֹת אֲבֹתֵיהֶם). G. Mayer notes that the short post-biblical confession implies that a private individual is speaking for him or herself extemporaneously, as opposed to citing a complex composition within the cult. This view helps to explain why ידה in *hitpaʻel* does not appear in the long penitential prayers we are studying. To confess sin, the long prayers use language distinct from the pithy ידה. Furthermore, Mayer notes a trend for such prayers to be framed by the short biblical confession, as in the two cases cited here and in Dan 9:4,20. If this framing were a literary convention, it would explain further why ידה in *hitpaʻel* is not attested in the prayers themselves, which reserve other language for the confession of sin. See G. Mayer, "ידה," *TDOT* 5:439–42.

[13] There is a structural similarity inasmuch as Ezra 9:1–5 and 10:1–8 are a conflation of sources while Neh 8:1–12 and 9:1–5 also appear to be a conflation of two strands. Re. the likelihood that C has composed both, see Blenkinsopp, *Ezra-Nehemiah: A Commentary*, 187, 294–95.

cannot argue for C's authorship of Nehemiah 9–10 as persuasively as we did for Ezra 9–10, it remains plausible that C stands behind Nehemiah 9–10.[14] Before further consideration of the question, however, we must study the prayer itself, Neh 9:6–37.

4.4 Structural Analysis: Neh 9:6–37

The question of prosody is different from that of structure and will be addressed here in preliminary fashion. Our translation of Neh 9:6–37 is in verse because several features of the prayer suggest that it is poetry.[15] The evidence, however, is not univocal.[16] Thus scholars describe the prayer as an amalgam of poetry and prose; it is said to be "rhythmic liturgical prose,"[17] "a penitential song in the form of a prayer,"[18] and "a liturgical prose prayer in Scripture."[19] It suffices to say that on a continuum between poetry and prose, the prayer is somewhere near the center.[20]

---

[14] In fact numerous scholars have recognized the hand of C or a Chronistic redactor in the prayer's context but discount C as the author of the prayer itself. See L. W. Batten, *The Books of Ezra and Nehemiah*, 365; Martin Rehm, "Nehemias 9," *BZ* nf. 1 (1957): 57–67; Kellermann, *Nehemia: Quellen, Überlieferung und Geschichte*, 36 n. 172; Blenkinsopp, *Ezra-Nehemiah: A Commentary*, 294–97, 302.

[15] Indications of poetic structure include parallelism (9:15aα,β), segments of discernible meter 9:6–7) and poetic syntax. Regarding the prayer's irregularity of meter and strophic structure, see A. Gunneweg, *Nehemia* (KAT 19.2; Stuttgart: Gerd Mohn, 1987), 124.

[16] Prose elements found in the prayer include the recurrence of the *waw* consecutive as well as the "prose particles" את, אשר and ה. Francis Andersen and David Noel Freedman have established a statistical standard of frequency for the three prose particles: in prose they constitute 15% or more of all words and in poetry 5% or less. By this standard, Neh 9:6–37 is closer to the prose end of the scale. The prose particles account for 14.5% (83 of 572) of all words. On the instrument of Andersen and Freedman, see their *Hosea: A New Translation with Introduction and Commentary* (AB 24; Garden City, N.Y.: Doubleday, 1980), 60–66.

[17] Ackroyd, *I & II Chronicles, Ezra, Nehemiah*, 301.

[18] F. C. Fensham, "Neh. 9 and Pss. 105, 106, 135 and 136: Post-exilic Historical Traditions in Poetic Form," *JNSL* 9 (1981): 37.

[19] Leon Liebreich, "The Impact of Neh 9:5–37 on the Liturgy of the Synagogue," *HUCA* 32 (1961): 227.

[20] The continuum between biblical poetry and prose is implied by Kugel, who speaks of poetry and prose as stylistic poles: "... there is nothing absolute about the stylistic poles distinguished – that, in this respect most of all, the very identifying of one extreme of parallelistic, terse, elliptical sentences as 'poetry' and their opposite as 'prose' is in some basic way misleading." *The Idea of Biblical Poetry: Parallelism and its History* (New Haven/London: Yale University Press, 1981), 83.

With regard to the text's *Gattung,* no *prima facie* determination is possible, and several alternatives exist.[21] Noteworthy, however, are the affinities between Neh 9:6–37 and the psalms of communal lament. The psalms and prayer exhibit a certain relationship of form that is not immediately self-evident. Thus, correlations between the prayer's elements and the form-critical repertoire of the communal lament are indicated in this section and elaborated in the next.

There are two parts to the prayer, the historical recital (9:6–31) and the prayer proper (9:32–37). The division is indicated at 9:32 with וְעַתָּה ("and now") followed by a second invocation to the "great, mighty and fearsome" God (הָאֵל הַגָּדוֹל הַגִּבּוֹר וְהַנּוֹרָא). These encomiums of God, based on Deut 10:17 and well attested in the later books of the Hebrew Bible (Jer 32:18, Dan 9:4, Neh 1:4–5), may have become liturgical formulas by the post-exilic period.[22] They also constitute an invocation in the manner of the psalms of communal lament. Specifically, they are hymnal attributes added to the name of God that appeal to God's power and willingness to help.[23]

After the invocation there begins the prayer proper, which involves a petition followed by a confession of sin and a complaint. The petition (9:32aβ) asks that God not make light of the hardship that has beset God's people. The intercessory language lacks certain hallmarks of the communal laments.[24] Also, in many communal laments the petition either contains words of poignant complaint[25] or is followed by a passage of complaint.[26] Neh 9:32aβ, however, merely alludes to travail, and does so only briefly ("Do not make light of all the hardship that has beset us" אַל יִמְעַט לְפָנֶיךָ אֵת כָּל הַתְּלָאָה אֲשֶׁר מְצָאַתְנוּ).

---

[21] Some of these alternatives relate to history writing. For example, von Rad refers to Nehemiah 9 in his discussion of the "short historical credo." He focuses on Neh 9:13–14, regarding Sinai, to maintain that "with this stage the *genre* falls apart, for the historical conspectus now includes the creation, the patriarchal history, Egypt, the exodus, Sinai, the desert wanderings, the settlement in Canaan, the time of the Judges and the monarchy right down to post-exilic times." "The Form-Critical Problem of the Hexateuch," 13. Neh 9:6–37 has also been linked form-critically to the historical psalms (Pss 78, 105, 106, 135, and 136), although most scholars resist merging these into a single *Gattung* because in each the historical recital and its purpose are varied. Thus, Fensham assigns each of these psalms as well as Nehemiah 9:6–37 its own *Gattung* specified by purpose (see n. 18 above). In another vein, Neh 9:6–37 has been associated generically with biblical praise; Rehm concludes: "In its foremost sense, the prayer is thus a litany of God's gracious deeds." ("Das Gebet ist also in seinem Hauptteil eine Aufzählung der Wohltaten Gottes.") "Nehemias 9," 67.

[22] This view is developed by Newman, *Praying by the Book,* 101–2.

[23] Cf. the following invocations with divine attributes: "Help us, O God of our salvation" (Ps 79:9), "Give ear, you who lead Joseph like a flock, you who are seated upon the cherubim" (80:2), "O God of vengeance" (94:1–2).

[24] Most communal laments petition God to "remember" and/or not to "forget" God's people in difficulty. Cf. Pss 44:25; 74:2,18,19,23; 79:8.

[25] Cf. Pss 44:25; 74:19a, 20b.

[26] Cf. Ps 79:1–4 as preceding 79:5ff; Ps 80:5–7 as preceding 80:8.

Rather than complaint, a confession of sin (9:33–35) is fused onto the petition. The confession is distinguished by its formulaic language (first person plural "we have done wicked deeds הִרְשָׁעְנוּ) and other features such as listing the prominent persons with whom the penitents are in solidarity (cf. Jer 44:17; Dan 9:6,8; Ezra 9:7). Fusing the petition and confession of sins in this manner is an exilic or post-exilic development that Edward Lipinski dates to Josiah's reform of sixth century B.C.E.[27] Johannes Kühlewein provides a precise account of the two elements' interrelationship: a confession of sins (vv. 34ff) along with the praise of God's righteousness (v. 33) is conjoined to the lament (v. 36) and the request (v. 32).[28] Similar to Lipinski, he locates this form-critical development in "an advanced traditio-critical stage of the communal lament."[29]

Concluding the penitential prayer proper is the complaint (9:36–37), which one would expect to be more proximate to the petition (9:32aβ) were this a conventional lament of the community. These final verses complain about the foreign kings who take the land's rich yield while exercising power over the Judeans and their livestock. The reference may be to Persian taxation that is indicated elsewhere in Ezra-Nehemiah (Ezra 4:13, 7:24; Neh 5:4). If so, the lament functions as a veiled call for Judean self-determination in the homeland. Inasmuch as the lament's background is one of national politics, 9:36–37 follows a convention of the psalms of communal lament.[30]

The material prior to 9:32 is the historical recital, whose principal divisions may be determined on the basis of content, structure and vocabulary: 9:6 Creation, 9:7–8 Abraham, 9:9–11 Exodus, 9:12–21 Wandering in the Wilderness, 9:22–31 Taking of the Land and Life Therein. The recital's sweep, from creation to life in the land, reflects a view of history consonant with the priestly composer, as it relates "the universal creaturely dimension of the

---

[27] In Edward Lipinski's view, during pre-exilic times, confession of sin was always a distinct phase apart from the penitential liturgy. During the time of the Deuteronomic reform, he holds, confession of sin entered the liturgy at the rite of supplication. In the sixth century B.C.E., he concludes, Israelite prayer began to evince a more intense need to confess the nation's sins to God. *La Liturgie Pénitentielle dans la Bible* (Paris: Les Éditions du Cerf, 1969), 39.

[28] "Das Prosagebet Neh 9 schliest in V 32–37 eindeutig mit einer KV, wobei mit der Klage (V 36f) und der Bitte (V 32) noch ein Sündenbekenntinis (V 34f) und das Lob der Gerechtigkeit Gottes (V 33) verbunden sind – Zeichen für ein bereits fortgeschrittenes überlieferungsgeschichtliches Stadium der Klage." Kühlewein, *Geschichte in den Psalmen*, 125.

[29] Ibid.

[30] As Gunkel states the matter: "Die Klagen der im Psalter erhaltenen Volksklagelieder sind fast sämtlich politischer Art Pss 44:10–17, 20, 23–25; 60:3–5, 12; 74:4–11; 79:1–4; 80:5–7, 13 ...." *Einleitung in die Psalmen*, 125. Mowinckel explains that "as a rule the national psalms of lamentation are concerned with national and political distress: defeat in war, attack and ravaging by external enemies, who are sometimes named.... The background of each psalm is some definite historical event." *The Psalms in Israel's Worship*, 1:197.

relationship with God to the particular historical relationship between God and Israel."[31] The initial focus upon creation occurs in two other biblical recitals of history, Pss 135:7 and 136:4–9. The taking of the land (Neh 9:22–31) is a standard terminus in the biblical accounts of history. In its entirety, Neh 9:6–31 is a rather complete rendition of events, as indicated by the overview of Israelite histories in Table 6.

TABLE 6

SEQUENCE OF EVENTS
IN THE HISTORICAL ACCOUNTS OF ISRAEL
INCLUDED IN THE HEBREW BIBLE

Event	Neh 9: 6–37	Ezek 20: 1–38	Ps 78: 12–32	Ps 78: 44–72	Ps 105	Ps 106	Ps 135	Ps 136
Creation	9:6	-	-	-	-	-	135:7	136: 4–9
Patriarchs	9:7–8	-	-	-	105: 8–15	-	-	-
Exodus	9: 9–11	20: 5–10	78: 13	78: 44–51	105: 28–37	106: 8–12	135: 8–9	136: 10–15
Wilderness	9: 12–21	20: 11–26	78: 14–24	78: 52–53	105: 43	106: 13–34	-	136: 16
Taking of the Land	9: 22–31	20: 27–30	-	78: 54–55	105: 44–45	106: 35–43	135: 10–11	136: 20–24

All the recitals in table six are Deuteronomistic in that they provide a theological perspective on past events. Because this dissertation aims to specify the Dtr character of Neh 9:6–37, let us note how the recital uniquely follows Dtr's version of Israelite history. The prominence of Abraham coincides with Dtr's choice of the patriarchs as religious models for Jews who returned from exile. Also, Sinai's centrality is likely a Dtr feature that is designed to reinforce the moral identity of "Israel" among post-exilic Jews.[32] In a later section of this chapter, we will distinguish further the relative influences of the priestly and Dtr tradents upon the prayer in Nehemiah 9. Now we proceed to a form-critical inventory of the historical recital (9:6–31).

---

[31] Albertz, *A History of Israelite Religion*, 490.
[32] Ibid., 472–73.

Like the prayer, the historical recital itself is bipartite, with Neh 9:6–16 forming the first half and 9:17–31 the second half.[33] The substantive difference between the two halves is the introduction of moral failure into the latter. For example, "they and our ancestors acted insolently and stiffened their necks (הֵזִידוּ וַיַּקְשׁוּ אֶת עָרְפָּם)" (9:16); "they had made a molten calf for themselves... and carried out great blasphemies (נֶאָצוֹת גְּדֹלוֹת)" (9:18); "they were rebellious and revolted against you (וַיַּמְרוּ וַיִּמְרְדוּ בָךְ)" (9:26); "[They] sinned against your ordinances" (וּבְמִשְׁפָּטֶיךָ חָטְאוּ בָם) (9:29). While the first half of the history never refers to Israelite wrongdoing, such language appears in 9:17–31 for two reasons. First, the second half of the history, especially 9:26–31, is structured on a sin-punishment-repentance-salvation cycle drawn from the book of Judges.[34] In this model, the classic Dtr formulation from Judg 2:11–23 is superimposed on Israelite history: After rebellion, punishment is inevitable. Thus, the second half of the history has a distinctively penitential tone due to the influence of a source, Judges 2, and a tradition, Dtr.

Consistent with this choice, moreover, is the description of Sinai at the center of the historical recital (9:16–17). Structurally, Sinai is a hinge and a moral threshold. After the law has been given, it is possible to transgress its precepts and turn away from God. Sinai thus marks a new era in this and other post-exilic prayers.[35] The Israelites at Sinai have aptly been compared to a boy at puberty undergoing initiation rites "whose role is to mark the boy's turning away from childhood and entrance into the world of social responsibilities."[36] With the promulgation of the community's sacred codes and customs, the people enter a new time with new responsibilities.

Recognition of the historical recital's bipartite structure invites a comparison of Neh 9:6–31 with Psalm 78, a communal lament that also incorporates two distinct sequences of Israelite history (78:13–32, 40–64). In

---

[33] In their analysis of literary design, scholars increasingly recognize that the five thematic divisions noted above do not follow pentateuchal chronology and reflect rather a different underlying principle. As yet there is no consensus as to the elusive structure of the historical recital. While my proposal of a bipartite structure with Sinai as the moral hinge is original, at least one other scholar propounds this schema. See Mark Throntveit, *Ezra-Nehemiah* (Louisville: John Knox, 1992) 102–6, esp. 104.

[34] Blenkinsopp, *Ezra-Nehemiah: A Commentary*, 306. The Dtr formulation of Judg 2:11–23 is easily distinguished from, for example, the priestly compendium of misdeeds in Lev 26:3–45.

[35] In a previous chapter we noted that within the communal lament of Isa 63:7–64:11, vv. 63:19b–64:3 form a discrete unit treating the Sinai theophany. The unit that follows, 64:4b–6, delivers the lament's principal confession of sin, in light of events at Sinai. In subsequent prayers of the Jewish liturgy, references to Sinai anchor the middle benedictions in several of the Sabbath *'Amidoth*. These include the morning service, the Musaf service, and the *'amidah* for Sabbath and the new moon, all available in Seligmann Baer's *Seder 'Avodath Yisra'el* (Rödelheim: 1868), 219, 238–39, 240.

[36] Ilana Pardes, *The Biography of Ancient Israel: National Narratives in the Bible* (Berkeley: University of California Press, 2000), 67–68.

Psalm 78, both presentations of historical traditions are based on a pattern of miracle-sin-divine anger-punishment much like that drawn from Judges 2 and applied to sections of Neh 9:6–31. Moreover, the historical cycles in both the psalm and the prayer include interludes of God responding mercifully to human misdeeds (Ps 78:33–39, 65–72;[37] Neh 9:17b,19–20,27b,28b,31a). Unlike the prayer in Nehemiah, both of the psalm's historical sequences include instances of rebellion, and there is no reference to Sinai as a hinge to distinguish the two parts (among the historical psalms, Sinai is mentioned only in Ps 106:19–20). Rather, the psalm is structured according to poetic principles.[38] Later in this chapter, we will see further correspondences, especially in terms of phrasing and diction, between Neh 9:6–37 and Psalm 78, a psalm with communal lament.

Finally, we must address the form-critical relationship between the two main parts of the prayer, the bipartite historical recital (Neh 9:6–31) and the petition/confession of sin (9:32–37). As we have seen, the latter reflects the genre of communal lament in a relatively late stage of development. The stage may also be observed in Psalm 106:

> Next to the confessions of sins there is found in Psalm 106 the petition regarding help (v. 4,47); the lament here merely resonates in the background. The combination of the confession of sins and petition in place of the former [convention]—lament, petition—shows that we are traditio-historically in an already advanced stage. In this, the other parts of the historical recital assume a new function, naturally primarily the parts which relate to the providential care of Yahweh; they hold up to Yahweh his early conduct, thus strengthening the accusation and supporting the petition.[39]

Kühlewein notes the fundamental transformation that has taken place in this late psalm, which he considers to be most comparable with Neh 9:6–37: petition is now joined with confession of sin. His point is important for this dissertation's study of the confession of sin as a catalyst of post-exilic prayer. Kühlewein also indicates the role of the historical recital that precedes the psalm. The events hold up to God his early conduct, thus strengthening the people's self accusation

---

[37] In his analysis of the psalm's structure, Clifford indicates two recitals "each followed by a sequel in which divine merciful response is depicted." "In Zion and David a New Beginning: An Interpretation of Psalm 78," 129.

[38] Ibid., 127.

[39] "Neben dem Sündenbekenntnis begegnet aber nun in Ps 106 die Bitte um Hilfe (V 4f.47)—die Klage schwingt hier lediglich in Hintergrund mit. Die Verbindung von Sündenbekenntnis und Bitte statt dem sonstigen: Klage—Bitte, zeigt, das wir uns traditionsgeschichtlich in einem bereits fortgeschritten Stadium befinden (s.o.). Damit können nun auch die anderen Teile de Geschichtsrückblicks eine neue Funktion bekommen, primär natürlich die Teile, die von Jahwes früherem Heilshandeln berichten (vgl. Die Tabelle): sie halten Jahwe sein früheres Tun von Augen, verstärken also die Anklage und unterstützen die Bitte." Kühlewein, *Geschichte in den Psalmen,* 124.

and supporting their petition for divine succor. Such are the historical grounds upon which the petition for mercy is based. Kühlewein's analysis finds support in the commentaries of Williamson and Blenkinsopp, both of whom characterize the history as a vehicle for the confession of sins.[40]

Common to all three scholars is the presumption that in Neh 9:6–37 the historical recital performs a standard function of the psalms of communal lament, the statement of motive. In the nomenclature provided by Mowinckel, "statement of motive" is an umbrella term for reasons why God should listen to the people and act on their prayer. Among the possible motives is calling to mind the cause of the distress, specified in terms of the people's righteous innocence or their enemies' wickedness and hate.[41] In the historical recital of Neh 9:6–31, the convention is altered such that the contemporary distress owes directly to the people's own wickedness and lack of righteous innocence. Since the giving of the law on Sinai, the people have too often lived lawlessly. They reiterate the dark chapters of Israelite history so as to acknowledge their sin and thus press God for a merciful response to their present distress. Their penitential posture recalls our study of prayers in Trito Isaiah and Ezra as these cull from the communal laments attributes such as deceit, shame and disgrace (Isa 63:8,10; Ezra 9:6). Both prayers apply the disreputable attributes to God's people much like Neh 9:6–31 witnesses to the people's wickedness and lawlessness in history.

To summarize this section, Neh 9:6–37 has two parts, a historical recital (9:6–31) and a prayer proper (9:32–37). The former is bipartite with a structure analogous to that of Psalm 78. Within the history, Sinai (9:16) is the hinge after which there appear numerous accounts of lawlessness. The cyclical nature of these accounts reflects the book of Judges, and the accounts' tone is decidedly penitential. Indeed the historical recital's primary function is to acknowledge Israelite sin so as to motivate God to act on the Judeans' petition. The prayer proper specifies the petition (9:32aβ), that God not make light of the Judeans' present travail. The petition is fused to a confession of sin and together these form the nucleus of the prayer proper. Two other elements, an invocation (9:32aα) and a lament/complaint (9:36–37), begin and conclude the prayer, respectively.

---

[40] Williamson follows Kühlewein and argues that the third-person litany of moral failure in Neh 9:17–31 renders the historical recital a basis for appealing to God's mercy and, specifically, a vehicle for the confession of sins. The human misdeeds indeed strengthen the self-accusation in Neh 9:33—and so add poignancy to the appeal for mercy. *Ezra, Nehemiah*, 307. Like Kühlewein, Blenkinsopp compares Neh 9:6–37 to Psalm 106 to show that the purpose of the former's historical recital is "the communal confession of a sinful history leading up to the 'great distress' in which the people now finds itself." *Ezra–Nehemiah: A Commentary*, 302.

[41] *The Psalms in Israel's Worship*, 1:206.

4.5 Form-Critical Inquiry: Neh 9:6–37 and the Psalms of Communal Lament

The preceding section allowed us to note points of contact between Neh 9:6–37 and the psalms of communal lament. The historical recital that begins the prayer is similar to Psalm 78 in structure, and, as we shall see, it echoes several of the psalm's expressions. The prayer proper approximates the communal laments in terms of their common, formal elements. The prayer's invocation and complaint/lamentation, we have seen, are consistent with those of the lament, and this section will demonstrate how the confession of sin, which has been joined to the petition, follows conventions of the lament genre. In short, to understand the composition of Neh 9:6–37, one must read it against Psalm 78 and against the communal laments (Pss 44, 74, 79, 80) as well as the form-critical studies to which they have given rise.[42] This section will provide such a reading with attention to both the form and content of Neh 9:6–37.

Similarities between the prayer's historical recital (9:6–31) and Psalm 78 are both structural and lexical. The lexical correlations are numerous and occur mostly in the history's treatment of the Exodus/Crossing of the Reed Sea (9:9–11) and the Wandering in the Wilderness (9:15–19).[43] When an expression in these episodes echoes Psalm 78, it is not necessarily evidence of literary dependency. Many of these references find a more exact parallel in the pentateuch, the prayer's principal source for historical events.[44]

The history also includes third-person references to misdeeds and iniquity (9:16,18,26,29). Although not in the first-person plural, these are *de facto* confessions of sin because they involve a frank admission of guilt on behalf of the people. We may defer discussion of 9:16,18, and 29, but 9:26aα should be read in light of Ps 78:40:

וַיַּמְרוּ וַיִּמְרְדוּ בָּךְ
= Nevertheless they were rebellious and revolted against you (Neh 9:26aα)

כַּמָּה יַמְרוּהוּ בַמִּדְבָּר יַעֲצִיבוּהוּ בִּישִׁימוֹן
= How often they rebelled against him in the wilderness and grieved him in the desert (Ps 78:40)

It is worth recalling that when forms of the root מרה are attested in the post-exilic period, at issue is Israel's rebelliousness in the face of God's public,

---

[42] Form–critical discussion of the psalms of communal lament is found in Gunkel, *Einleitung in die Psalmen*, 117–39; Mowinckel, *The Psalms in Israel's Worship*, 1:193–224; Westermann, *Praise and Lament in the Psalms*, 173–81; Paul Ferris, *The Genre of Communal Lament in the Bible and the Ancient Near East* (SBLDS 127; Atlanta: Scholars Press, 1992), 89–100.

[43] For example, אֹתֹת וּמֹפְתִים (Neh 9:10; Ps 78:43); וְהַיָּם בָּקַעְתָּ (Neh 9:11; Ps 78:13); לֶחֶם מִשָּׁמַיִם (Neh 9:15; Ps 78:25); לֹא זָכְרוּ נִפְלְאֹתֶיךָ (Neh 9:17a; Ps 78:11).

[44] For example, Neh 9:10//Deut 34:11; Neh 9:11//Exod 14:6; Neh 9:15//Exod 16:4.

A TRANSFORMATION OF THE LAMENT   117

historical deeds.⁴⁵ The triliteral root appears predominantly (seven times) in Psalms 78 and 106 and is often parallel to a synonym of Dtr or sapiential origin. Both of the quotations above match מרה with contemporary synonyms for sin, מרד (Neh 9:26aα) and עצב (Ps 78:40). The compound verbs of Ps 78:40 also appear in Isa 63:10 and may represent a standardized expression; the verbs in Neh 9:26aα replicate the pattern but are themselves *sui generis*.

Furthermore, מרה paired with a synonym indicates rebellious conduct during the wilderness period except in the case of Neh 9:26aα, where it describes Israelites who have become indolent *in the promised land*. Their rebellion and revolt involve casting God's law behind their backs, killing the prophets sent to warn them, and committing acts of great contempt (Neh 9:26aβ,b). Thus, Neh 9:26 contains four expressions for lawlessness, each based inexactly upon an earlier portion of scripture. Neh 9:26aβ, about casting back God's law, reflects 1 Kgs 14:9 and Ezek 23:35 where *God* is cast behind the back. Neh 9:26bα, about killing the prophets, approximates 1 Kgs 19:10,14, although in 1 Kings the perpetrator is Jezebel. Finally, the acts of great contempt, נֶאָצוֹת גְּדוֹלֹת, serve as a summary statement in Neh 9:26bβ but are otherwise agent-specific; God pronounces this misfortune against humans (2 Kgs 19:3) while humans pronounce it against the mountains of Israel (Ezek 35:12). The overriding principle in the composition of Neh 9:26 is that scriptural allusions are set in new contexts, as is the case with Neh 9:26aα, "Nevertheless they were rebellious and revolted against you." That the expression recalls the promised land rather than the wilderness reflects not an artless adoption of Ps 78:40 but the tendency, evidenced throughout Neh 9:26, to contextualize scriptural material in novel ways.⁴⁶

In the prayer proper, Neh 9:32–37, there continues the creative application of confessional language drawn from the psalms of communal lament. The verse in question, 9:33, will be examined presently as a confession of sin analogous to 9:16–17, 9:18, 9:26 and 9:29. First, however, it is helpful to establish how the prayer's structure derives from the psalms of communal lament. To do so we will combine conclusions from the prior section with others drawn here.

Gunkel has established the communal lament's three principal parts,⁴⁷ and Mowinckel has added other primary elements.⁴⁸ Although the sequence of elements varies from psalm to psalm,⁴⁹ their general pattern is quite stable and remains serviceable to scholars.⁵⁰

---

⁴⁵ Knierim, *TLOT* 2:688.

⁴⁶ Further analysis of the exegetical dimension in Neh 9:26 is available in Newman's *Praying By the Book*, 95–98.

⁴⁷ *Einleitung in die Psalmen*, 125.

⁴⁸ *The Psalms in Israel's Worship*, 1:195–219.

⁴⁹ Mowinckel observes: "There is no definite sequence; these different items alternate in any order, and often recur several times." Ibid., 1:196. Ferris adds: "The structural elements are variously represented and variously placed from composition to composition. The structure of the laments is notably flexible and is subject to the issues

TABLE 7

FORM-CRITICAL STRUCTURE OF THE PSALMS OF COMMUNAL LAMENT

GUNKEL	MOWINCKEL	NEH 9:6–37
	Address	Address (9:6aα)
Complaint =	Lament =	Historical Recital (9:6–31)
		Address (9:32aα)
Petition =	Request =	Request (9:32aβ,b)
Self-Reproaches for Motivational Effect =	Statement of Motive =	Confession of Sin (9:33–35)
		Lament (9:36–37)
	Individual's Vow of Confidence	
	Confidence of Being Heard	

The first two columns of table seven show that the core of the communal lament is the petition framed by a complaint and a statement of motive. The third column suggests that the communal lament's three principal parts are realized in Neh 9:6–37, but that generic transformations have occurred. The petition or request is now framed by a historical recital and a confession of sin. Both elements, however, function in the standard manner of a frame comprising a lament and a statement of motive.

The point of the frame is to provide God with added incentive for acting upon the petition at the center of the prayer. This is exactly what takes place in Neh 9:6–37. Earlier we noted that the historical recital (9:6–31) as punctuated by the people's self-accusations is the grounds for the petition that God take seriously their present plight (see footnotes 39, 40). That is to say, the historical

---

being treated and all the emotions which are brought to bear upon their being brought to the LORD. The national laments refuse a formal structure to which they must conform." *The Genre of Communal Lament*, 92.

[50] For example, in his 1984 study *Psalmody and Prophecy*, W. H. Bellinger Jr. presents the psalms of lament as comprising an invocation, lament, petition, motivation(s), certainty of a hearing and vow. His schema is essentially that of Mowinckel. *Psalmody and Prophecy*, 22–24. In form-critical studies, innovation has come rather in construing anew the relationships between psalmic genres, as with Westermann's studies of lament and praise. For commentary on Westermann's initiatives and those of Walter Brueggemann, see Harry Nasuti, *Defining the Sacred Songs: Genre, Tradition and the Post-Critical Interpretation of the Psalms* (JSOTSup 218; Sheffield: Sheffield Academic Press, 1999), 57–62.

recital is a motivating element leading directly into the petition (9:32). Another motivating element follows the petition. We have established that the confession of sin (9:33–35) has been fused into its place immediately after the petition (see footnote 28). As a result, the petition is further strengthened as the people again confess their sin and the sin of their ancestors. In Neh 9:6–37, as in the communal laments, the petition is framed by motivating elements now oriented to the confession of sin.

The exigencies of form and function thus explain why the confession of sin was accorded an integral relationship with the petition of this post-exilic prayer. Previously the confession was a minor element of the communal lament that was often not even included.[51] Thus, the confession of sin rose in stature within the genre's form-critical repertoire. It is incomplete to hold that the confession of sin simply replaced one sub-element of the petition, the prayer for revenge.[52] Such substitution coincides with a larger transformation whereby the confession of sin is fused onto the petition as a motivating element. In turn, the petition employs the confession as part of its framework.

In light of these form-critical developments, the confession of sin in Neh 9:33–35 warrants close study. The focus is 9:33aα and 33bβ:

9:33aα: You have been just וְאַתָּה צַדִּיק

9:33aβ: In all that has come upon us עַל כָּל הַבָּא עָלֵינוּ

9:33bα: For you have acted faithfully כִּי אֱמֶת עָשִׂיתָ

9:33bβ: Yet we have acted wickedly וַאֲנַחְנוּ הִרְשָׁעְנוּ

Because צדיק and רשע are binary categories in the psalms of communal lament, they are an obvious vehicle for interpreting the confession.[53] Specifically, the tone of lament psalms such as 44 and 74 implies that the people are *righteous* and have not failed God's covenant (44:17–18).[54] In related psalms, the evildoers are the "gentile enemies and oppressors of Israel."[55] Indeed, a

---

[51] Ps 79:8–9 is one of the few confessions of sin in the psalms of communal lament. See Mowinckel, *The Psalms in Israel's Worship,* 1:214.

[52] Westermann notes that in both of the communal laments in Jeremiah 14, references to an enemy are "naturally absent" while a confession of sins appears in their place. *Praise and Lament in the Psalms,* 174.

[53] Mowinckel provides an extended discussion of צדיק and רשע in the psalms of communal lament. See his *The Psalms in Israel's Worship,* 1:206–14. Also see Pius Drijvers, who designates many of the so-called wisdom psalms (e.g. Pss 1,10,11,37,52,53,73,75,94,125,127) as psalms about a just person and a sinner (*The Psalms: Their Structure and Meaning* [London: Burns & Oates, 1965], 126–28).

[54] Ibid., 206.

[55] Ibid., 208.

reference to the רשע could indicate that a call for vengeance has been issued, as in Ps 58:7–9. In Neh 9:33, however, subjects and predicates have shifted such that the people penitently assert their own wickedness while imputing all justice to God. Form-critically the shift is not particularly remarkable as the three subjects of the communal lament (God, the people and the evildoers) are a standard means of devising structure.[56] At a less technical level, however, the shift in subjects and predicates involves a radical change in perceptions.

Whereas the psalms of communal lament maintain that the speaker's people are innocent, here the people's wickedness is asserted. Such a move has been stereotyped thus: The legal opponent who admits his own guilt declares that he is רשע and that his opponent is צדיק.[57] Subsequently he offers a reason for this admission, such as "in all that has come upon us you have acted faithfully." (Neh 9:33aβ,bα) The proponent of this view, Hans Boecker, lists Neh 9:33 among his examples,[58] and his explanation is tenable if one considers only the people and their self-accusation. It requires more nuance, however, to equate God with the people's legal opponent, a role typically reserved for gentile enemies oppressing Israel. One must specify, as do the psalms of communal lament, that God is an opponent in the sense of being culpably indifferent to the people's plight (Pss 44:9–14,19; 74:1,11,19–21; 77:9–10; 80:12–13). When God is construed thus, a declaration of God's righteousness (9:33) is a reversal of sorts. In a qualified sense, the assertions within 9:33 indeed reverse the צדיק and רשע convention in the psalms of communal lament.

Neh 9:33 not only plays on the traditional subjects of צדיק and רשע, but also departs from certain facts established earlier in the composition. Whereas Neh 9:8 called God just in light of Abram's faithfulness (a reference to Gen 15:6), 9:33 uses the people's wickedness as the foil to God's justice. In the later verse, the faithfulness once attributed to Abram has slipped from the human realm and now refers to God (9:33bα). Moreover, another confession of sin is predicated on the reversal of an earlier term. In 9:10 it is said that Israel's foes, the Egyptians, acted insolently (הֵזִידוּ), but in time the Israelites themselves act insolently before God (9:16, 29). Again, the stereotypical subjects of the communal lament are reversed; God's people embrace an ignominious predicate, from the root זיד, to effect their confession of sin. Although reversal

---

[56] The three subjects of the psalms of communal lament may serve as an organizing principle for the genre, as with Westermann's overview of Psalms 79, 74, 44, 80, 89, 83, and 60. His analysis of passages in Second Isaiah is also keyed to the three subjects. *Praise and Lament in the Psalms,* 173–76.

[57] Hans Boeker supports this interpretation with texts such as Deut 25:1, 1 Kgs 8:31, and Exod 22:7–8. *Redeformen des Rechtslebens im Alten Testament* (WMANT 14; Neukirchen-Vluyn: Neukirchener, 1964), 122–23.

[58] Ibid., 130.

involving the expression הֵזִידוּ is not original to this prayer,⁵⁹ here its triggering the confession of sin is a novel twist.

A focal point in the prayer, Neh 9:33 is like the earlier confessions of sin in that it shifts subjects and predicates to render ethical judgments. Among the prayer's confessions, however, only 9:33 publicly confesses that God is just despite the travail that now besets the people (9:36–37). Earlier, the people's sin elicited talk of God's mercy (9:17,19,27,30). Only with 9:33 is it clear that God is also just, thereby demonstrating that the people realize that their own evildoing is the root cause of their trouble. There follows a substantiation of the admission of guilt with reference to ancient history (9:34–35). Because this expression of solidarity with the forebears lacks self-justification or excuse, it further acknowledges the crisis at hand as principally the people's own doing. Such a thoroughgoing admission of guilt, we noted above, serves as motive for God to act on the prayer's petition and help the beleaguered people.

The relationship between Neh 9:6–37 and the psalms of communal lament may be summarized in terms of form and content. Analysis shows that as a result of certain generic transformations, the three principal parts of the lament psalms are realized in Neh 9:6–37. The prayer's petition (9:32) is now framed by two motivating elements that have been oriented to the confession of sin. Preceding the petition is the historical recital, which reflects the structure of Psalm 78 while delivering four confessions of sin that include a strong lexical parallel between 9:26a and Ps 78:40. Following the petition is the prayer's most complex confession of sin, 9:33–35, built on a reversal of subjects that in turn redefines the binary opposition of צדיק and רשע as it is found in the communal laments. The prayer thus represents a transformation of the psalms of communal lament, while exemplifying how the confession of sin became increasingly important in the genre's form-critical repertoire after the exile.

4.6 Neh 9:6–37: *Sitz im Leben*

The literary context of Neh 9:6–37 provides indications about the situation in life that it presumes. The prayer marks a penitential service taking place on the twenty-fourth day of the seventh month, two days after the conclusion of the weeklong feast of Sukkoth (Neh 8:18, 9:1). Thus, no new setting need be presupposed. It is possible that the prayer has come from a rite of Sukkoth or some other special occasion in the festal year.⁶⁰ These would include Yom

---

⁵⁹ In the pentateuchal narrative, the Egyptians act insolently (Exod 18:11, 21:14). But in the preaching of Deuteronomy, the subject changes and it is the Israelites who act insolently toward God (Deut 1:43, 17:13, 18:20).

⁶⁰ One of the psalmic forms identified by Marina Mannati and E. de Solms is collective supplications offered by the people. They maintain that this form's cultic setting is the fixed occasions in the liturgical year, such as the feasts of Tabernacles or Booths. *Les Psaumes* (4 vols.; Cahiers de la Pierre-qui-Vire, 26–29; Paris: Desclée de Brouwer, 1966–68).

Kippur, a candidate in that it too occurs in the seventh month.⁶¹ The prayer's acts of self-affliction (Neh 9:1) reflect the ethos of Yom Kippur, whose injunction to "afflict yourselves" (תְּעַנּוּ אֶת נַפְשֹׁתֵיכֶם Lev 16:29,31; 23:27,32; Num 29:7) is a technical term for fasting in the priestly law. More broadly, Nehemiah 9 has affinity with the penitential liturgy that arose at the onset of the exile when a Temple-based rite of atonement was no longer available.⁶²

Another indication of the situation in life comes from the prayer's functions or aims. We have noted one primary function or aim of Neh 9:6–37, to motivate God to act on the people's behalf. The prayer takes seriously the people's plight and directs itself as much to them as to God. A consideration of those involved in the prayer's composition and reception is in no way secondary to its treatment of God. There are at least two primary functions that may be assigned to the prayer on the basis of its intended effect upon the people with whom it originated.

Mark Throntveit rightly suggests that the prayer in Nehemiah 9 is designed both to console the people in their difficulty and to exhort them to live wholly by the law. Consolation comes as the prayer leads the people "to expect an immanent manifestation of divine activity."⁶³ On the other hand, the prayer also serves "to motivate the people into making the proper response so woefully lacking in the historical survey."⁶⁴ These two functions or aims may be explored simultaneously as they are not mutually exclusive.

The liturgy of repentance is a logical setting for a prayer that seeks to console the unfortunate by associating divine succor with their confessing sin. Liturgical expressions of repentance in practice at the time of the exile included fasting (Zech 7:3,5; 8:19), mourning (Lam 2:10–11), and perhaps even self-laceration (Jer 41:5).⁶⁵ These practices became increasingly commonplace in the exilic period, as indicated by the four days of fasting in Zech 8:19, in contrast to the one fast day, Yom Kippur, that is prescribed by biblical law.⁶⁶ Even after the

---

⁶¹ Although the celebration of Yom Kippur may well predate the exile, its association with the tenth day of the seventh month probably is not ancient. In fact, the inconsistency between Nehemiah 8–9 and the pentateuchal law dating Yom Kippur (Lev 16:29, 23:27; Num 29:7) "is one of several indications that the latter had not yet attained its final form." Blenkinsopp, *Ezra-Nehemiah: A Commentary*, 291.

⁶² Ackroyd presents the evidence for public occasions of mourning in the post-exilic period. See his *Exile and Restoration*, 47.

⁶³ Throntveit, *Ezra-Nehemiah*, 106.

⁶⁴ Ibid.

⁶⁵ The liturgy may have included the following penitential practices, which are documented in Ezra 9–10 and Nehemiah 9: tearing clothes, pulling out hair, sitting down, weeping, fasting, wearing sackcloth, placing dust on heads, and offering the evening sacrifice.

⁶⁶ Interestingly, after the fall of the Second Temple penitential rites such as Yom Kippur were expanded with more detail. A comparison of *m.Yoma* and its source, Leviticus 16, shows that the former alone specifies where the bull and goats initially stand, what direction they face, and to which points they are dispatched. The mention of

completion of the Second Temple and the restoration of national rites, penitential practices remained vital to the local liturgy, as with the fasting, sackcloth and dust cited in Neh 9:1. Like these penitential practices, the confession of sin also became increasingly commonplace in the post-exilic period. It is worth noting that the liturgical gestures and the confession constituted worship. Said worship proclaimed the people's salvation rather than their condemnation, even as it included penitential practices, the confession of sin and various forms of reproach.

A contemporary example of reproach punctuating an ultimately hopeful text is the liturgical expansion of Jer 32:17–24. Despite Judah's being overtaken by foreign invaders, Jeremiah buys a field (32:6–25,42–44), and does so against a historical backdrop keyed to contrast statements. Contrasting God's greatness (32:17–22) with the people's waywardness (Jer 32:23–24), the statements provide a dimension of reproach in an ultimately hopeful recital. Blenkinsopp has noted that the contrastive structure of Jer 32:17–24 approximates that of Neh 9:6–37: God's beneficence from creation to the promise of land (9:6–15) stands in sharp contrast with the people's ingratitude (9:16–17).[67] In both compositions, Blenkinsopp adds, there follows a series of contrasts that conclude with mercy rather than condemnation.[68] In sum, in Nehemiah 9 the prayer's trajectory of consolation reflects post-exilic penitential liturgy but is indebted literarily to both the psalms of communal lament and to prophecy as a genre of warning.

Warning also figures in the second function of Neh 9:6–37, motivating the people to live lawfully. The message that ethical purity must complement cultic purity came especially from the prophets. The post-exilic prophets stress that fasting must be accompanied by sincerity and charity rather than oppression (Isa 58:3–9; Joel 2:12–13). Their point is that the liturgy of repentance must have real effects in the world lest the people fall under God's judgment. Isa 58:3 underscores the point by punning on the words for fast and day (בְּיוֹם צֹמְכֶם), with "day" connoting as well the day of God's judgment, as in Amos 5:18.

Form-critically, we are dealing not with the classical prophets' warning but rather with an expansion of that form that is keyed to contrast.[69] The expansion, however, is attested in books that originated with the classical prophets (e.g. Amos 4:6–12) and becomes more clearly evident in exilic and post-exilic prophecy that is structured around contrast statements of reproach in *oratio recta*. Illustrative of this is Ezekiel 20, a historical recital with the refrain: "I thought I would pour out my wrath upon them, but I acted for the sake of my

---

the crimson cord is uniquely rabbinic. It is as if *m. Yoma* presumes the scriptural version and aims for a composite account that is fuller and more precise.

[67] Joseph Blenkinsopp, "The Prophetic Reproach," *JBL* 90 (1971): 277.
[68] Ibid.
[69] Attested in all the prophets from Amos to Ezekiel, the expansion typically achieves contrast by introducing historical material (Amos 2:9–11; Hos 9:10; Isa 5:1–7; Jer 2:4–13; Mic 6:3–5). For further description of the expansion, see Claus Westermann, *Basic Forms of Prophetic Speech* (Louisville: Westminster/John Knox, 1991), 182–86.

name." (20:8b,13b,21b) Words to warn of God's imminent wrath become part of a complex statement about divine mercy. Thus, the recital of Ezekiel 20 ends not in condemnation but in a salvation oracle (20:33–34). Ostensibly, this construction encouraged people to follow the law as it evoked a milieu of prophetic preaching.

The later books of the Bible include texts analogous to Ezekiel 20, including Neh 9:6–37.[70] The warning motif is first thematized in 9:26, "They killed your prophets, who had warned them to turn back to you," and further established at 9:29,30,34. The rejection of the prophet is *de facto* a rejection of the law, whose emissaries are the prophets. As well, the prayer's word reversals and puns represent, in post-exilic discourse, a prophetic convention of warning. Earlier we saw that the persons responsible for the prayer highly valued reversal and contrast. To this evidence we may add other examples[71] that show the character of late Israelite prophecy: "Unlike the case in monarchic Israel, when a prophet might give a new oracle, whoever now inquires of a prophet is to be confounded by a pun. Claiming to possess new oracles from Yahweh is no longer allowed."[72] The lexical dislocations that reshape prophecy in the post-exilic era are a significant feature of Neh 9:6–37.

With regard to the people, the prayer in Neh 9:6–37 has two principal functions or aims, to console and to exhort. Remarkably, both may reflect a situation of prophetic figures issuing reproaches and warnings. Although these indications are not indubitable, they are too numerous to be coincidental and so give nuance to the view that the prayer reflects the penitential liturgy exclusively. Perhaps Neh 9:6–37 arises from the penitential liturgy under the influence of exilic and post-exilic prophetic speech, especially the warning that is built on principles of contrast. In any historical reconstruction, certainty is elusive and degrees of plausibility must suffice. Nonetheless, the prophetic warning in Neh 9:6–37 requires a rethinking of Japhet's view that the post-exilic prophet who preaches reform has no ties to classical prophecy; she implies that the warning function in post-exilic prophecy appeared *de novo* in late biblical

---

[70] Among the recent attempts to compare Nehemiah 9 and Ezekiel 20, Waldemar Chrostowski presents the relevant data but overstates his case: "The affinities are so striking that it is probable that Neh 9:6–37 is a careful interpretation of the prophetic oracle preserved in Ezekiel 20 ... composed in the circles directly connected with the prophet Ezekiel." "An Examination of Conscience by God's People as Exemplified in Neh 9:6–37," *BZ* nf 34 (1990): 259.

[71] The Israelites do as they please with the Canaanites (כִּרְצוֹנָם 9:24), but later foreign kings do as they please with the Israelites (9:37). While רצון typically indicates a sentiment of pleasure, in LBH there is a shift in meaning such that the word can refer to a capricious decision (G. Gerleman, "רצה," *TLOT* 3:1260). Also, the Israelites would return to slavery in Egypt (לְעַבְדֻתָם 9:17) but ultimately are slaves in their own land (9:36). Neh 9:17 draws attention to עבדות in that it is a word wholly absent from the source text, Num 14:4: וַיֹּאמְרוּ אִישׁ אֶל אָחִיו נִתְּנָה רֹאשׁ וְנָשׁוּבָה מִצְרָיְמָה.

[72] David L. Petersen, *Late Israelite Prophecy: Studies in Deutero-Prophetic Literature and in Chronicles* (SBLMS 23; Missoula: Scholars Press, 1977), 28.

A TRANSFORMATION OF THE LAMENT   125

literature sometime after the sixth century B.C.E.[73] In this era, rather, warning reflects earlier forms that have undergone evolution. Specifically, Neh 9:6–37 reflects warning based on a reproach that goes back to the *rib*-form,[74] thereby implying that a situation of prophetic preaching as well as penitential liturgy may stand behind the prayer.

4.7 Neh 9:6–37 and Pentateuchal Sources

The relationship of the prayer in Neh 9:6–37 to the pentateuchal sources is complex. While there is ample evidence to link the prayer in Nehemiah 9 with Deuteronomy (D) as well as the Deuteronomistic view of history (Dtr),[75] since the end of the nineteenth century there has been recognition of complementary material from the priestly tradition (P).[76] Johannes Geissler, reflecting the contemporary interest in source criticism, identified in Neh 9:6–37 three points of literary confluence with P.[77] Despite Geissler's initiative, few modern commentators have addressed P's influence upon the prayer, the exception being Blenkinsopp, who highlights the priestly references to heaven and its host (9:6), Abram's name changed to Abraham (9:7), and the sabbath as holy (9:14).[78] Citing Blenkinsopp, Newman tracks P's influence in the prayer but does not specify P's role in the "reinterpretation of scriptural tradition" that, Newman

---

[73] *The Ideology of the Book of Chronicles and Its Place in Biblical Thought*, 187. Japhet's view is endorsed by Newman, who further considers the prophet as warner in Second Temple literature such as the book of *Jubilees*. *Praying by the Book*, 97 n. 62, 104–5.

[74] See Buis, "Notification de jugement et confession nationale," 204.

[75] In the previous chapters we introduced the school of thought that has drawn directly on Deuteronomic language and law to generate much of the history writing in the Hebrew Bible. The school is responsible for the books of Joshua, Judges, Samuel and Kings as we now have them, a collection referred to as Dtr. Along with this school, most survivors of the exile interpreted history thus: The disasters that have beset Israel are divine punishment for faithlessness to God since "the days of our fathers" (Judg 2:11–23). A whole pattern of history is thus portrayed in rebellion and forgiveness, and the author of Nehemiah 9 is especially keen to the cycles of human sin and divine retribution.

[76] P is an alternative account of founding events with its own linguistic and structural particularities. At a secondary level, the tradition contains a large quantity of ritual and legislative material, some of which is pre-exilic. P's historical construct, on the other hand, may reflect a later, post-exilic date coinciding with one of the final redactions of the Pentateuch. See Joseph Blenkinsopp, *The Pentateuch: An Introduction to the First Five Books of the Bible* (New York: Doubleday, 1992), 217–25, 237–42.

[77] Geissler posits an analogous relationship between Neh 9:28 (רַבּוֹת עִתִּים) and Lev 25:51; direct influence ("unmittelbaren Einfluß") between 9:29 (אֲשֶׁר יַעֲשֶׂה אָדָם וְחָיָה בָהֶם) and Lev 18:5/Ezek 20:11; and a rhetorical alliance ("die Redensart verbunden ist") between 9:32 (אַל יִמְעַט) and Josh 22:17. See his *Die literarischen Beziehungen der Esramemoiren insbesondere zur Chronik und den hexateuchischen Quellschriften* (Chemnitz: Pickenhahn, 1899), 21.

[78] *Ezra-Nehemiah: A Commentary*, 303–4.

claims, guides the prayer's composition.[79] Others have attempted to specify P's influence on Neh 9:6–37 by way of the book of Ezekiel. Although there are significant correlations between Ezekiel 20 and Nehemiah 9, Chrostowski argues the matter too generally to be persuasive.[80] On the other hand, Boda's case for Ezekiel as a primary influence on Neh 9:6–37 and other penitential prayers is focused in a manner that does not include data from other sources. Specifically, he explains the resonant opposition of צדיק and רשע in Neh 9:33 in terms of one verse, Ezek 18:9.[81] P's stamp upon Neh 9:6–37 is not easily deduced, and we will approach the task by exploring P's interrelationship with the prayer's other salient tradition, Dtr.

The prayer draws on both traditions but does so unevenly. There are eight verses that reflect the language or thought of both Dtr and P, and these occur rather evenly throughout the historical recital (9:6,7,8,13,14,18,24,29). Additionally, 12 verses have linguistic ties to Deuteronomy or Dtr alone, and these are spread across both the recital and the prayer proper (9:10,12,15,16,19,21,25,27,28,32,34,35). Finally, three verses in the historical recital contain phrases uniquely dependent on P (9:11,15,23).

The raw data are not conclusive, even though there is indicated a preponderance of Dtr references as well as the use of P material strictly within the historical recital. The relationship between Dtr and P may conform to one of several scenarios. One possibility is that the prayer has a Dtr substructure that has incorporated P material through redaction. In this scenario, after the emergence of Dtr and P as two "schools of crystallized theological thought," the former adopted elements of the latter.[82] Albertz presents evidence that a merger occurred in this manner among the exiles in Babylon.[83] A second possibility is that a P substructure has included Dtr language understood as a generic stock of

---

[79] *Praying By the Book*, 65.

[80] See n. 70.

[81] *Praying the Tradition*, 63. We demonstrated above that צדיק and רשע is a binary opposition in the psalms of communal lament, whence it comes to the prayer in Nehemiah 9. Similarly, on p. 69 Boda maintains that the reference to disgrace (וְנִכְלַמְתִּי) in Ezra 9:6 is uniquely dependent on Ezek 16:61,63, whereas Psalm 44 (44:16) has informed this penitential expression, as demonstrated in the previous chapter (see p. 72).

[82] Weinfeld maintains that there are "no significant ideological or linguistic ties between the two corpora," which he designates as D and P. *Deuteronomy and the Deuteronomic School*, 180. Richard D. Nelson also argues for the mutual autonomy of Dtr and P, despite the former's depiction of priests in its narrative. Dtr, he claims, did not concern itself with priests *per se* but used them in order to make a theological point and to reinforce ideological truths. "The Role of the Priesthood in the Deuteronomistic History," pp. 132–47 in *Congress Volume: Leuven, 1989* (ed. J. A. Emerton; Leiden/New York: Brill, 1991).

[83] Albertz lists prayer in the direction of Jerusalem (1 Kgs 8:48) among the evidence that Dtr was redacted in Babylon. See his "Le Milieu des Deutéronomistes," pp. 377–407 in *Israël construit son histoire* (ed. A. de Pury, et al.; Geneva: Labor et Fides, 1996), 406.

A TRANSFORMATION OF THE LAMENT 127

religious idiom.[84] After analyzing the "abundant" Deuteronomistic phraseology in Nehemiah 9, Anderson concludes that the prayer is not the result of Dtr redaction but took the phrases from "the vast treasury of general religious language upon which one would draw in worship."[85] Perhaps the composer of Neh 9:6–37 was committed rather to a priestly point of view and employed Dtr cursorily. Finally, we must allow the possibility that Neh 9:6–37 is harmonizing the two views of Dtr and P, a scenario that is discussed by André Lacocque but without reference to the prayer under study here.[86] Thomas Römer and Marc Brettler also posit such a scenario in arguing that a post-exilic redactor employs both Dtr and P in an attempt to create a hexateuch as the official document of Judaism.[87] According to Römer and Brettler, the redactor draws on both Dtr and P to compose Joshua 24 as the conclusion to his hexateuch, which includes redactional verses such as Gen 35:2–5 and Deut 34:1b, 7–9.

Outside of the hexateuch, Römer and Brettler focus on Neh 8:17–18 and attempt to demonstrate that these verses combine elements of Dtr and P very much in the manner of the redactor whom they posit.[88] As they broaden their focus, they cite similarities between Joshua 24 and Nehemiah 8–9 and imply that the composers of these texts are related if not identical. In light of these remarks, it is well worth considering the comparability of the composer of Nehemiah 9 and the hypothetical redactor of Römer and Brettler. To make this judgment, we shall focus on Nehemiah 9 and examine the eight passages in Neh 9:6–31 that draw on both schools of thought, Dtr and P.

> Neh 9:6aα "You alone are LORD;
> You have made the heavens, the heaven of heavens, and all their host,
> The earth and all that is on it,
> The seas and all that is in them."
>
> אַתָּה הוּא יְהוָה לְבַדֶּךָ
> אַתָּה עָשִׂיתָ אֶת הַשָּׁמַיִם שְׁמֵי הַשָּׁמַיִם וְכָל צְבָאָם
> הָאָרֶץ וְכָל אֲשֶׁר עָלֶיהָ
> הַיַּמִּים וְכָל אֲשֶׁר בָּהֶם

---

[84] In the exilic and post-exilic periods, mainstream literature was flavored with the pietistic and political expressions of Dtr; one could use such language cursorily without being a deuteronomist. This point is made by Mark Biddle in his *A Redaction History of Jeremiah 2:1–4:2* (ATANT 77; Zürich: Theologischer Verlag Zürich, 1990), 63 n.39.

[85] Anderson, "The Formation of the Levitical Prayer in Nehemiah 9," 253, 259.

[86] See his "The Land in 'D' and 'P'," pp. 91–100 in *"Dort ziehen Schiffe dahin ..."* (ed. M. Augustin and K.D. Schunck; Frankfurt: Lang, 1996).

[87] Fundamentally, Römer and Brettler associate the redactor with "block[s] of P material well integrated with D material." See their "Deuteronomy 34 and the Case for a Persian Hexateuch," *JBL* 119 (2000): 411, 414–15.

[88] Ibid., 415–16.

Clearly, the prayer's invocation recalls Gen 1:1, the keynote to P's creation account. Gen 1:1 refers to God's creating the heavens and the earth (אֵת הַשָּׁמַיִם וְאֵת הָאָרֶץ). The stronger parallel, however, is to the Dtr prayer of 2 Kings 19, where King Hezekiah avows "you alone are God" (אַתָּה הוּא הָאֱלֹהִים לְבַדְּךָ 2 Kgs 19:15), and "you made heaven and earth" (אַתָּה עָשִׂיתָ אֶת הַשָּׁמַיִם וְאֶת הָאָרֶץ 2 Kgs 19:15). God's uniqueness has precedent in Deut 6:4, and the expression "alone" (לְבַדְּךָ) is from Deut 4:35 as well as the Asaphite psalms (Pss 83:19, 86:10), a collection that features psalms of communal lament (Psalms 74,79,80). The reference to heaven and earth as God's possessions finds support in Deut 10:14, whose conclusion (וְכָל אֲשֶׁר בָּהּ) is identical to the portion of Neh 9:6 quoted above albeit in Deuteronomy the referent is the earth rather than the seas. Including the seas among the elements of creation is unique to Neh 9:6 (cf. both Deut 10:14 and 2 Kgs 19:15), perhaps to correct the suggestion in P that the seas predated God's creation (Gen 1:2). In sum, 9:6 draws primarily on phrasing from Deuteronomy and Dtr while engaging critically certain notions in P.

> Neh 9:7 "You are the LORD, the God who chose Abram
> And brought him out of Ur of the Chaldeans
> And gave him the name Abraham;"

אַתָּה הוּא יְהוָה הָאֱלֹהִים אֲשֶׁר בָּחַרְתָּ בְּאַבְרָם
וְהוֹצֵאתוֹ מֵאוּר כַּשְׂדִּים וְשַׂמְתָּ שְּׁמוֹ אַבְרָהָם

This exact expression for "chose" (בחר + ב) arises from Deuteronomic and Dtr circles, where it denotes the election of the people of Israel (Deut 4:37; 7:6–8; 10:14; 14:2; 1 Kgs 3:8).[89] Deut 7:6–8 pairs this sense of the verb and the expression "brought out" (הוֹצִיא Deut 7:8) with reference to the Israelites in exodus from Egypt. In short, Neh 9:7 points back directly to Deut 7:6–8. During and after the exile, moreover, יצא in *hifʿil* with YHWH as subject served the idea that "deliverance from Egypt stands transparently for deliverance from ... the exile in Babylon."[90] H. D. Preuss adds that this idea is found only "in the Holiness Code, P, and the Deuteronomic/Deuteronomistic History" because "the *Sitz im Leben* was where such theological argumentation was needed: oral and written 'preaching' to the exilic community."[91] Thus we find acknowledgment of P's perspective, especially with the patriarch's change of name (cf. Gen 17:5), in a treatment of Abraham that is otherwise based in the discourse of Deuteronomy and Dtr.

---

[89] Horst Seebass elaborates: "These passages may be compared to the Deuteronomic cult formula and its concept of choosing someone or something out of a whole (Deut 12:5,14). Israel, which was chosen as a peculiar people from among the peoples of the world, cannot adopt those people's superstitious practices because Israel is to be distinguished by the unique inalterability of its God." "בחר," *TDOT* 2:83.

[90] H. D. Preuss, "יצא," *TDOT* 6:247.

[91] Ibid., 6:248.

Neh 9:8 "And you found his heart faithful before you,
And made with him a covenant to give the land of the Canaanites, the
   Hittites, the Amorites,
The Perizzites, the Jebusites, and the Girgashites to his descendants;
And you have fulfilled your promise, for you are just."

וּמָצָאתָ אֶת לְבָבוֹ נֶאֱמָן לְפָנֶיךָ
וְכָרוֹת עִמּוֹ הַבְּרִית לָתֵת אֶת אֶרֶץ הַכְּנַעֲנִי הַחִתִּי הָאֱמֹרִי
וְהַפְּרִזִּי וְהַיְבוּסִי וְהַגִּרְגָּשִׁי לָתֵת לְזַרְעוֹ
וַתָּקֶם אֶת דְּבָרֶיךָ כִּי צַדִּיק אָתָּה

This lengthy verse is structured like an envelope based on צַדִּיק and נֶאֱמָן, which are the first and final words of Gen 15:6a and 15:6b. While von Rad maintained that the pentateuchal verse reflects a cultic *Sitz im Leben*, this is doubtfully so.[92] Thus Gen 15:6 itself provides interpreters of Nehemiah 9 no link to the priestly composition. Rather, a priestly hand may be detected in the expression for fixing a covenant, וַתָּקֶם אֶת דְּבָרֶיךָ. The verb is that used by P for establishing a covenant (Gen 17:7), whereas וְכָרוֹת עִמּוֹ הַבְּרִית is indicative of a different source, the Yahwist (cf. Gen 15:18).[93] Evoking P and Gen 17:7, וַתָּקֶם אֶת דְּבָרֶיךָ also points to D/Dtr, which refer to prophecy's fulfillment as הקים דבר יהוה (Deut 9:5; 1 Kgs 2:4,8:20,12:15). Weinfeld remarks that in the Deuteronomistic literature the phrase always occurs "in connection with the fulfillment of a divine promise of a national nature," such as the promise to Abraham in Neh 9:8.[94] In Neh 9:8, however, the Abrahamic covenant has equally strong priestly connotations of an absolute promise of the land by the God who is just and delivers on his word. To render God thus, the prayer relies on phrasing that is akin to הקים דבר יהוה, and which thereby intimates P and D/Dtr simultaneously. This same technique may be observed in 1 Kgs 6:12, which is part of a Deuteronomistic interlude (1 Kgs 6:11–13) in a priestly section of temple description (6:1–8:11).

Neh 9:13 "You came down upon Mount Sinai, and spoke with them from
   heaven,
And gave them just ordinances and true laws, good statutes and
   commandments,

---

[92] Von Rad linked the verb וַיַּחְשְׁבֶהָ to priestly contexts where the trilateral root חשב is attested (Lev 7:4,18b; Num 18:27); Manfred Oeming has pointed out that in von Rad's prooftexts the verb is in the *nif'al* whereas it is in the *qal* in Gen 15:6. See von Rad's "Die Anrechnung des Glaubens zur Gerechtigkeit," *TLZ* 76 (1951): 129–32 and Oeming's "Ist Genesis 15:6 ein Beleg für die Anrechnung des Glaubens zur Gerechtigkeit?" *ZAW* 95 (1983): 185.

[93] Blenkinsopp, *Ezra-Nehemiah: A Commentary,* 304.

[94] *Deuteronomy and Deuteronomic School,* 350.

9:14 And you declared your holy sabbath to them
And gave them commandments and statutes and a law through Moses your servant."

וְעַל הַר סִינַי יָרַדְתָּ וְדַבֵּר עִמָּהֶם מִשָּׁמָיִם
וַתִּתֵּן לָהֶם מִשְׁפָּטִים יְשָׁרִים וְתוֹרוֹת אֱמֶת חֻקִּים וּמִצְוֹת טוֹבִים
וְאֶת שַׁבַּת קָדְשְׁךָ הוֹדַעְתָּ לָהֶם
וּמִצְוֹת וְחֻקִּים וְתוֹרָה צִוִּיתָ לָהֶם בְּיַד מֹשֶׁה עַבְדֶּךָ

Above we indicated that Sinai inaugurates a new era marked both by God's gift of the law and the people's potential for transgressing the law. In Deuteronomic fashion Neh 9:13–14 enshrines the law with references such as "ordinances, laws, statutes and commandments." Twice mentioning "statutes" and "commandments" in succession echoes clearly the standard Deuteronomic phrase, "commandments, statutes, and judgments" (Deut 5:28,6:1,7:11). Deuteronomic parlance stands behind both 9:13, which indicates the Decalogue directly ordained by God, and 9:14, a reference to the entire corpus of law that Moses is to promulgate.[95]

The prayer's reference to Sinai involves some circumlocution in order to maintain both God's immanence and transcendence. So Neh 9:13a: "You came down upon Mount Sinai, and spoke with them from heaven." The verse locates God on Sinai *and* in heaven, a contradiction that may be resolved if one envisions Sinai's summit extending into heaven, in the manner of the seventh level of the ziggurat, which reached above the clouds into the next realm.[96] Another text that makes Sinai a vehicle of theophanic speculation is Deut 4:36: "From heaven he made you hear his voice to discipline you. On earth he showed you his great fire, while you heard his words coming out of the fire." This verse, in Weinfeld's words, is designed "to eliminate the inherent corporeality of the traditional imagery" of God.[97] That is, there is no longer even the possibility of seeing God (Gen 32:31, Exod 33:20) while contact with the divine is now a matter of words issued from heaven. The shift initiated in Deuteronomy is operative in Neh 9:13a, which merges Sinai and heaven so that God speaks from the latter even after descending upon the former.

---

[95] This distinction is applied to Neh 9:13–14 by Maurice Gilbert, "La place de la Loi dans la prière de Nèhèmie 9," pp. 307–16 in *De la Tôrah au Messie* (ed. M. Carrez et al.; Paris: Desclée, 1981), 311.

[96] According to Mesopotamian myth, the high priest climbed to the seventh level of the ziggurat once every year, thus allowing him contact with the transcendent and immanent gods. The myth was later transferred to Jerusalem, the pre-Israelite city of the Jebusites, and it subsequently influenced the composition of the biblical psalms, according to Julio Trebolle Barrera. See his *Libro de los Salmos: Religión, Poder y Saber* (Colección Estructuras y Proesos, Serie Religión; Madrid: Editorial Trotta, 2001), 124–25.

[97] *Deuteronomy and Deuteronomic School*, 208.

The one law that is mentioned concerns "holy sabbath," a term associated with P. Israel Knohl observes that "holy sabbath" is especially prominent in transition passages that link Priestly and non-Priestly writing (Exod 31:12–18, 35:1–3).[98] These passages are stylized and have an anthropomorphic tone in that God is said to rest. Three other mentions of holy Sabbath (Exod 16:23, 20:11 and Lev 23:3) fit his criteria and fall into this group of passages that he ascribes to the Holiness School. [99] The "school" is a priestly cohort whom Knohl distinguishes from the composers of the priestly Torah. In the priestly Torah, mentions of sabbath lack the adjective "holy" as well as the anthropomorphic image of God resting (Gen 2:2–3, Num 28:9–10). Thus Neh 9:13–14 poses a *coincidentia oppositorum*. On the one hand it underscores the priestly view of the Holiness School, which dramatizes God at rest on the sabbath. On the other hand, it adopts the Deuteronomic treatment of Sinai that mitigates God's corporeality. The influences of P and D/Dtr upon this verse are apposite and equally direct.

> Neh 9:18 Even when they had made a molten calf for themselves
> And said, 'This is your god who brought you up from Egypt,'
> And had carried out great blasphemies,"

> אַף כִּי עָשׂוּ לָהֶם עֵגֶל מַסֵּכָה
> וַיֹּאמְרוּ זֶה אֱלֹהֶיךָ אֲשֶׁר הֶעֶלְךָ מִמִּצְרַיִם
> וַיַּעֲשׂוּ נֶאָצוֹת גְּדֹלוֹת

The prayer alludes to the incident of the golden calf as presented in Exodus 32, which also refers to the idol as a עֵגֶל מַסֵּכָה (32:4a) and includes the quotation: וַיֹּאמְרוּ אֵלֶּה אֱלֹהֶיךָ יִשְׂרָאֵל אֲשֶׁר הֶעֱלוּךָ מֵאֶרֶץ מִצְרָיִם (32:4b). The two quotations are identical except that Neh 9:18 omits the vocative "O Israel" as well as "the land" of Egypt and changes the finite verb from plural to singular. The base text, Exod 32:4, is part of Exod 32:1–6, a pentateuchal unit that echoes Deuteronomy 9 and most exactly parallels 1 Kgs 12:26–32, a Dtr polemic against Jeroboam as founder of the northern cults.[100] The links between Dtr and Neh 9:18 are further established by the reference to "great blasphemies," נֶאָצוֹת, a word whose nominal form is otherwise attested only in 2 Kgs 19:3, of Dtr origin. Neh 9:18 is, however, not wholly Deuteronomistic in its view of Aaron. First, it attributes

---

[98] Knohl holds that the transition passages combine P language with that from other pentateuchal sources and are indicative of an "editing project." *The Sanctuary of Silence: The Priestly Torah and the Holiness School*, 66–67.

[99] Ibid., 15–17, 67.

[100] Moses Aberbach and Leivy Smolar establish the link between Exodus 32 and 1 Kings 12 by demonstrating 13 similarities between the two texts. They explain the correspondences as the result of southern Zadokites polemicizing against the rival sanctuaries at Bethel and Dan; specifically the Zadokites attacked Jeroboam through the figure of Aaron and made him primarily responsible for the calf incident (Exod 32:35). "Aaron, Jeroboam and the Golden Calves," *JBL* 86 (1967): 129–35.

the deictic expression "This is your god" to the people rather than their leader, a departure from 1 Kgs 12:28 that is also reflected in Exod 32:4b and may indicate the hand of the pentateuchal writer. More to the point, Neh 9:18 states that the people made the molten calf whereas both Exod 32:4a and 1 Kgs 12:28 agree it was the work of their leaders, Aaron and Jeroboam respectively. The suppression of Aaron's role in the idolatry of Neh 9:18 could stand on literary grounds or represent some sort of attempt to shield the preeminent priest, Aaron, from criticism.[101] The verse is clearly indebted to Dtr thought and language, but its treatment of Aaron may be sympathetic to a priestly agenda as well.

> Neh 9:24 "So the descendants entered and possessed the land,
> And you subdued before them those dwelling in the land, the Canaanites,
> And gave them into their hands, with their kings and the peoples of the land,
> To do with them as they pleased."

וַיָּבֹאוּ הַבָּנִים וַיִּירְשׁוּ אֶת הָאָרֶץ
וַתַּכְנַע לִפְנֵיהֶם אֶת יֹשְׁבֵי הָאָרֶץ הַכְּנַעֲנִים
וַתִּתְּנֵם בְּיָדָם וְאֶת מַלְכֵיהֶם וְאֶת עַמְמֵי הָאָרֶץ
לַעֲשׂוֹת בָּהֶם כִּרְצוֹנָם

We earlier discussed the rhetorical interplay between Neh 9:37 and the final expression of this verse, pegged as it were to כִּרְצוֹנָם (see footnote 71). The victor's pleasure results from the conquest described earlier in 9:24a. The land is entered and possessed, וַיִּירְשׁוּ, an expression that is wholly Deuteronomic (Deut 4:1,5; 6:18; 7:1; 8:1; 9:1,5; 11:8,10,29,31; 12:29; 28:21,63; 30:16) and extends into Dtr (Josh 1:11; 18:3). When P describes land gained through conquest, it speaks of נחלה ("inheritance" Josh 14:1,2,3;19:51) to underscore that "the land belongs to God, who allots it to whom he pleases."[102] P's perspective is epitomized in Lev 25:23, an assertion that God alone possesses the land, upon which God's people reside as tenants. God's sovereignty is also connoted by P's expression for subduing the land, כבש (Gen 1:28, Josh 18:1). That Neh 9:24 denotes conquest with the expression וַתַּכְנַע again suggests that its source is not P but the Deuteronomistic writings. Deut 9:3 depicts conquest as כנע in the *hif'il* with God as the subject. At the level of diction, Neh 9:24 exhibits contacts with Dtr over and against P. One explanation for this uncharacteristically exclusive use of tradition is that the prayer is following Dtr's narrative of conquest and occupation over and against P's account of conquest and occupation. If this is

---

[101] In priestly literature after the exile, Aaron becomes Israel's chief cultic officiant with putative roots to a northern shrine. See H. G. Judge, "Aaron, Zadok and Abiathar." *JTS* 7 (1956): 70–74. Others maintain that P established its connection with Aaron via his southern origins in a town south of Jerusalem as indicated in Josh 21:4,13, a priestly interpolation. This is the view of Aelred Cody, *A History of the Old Testament Priesthood* (Rome: Pontifical Biblical Institute, 1969), 159–64.

[102] Lacocque, "The Land in 'D' and 'P'," 95.

the case, it explains the concentration of Dtr language in the surrounding verses as well.[103]

> 9:29 "You warned them so that they would turn back to your law.
> Yet they acted insolently and did not obey your commandments,
> But sinned against your ordinances, by the observance of which one will live.
> They turned a stubborn shoulder and stiffened their neck and would not obey."

וַתָּעַד בָּהֶם לַהֲשִׁיבָם אֶל תּוֹרָתֶךָ
וְהֵמָּה הֵזִידוּ וְלֹא שָׁמְעוּ לְמִצְוֹתֶיךָ
וּבְמִשְׁפָּטֶיךָ חָטְאוּ בָם אֲשֶׁר יַעֲשֶׂה אָדָם וְחָיָה בָהֶם
וַיִּתְּנוּ כָתֵף סוֹרֶרֶת וְעָרְפָּם הִקְשׁוּ וְלֹא שָׁמֵעוּ

Earlier we discussed the warning function evident in 9:29a and other verses in the prayer (9:26,30,34). As well, the Israelites' "acting insolently" was discussed as part of the prayer's contrasts and reversals (9:17,36; 9:24,37). Novel to this verse is a view that if ordinances are followed one's life will be sustained. On the one hand, this is a Deuteronomic theme (Deut 30:15–20) with roots in the Bible's sapiential literature (Prov 2:19,5:6,6:23,10:17,15:24). Deut 30:16 promises that obeying the commandments will bring life, numerous descendants and blessing in the land to be possessed (cf. Neh 9:8,15,24). On the other hand, the view is also attested in the priestly source (Lev 18:5) and in Ezekiel (20:11,13). Knohl credits the Holiness School for Lev 18:5: "You shall keep my statutes and my ordinances; by doing so one shall live: I am the LORD."[104] Knohl relates the verse to P's list of rewards that people gain by following the commandments (Lev 26:3–13) and punishments they receive for failing to follow the commandments (Lev 26:14–45).[105] As in Deut 30:15–20, the people face a fundamental choice that will extend or curtail life as they know it. Thus, "ordinances, by the observance of which one will live" comes to this prayer from the Deuteronomic and Priestly writings. Both corpora connect lawfulness and the granting of life in an integral manner.

To summarize this section, an analysis of eight verses indicates that the prayer in Neh 9:6–37 consolidates the traditions of Dtr and P while employing each to differing degrees. The prayer appears to be partial to Dtr's language and

---

[103] For example, when Neh 9:25 describes the Israelites' bounty in the land, the sources are Deut 6:11 and 32:15, with טוב the generic term for foodstuffs. P has a different term for the land's yield, מְעֲבוּר (Josh 5:11,12). Also, the reference to destruction כָּלָה in Neh 9:31 reflects the Dtr stratum of Jeremiah (Jer 4:27;5:18;30:11;46:28). In contrast, P's conquest narrative describes decimation as שמד and חרם (Josh 11:20). P's conquest narrative is attested fragmentarily in the Book of Joshua; its reconstruction is presented in Joseph Blenkinsopp, "The Structure of P," *CBQ* 38 (1976): 287–92.

[104] *The Sanctuary of Silence: The Priestly Torah and the Holiness School*, 174.

[105] Ibid.

presentation of events in the matters of creation (9:6), Abraham and exodus (9:7) and the golden calf (9:18). Yet in each case the prayer acknowledges P's view of the matter. In other verses, an interpenetration of the two traditions allows both to be represented significantly at the levels of language and ideas. Examples include the covenant described in 9:8, the ultimately ambivalent view of God's corporeality in 9:13–14, and the connection between lawfulness and life in 9:29. These *realia* become especially complex through the recombinant use of Dtr and P traditions in their representation. One effect of the complexity is a challenge to "the simplistic systems of theodicy that associated physical comfort with devoutness and suffering with evil" and were derivative of Dtr.[106] The challenge is especially evident in verses such as Neh 9:29, which draws on P as well as Dtr to assert an integral connection between lawfulness and the granting of life that is in no way reductive.

The above investigation produces largely negative data for comparing the composer of Nehemiah 9 and the post-exilic redactor of Römer and Brettler. Although both the composer and redactor draw liberally on Dtr and P, there are scant grounds to interrelate them. It would appear that coincidence alone accounts for the noteworthy link between the books of Joshua and Nehemiah, the recurrence of בְּסֵפֶר תּוֹרַת אֱלֹהִים in Josh 24:26 and Neh 8:18. No other lexical data is forthcoming. The above analysis of eight verses from Neh 9:6–31 does not point to the hypothetical redactor, whose compositional hand is in turn evidenced nowhere in Neh 9:6–31.[107] The inability to make this or any such identification, however, does not lessen the merit of establishing that the

---

[106] The full quotation, from Stefan Reif, connects source-critical issues with liturgical practice: "... patterns of thought that had already questioned the simplistic systems of theodicy that associated physical comfort with devoutness and suffering with evil... had thereby driven a philosophical wedge between appeals to God and actual human experience, between petitions and the response to them. Perhaps scholastic circles were in this way opting for a novel view of man's communication with the Divine. Expressed in different terms, what is here being suggested is a religious ferment among the majority of the people which provided the opportunity for liturgical innovation that took diverse forms in a variety of contexts." *Judaism and Hebrew Prayer: New Perspectives on Jewish Liturgical History* (Cambridge: Cambridge University Press, 1993), 70–71.

[107] Rather, there are several points of contrast between Neh 9:6–37 and Joshua 24, the signature of the redactor hypothesized by Römer and Brettler. First, whereas Joshua 24 begins history with the patriarchs and concludes with the conquest of the land, Neh 9:6–37 begins with creation and concludes with the situation of post-exilic colonialism. Repentance and the confession of sin are integral to the prayer (Neh 9:33–35), but Josh 24:18 rules out the possibility of repentance. Finally, expressions that Römer and Brettler hold to be distinctive of their redactor are not employed in Neh 9:6–37. Specifically, Neh 9:13 does not replicate the singular forms of חקים or משפטים that are found in Josh 24:25. Also, the redactor's preference for גרש to depict God's driving from the land its prior inhabitants (Josh 24:12,18) is different from the root כנע found in Neh 9:24 and discussed above. On these points of the redactor, see Römer and Brettler, "Deuteronomy 34," 411–12.

traditions of both Dtr and P figure significantly and at times symbiotically in the composition of Neh 9:6–37. As scholars devote increasing attention to P's influence upon the prayer, they need not overlook the contribution of Deuteronomy and the Deuteronomistic schools operative during and after the exile.

4.8 Conclusion

In concluding, we may press two questions: Who is responsible for the prayer in Neh 9:6–37 and what were the circumstances of its composition? We have shown the reasonable plausibility that C stands behind Nehemiah 9–10. The prayer itself, however, exhibits features that do not match well with C. The differences are especially evident if we focus on 2 Chr 36:15–23, the book's final verses and a window on C's idealization of Israelite history.

In Neh 9:6–37, the historical portion adopts the priestly view of sabbath that emphasizes its holiness, traced back to God's resting from the work of creation. Neh 9:14 understands sabbath as a law treating forbidden labors. In contrast, C's references to sabbath typically note the day's required sacrifices (1 Chr 9:32,23:31; 2 Chr 2:3,8:13,31:3) or the labor required of the Levites at the temple (2 Chr 23:4,8). C's final reference to sabbath, which explains the exile as a fulfillment of Jeremiah's prophecy of desolation, speaks of the land paying off its sabbaths for 70 years (2 Chr 36:20). Based upon Lev 26:41–43, the image is one of the land "in its desolated state... enjoying its sabbaths, and hence ... being made acceptable to God."[108] In C's final analysis, sabbath is a key to the recuperation needed for living in a new era that coincides with the post-exilic time. This view, which supports a certain idealization of history, is in no way connoted in Neh 9:14's reference to holy sabbath as the prohibition of labors.

The second half of Neh 9:6–37, the prayer proper, laments the loss of chattel and personal liberty to the occupying kings of Persia (9:36–37). The prayer implies that "an aspiration toward political emancipation" is required so that the prayer's promises, especially that of land, might be fulfilled.[109] In C's idealized history, however, the Persian empire enjoys legitimacy and plays a divine role in reestablishing Israel after its exile (2 Chr 36: 22–23). C displays no chagrin with Persian hegemony and posits instead an idealized, alternative world wherein Israel enjoys cultic sovereignty. Neh 9:6–37 never appeals to C's idealization of history and indirectly calls for an end to oppressive rule *in the age at hand*. In this the prayer echoes the psalms of communal lament, which routinely call for vengeance upon the gentile enemy.

With C's authorship discounted, the origins of Neh 9:6–37 remain uncertain. In the parallel case of Ezra 9:6–15, C adopted the prayer but did not

---

[108] Ackroyd holds that C purposefully adopts from Lev 26:41–43 two diverse senses of the root רצה: while the people "pay off" their sin, the land "enjoys" its sabbaths. *Exile and Restoration*, 242.

[109] Blenkinsopp, *Ezra-Nehemiah: A Commentary*, 307–8.

actually compose it. Rather, Ezra 9:6–15 probably originated with the Ezra memoir. It is much less likely, however, that Neh 9:6–37 comes from the Nehemiah memoir, for the simple fact that the prayer nowhere mentions Nehemiah. Curiously, the list of signatories that follows the prayer immediately begins with "Nehemiah, the governor" (10:2). As Lester Grabbe observes, "Considering Nehemiah's penchant for getting involved in every religious or political issue of significance, his omission here is doubly strange."[110]

The prayer's authorship is lost to history, but its origins are not. We have seen indications that Neh 9:6–37 arises from the penitential liturgy under the influence of exilic and post-exilic prophetic speech, especially the warning that effects contrast. Thus the prayer reflects prophecy understood not as the "canonical variety" but as an oracular, priestly genre that emerged in the post-exilic period.[111] Such prophecy contained a dimension of cultic hymnography and music, recalled in the stichometric and strophic arrangement of Neh 9:6–37.[112] Such prophecy understood its own inner dynamism to be nothing less than the Holy Spirit, exemplified in the Spirit's descent upon the 70 elders in the wilderness (Num 11:25),[113] an incident alluded to in Neh 9:20. Such prophecy construed anew its antiquated functions, such as the Urim and Thummim, which in the post-exilic era became a means for priests to establish their sacerdotal lineage (Ezra 2:63=Neh 7:65).[114] Similarly, Neh 9:26,29 and 30 retrieve the warning function of classical prophecy in order to exhort the people to live wholly by the law. In this context, fidelity to the law is what the ancestors lacked, and a return to fidelity completes the consolation begun with the people's penitence and confession of sin.

---

[110] Grabbe concludes that Nehemiah 9 was perhaps "compiled by someone who was not necessarily a great admirer of Nehemiah and certainly not by Nehemiah himself." *Ezra-Nehemiah*, 178.

[111] The definition and description of oracular, priestly prophecy as a phenomenon that began with the reign of Artaxerxes I and ended with the death of John Hyrcanus are taken from Joseph Blenkinsopp, "Prophecy and Priesthood in Josephus," *JJS* 25 (1974): 253.

[112] Ibid., 242.

[113] Ibid., 261.

[114] Ibid., 253.

5

THE FORM-CRITICAL LEGACY OF THE COMMUNAL LAMENT IN THE HELLENISTIC AND ROMAN PERIODS

5.1 Introduction

In his *Einleitung* to the psalms, Gunkel stipulates three criteria that must be met in order to establish a *genre* of truly comparable texts, such as the psalms of communal lament.[1] First, the poems in question must belong to or derive from a specific cultic occasion, that is, a common *Sitz im Leben*. Second, the poems must evince a common manner and tone that derive from the *Sitz im Leben* or could easily be related to it. Finally, the poems must employ a common language that is related to their form. The last point is the most fundamental: truly comparable literary structures must issue comparable expressions. We are acquainted with Gunkel's criteria inasmuch as they have guided our investigations in chapters two, three and four. Our studies of three significant penitential prayers from the post-exilic period have been subdivided with respect to form and expression, manner and tone, and situation in life. The evidence indicates that Isa 63:7–64:11, Ezra 9:6–15 and Neh 9:6–37 are all expressive of the form-critical ideal that inheres in the psalms of communal lament and gives rise to Gunkel's three criteria.

The prayers, however, satisfy the psalmic criteria partially and unevenly. These discrepancies result when the prayers take a different perspective than do the psalms on points of historical interpretation and theology. The prayers and psalms also diverge because the latter, during and after the exile, underwent transformation and even disintegration such that it was difficult and not always desirable to replicate them. From a form-critical viewpoint, we have been

---

[1] Gunkel addresses genre and the criteria for establishing a genre in the first chapter of *Einleitung in die Psalmen*, 22–24.

working with a genre in its final stages. Nonetheless, we have pressed the investigation in order to determine as exactly as possible how a given prayer resembles a psalm of communal lament in its ideal. The study has yielded a wealth of data that may now be culled for synthesis.

In this chapter Gunkel's criteria will again direct the investigation for two basic reasons. His criteria provide a convenient, tri-partite way of organizing this final chapter and they reflect an understanding of the psalms that subsequent scholarship has refined considerably but not superseded.[2] We will, however, reverse Gunkel's order to begin with the most fundamental matters of form and expression. As in the previous chapters, the dominant expression, the confession of sin, will receive special attention. We will conclude with the manner and tone and the situation in life as these further characterize the penitential prayers of the Second Temple Period deriving from the psalms of communal lament. Additionally, we will focus on aspects of the prayers that prove salient because they recur in later compositions, namely the Jewish penitential prayers of the Hellenistic and Roman periods.

5.2 Structural Transformations Related to the Petition

Thus far in our study, structural continuity and discontinuity have typified the relationship between the psalms of communal lament and the Bible's post-exilic penitential prayers. This is true especially of the lament psalms' three principal parts, the lament, petition and motivating element, which function like parts of a single cell with the petition serving as the nucleus. While the lament psalms' three parts are realized in the post-exilic penitential prayers, the lament, petition and motivating element cohere differently than they do in the psalms. The petition remains central, but the other two elements support it in a manner that fosters penitence. Both the lament and the motivating element have become infused with the confession of sin, as has an additional element, the historical recital. A minor element in the psalms of communal lament, the historical recital functions penitentially only in Psalm 78 (Ps 78:9–11, 17–19, 32, 56–58; contrast

---

[2] For example, Gunkel assumed that psalmic traditions, conventions and individual works had been accurately transmitted orally over a period of several centuries. Gunkel's theory of borrowing has been supplanted by more sophisticated approaches that do not assume direct, oral transmission of material between generations of psalmists. Specifically, Culley's work on oral formulaic language allows him to judge whether a psalm is an oral or literary composition based on the amount of formulas and formulaic phrases that it contains. Culley, however, notes that his judgment may be fallible; certain psalms contain repeated phrases and formulas to the degree that one *might* describe and define them as traditional language, *possibly* with an origin in oral, formulaic composition. Furthermore, Culley notes that a high percentage of oral formulaic language in a psalm is not insuperable evidence that the text is an oral composition because traditional language "does not disappear from a poetic tradition the moment oral formulaic composition ceases to be practiced." See his *Oral Formulaic Language in the Biblical Psalms*, 14 and 22, 112–16.

the non-penitential recitals in Pss 44:1–8, 74:12–15). The historical recital becomes a vehicle for confessing sins in the post-exilic prayers. The following analysis of structure will consider the three, newly penitential elements that revolve around the petition and will do so according to the order in which they typically occur: historical recital, lament, motivating element.

The Historical Recital

The historical recital introduces the confession of sin in the post-exilic prayers of penitence, as our study of Isa 63:7–64:11 has shown us. Preceding both the petition and the lament, a historical recital (63:7–14) has been appended to the psalm relatively late in its composition, according to the diachronic analysis adduced above in chapter two. When the historical recital strikes penitential chords in 63:8,10 with admissions of being untrue to the covenant and obstinate toward God's spirit, it introduces the lament and prepares for the petition. As well, historical recitals in both Neh 9:6–37 and Ezra 9:6–15 include confessions of sin that prepare for the petition; in these prayers the lament proper is indeed jettisoned. Neh 9:26 describes the people in the wilderness as rebellious and revolting against God, and the verse forms one cycle in the series of sinful events (9:16–31) leading to 9:32, the petition that God consider the people's hardship. Ezra 9:8 enumerates the sufferings that have resulted from the people's iniquity and guilt (9:6–7). Whether prefixed to the lament or used in lieu of it, the historical recital becomes a standard vehicle for the confession of sin in the post-exilic period's psalms of lament and in related genres.[3]

Later in the Second Temple Period, prayers and speeches continue to incorporate a historical prologue but de-emphasize penitential motifs such as the confession of sin. 1 Macc 2:49–70 is a speech not unlike Ezra 9:6–15 in that certain Jews have flouted God's law and brought on a time of arrogance and rebuke (ὑπερηφανία καὶ ἐλεγμός 1 Macc 2:49). Like Ezra, Mattathias exhorts loyal Jews to follow the law zealously, and he begins his speech by recalling the ancestors. The ancestors, however, are remembered for their virtue alone, and the only "sinners" mentioned are the contemporary enemies of the Maccabees (2:62–63). Similarly, the Prayer of Manasseh begins with a historical recital touching on creation (vv. 2–4) and the patriarchs (vv. 1,8).[4] The prayer implies that Abraham, Isaac and Jacob were sinless and that grace has been devised for sinners such as the speaker. In addition to contrasting the post-exilic prayers of penitence, the claim that the patriarchs were sinless is itself a theological innovation inasmuch as sinfulness has to this point been understood as endemic

---

[3] In the Pentateuch, Deuteronomy begins with a historical overview (1:1–3:29) that includes the rebellion in the wilderness (Deut 1:43). In prophecy, Ezekiel 20 relates Israel's history as punctuated by episodes of rebellion (20:8,13,16,21).

[4] The text of of this prayer, edited by James Charlesworth, is available in *Old Testament Pseudepigrapha* (ed. J. H. Charlesworth; New York: Doubleday, 1985), 2:634–7.

to humanity.⁵ A further innovation may be observed in 4Q504, a prayer text found at Qumran but not necessarily original to the community there. The prayer, which has been compared form-critically to the psalms of communal lament,⁶ comprises daily recitations that begin with a vignette from Israel's history.⁷ While the subsequent petitions are profusely penitential, the prologues do not emphasize the forebears' wrongdoing except to establish a contrast between the wilderness generation and the covenanters at Qumran. This contrast, in 4Q504 frag. 3 2:6–19 and frags. 1–2 2:7–11, will be examined below in an analysis of penitential expressions.

In summary, the historical recital becomes and remains a fixture in Second-Temple penitential prayers, but it does not necessarily retain its post-exilic function of facilitating penitence directly via the confession of sin. On the contrary, history's figures come to serve as moral models for penitent sinners to emulate.⁸ Among select texts of the Hellenistic and Roman periods, however,

---

⁵ Alan Avery-Peck explains that "through God's affirmation that 'I will never again curse the ground because of man, for the imagination of man's heart is evil from his youth; neither will I ever again destroy every living creature as I have done (Gen 8:21),' scripture expresses early Israel's keen awareness that sinfulness is an inherent trait of humankind. It is a necessary result of the intellectual and physical freedoms that make people human, and hence a trait that even God cannot change." "Sin in Judaism," *EJ* 1320. Like the Prayer of Manasseh, some deuterocanonical works hold that a few persons have been free from sin, such as Tob 3:14, Jub 27:18, TLevi 10:2, 2 Bar 9:1.

⁶ Esther G. Chazon identifies the prayers of 4Q504 with Gunkel's genre of the communal laments. She holds that the prayers have been modified so that everyday spiritual needs are at times substituted for the plea for deliverance from evildoers; in certain prayers, however, the plea remains current and no spiritual needs are voiced. See her "A Liturgical Document from Qumran and its Implications: 'Words of the Luminaries' (4QDibHam)," Ph. D. Dissertation, The Hebrew University of Jerusalem, 1991, 63. According to Daniel K. Falk, Chazon's analysis is questionable inasmuch as "all of the weekday prayers from the *Words of the Luminaries* combined concern for spiritual and physical [deliverance] assistance to varying degrees," but Falk does not dispute the more general identification of 4Q504 with the psalm genre of communal lament. See his *Daily, Sabbath, and Festival Prayers in the Dead Sea Scrolls* (*STDJ* 27; Leiden/Boston/Cologne: Brill, 1997), 71.

⁷ Translations of 4Q504 are based on the Hebrew text established by Maurice Baillet, "Paroles des Lumieres," pp. 137–68, pls. 49–53 in *Discoveries in the Judaean Desert* 7 (Oxford: Clarendon Press, 1982). Baillet's remarks on the original order of the fragments (p. 138) are to be supplemented with the more detailed reconstruction of Émile Puech in his review of DJD 7, *RB* 95 (1988): 404–16, esp 407–9.

⁸ In the course of Second-Temple Judaism, Abraham became such a model. In the second century B.C.E., writers celebrated Abraham's constancy in trial, as in Jub 17:18 and 19:9. Abraham's faithfulness in keeping covenant with God also leads to his being called friend of God in CD 3:2. These two references are both from programmatic literature of Jewish sects in the second century, and both represent theological attempts to gauge God's approval of Abraham's faithfulness. A century later Philo, in exegeting Gen

one finds recitals with vestiges of the penitential motif. Notably, Qumran's Community Rule describes the annual covenant renewal thus:

והכוהנים מספרים את צדקות אל במעשי גבורתום ומשמיעים
כול חסדי רחמים על ישראל והלויים מספרים את עוונות
בני ישראל וכול פשעי אשמתם וחטואתם בממשלת בליעל [ ]
העוברים בברית מודים אהריהם לאמור נעוינו [ ]נו הרשענו
אנו [ ]ואתינו מלפנינו בלכתנו [ ]אמת וצד [ ] משפטו בנו ובאבות
(1QS 1:21–26)⁹

The penitents join in solidarity with their forebears, whose iniquities, rebellions and sins are enumerated by the Levites. "The dominion of Belial" (ממשלת בליעל) is a temporal construct that signifies the world outside of the covenant; Belial's wicked dominion is opposed by the Qumran community, whose founding inspiration is rather the holy persons whom God will forgive so that they in turn might instruct the upright in knowledge and wisdom (cf. 1 QS 4:21–22). Clearly, 1QS is a witness to the historicizing of penitence at Qumran, and it stands to reason that this document would locate sin's origin in prehistory, when God is said to have created the spirits of light and darkness (1QS 3:25). While this witness to a sinful history is consistent with the post-exilic prayers we have studied, it is somewhat anomalous among contemporary texts such as 4Q504, in which people emulate their ancestors' perfections. Nonetheless, the historical allusions to sinfulness in 1QS have influenced scholarly presuppositions about prayer at the time of Qumran. For example, Bilhah Nitzan cites 1QS when she endeavors to identify a parallel section of historically based penitence at the start of the prayer 4QBer[a-e].[10]

15:6, provides the most complete and definitive articulation of Abraham's faithfulness and friendship with God (*De Abr* 270–74).

[9] The text is that of Millar Burrows, *The Dead Sea Scrolls of St. Mark's Monastery* (New Haven: American Schools of Oriental Research, 1951), 2. pl. 1. The author's translation: "The priests shall recount God's righteous acts manifested in deeds of strength, and shall make known to Israel the steadfast love of [God's] mercy. And the Levites shall recount the iniquities of the children of Israel, all their guilty transgressions and their sins during the dominion of Belial. And all those crossing over into the covenant shall confess after them and say: 'We have committed iniquity, we have [transgressed], we and our fathers before us have done evil in walking [counter to the precepts] of truth and righteousness, [and God has] made his judgment against us and our fathers also.'"

[10] The five manuscripts of *Berakhot* from cave four are described by Bilhah Nitzan as a series of liturgical blessings and curses and a series of laws. She surmises that the prayers reflect a covenantal ceremony in the third month, on the day of Pentecost. In her reconstruction of the prayer's form, Nitzan suggests that the first element was a confession of sin, followed by the blessings, curses and laws. The manuscript evidence for the confession of sin is marginal: "4QBer[a] 1 i 7–8 and frg. 9 may perhaps contain slight references to communal confessions of sins, which may be considered as a ritual of

The Lament

Especially after the exile, the confession of sin supplants the lament as the element preparatory to the petition in a psalm of communal lament. Prior to this development, the lament proper had described a situation of distress and rooted it in a historical event of national or political import, such as the destruction of the sanctuary in Ps 74:3–9. The lament had stereotyped enemies as evildoers (74:3, 4) and reviled them as impious fools (74:18, 22). After the exile, the lament undergoes change; in the words of Westermann, "The lament is replaced by the confession of sins, thus transforming the psalms of communal lament in which the lament recedes to the background and in its place another motif comes to dominate the psalm."[11] Westermann is, on the one hand, accurate in that the confession of sin indeed comes to dominate the psalm. In this development, confession of sin is analogous to the concept of "the dominant" in modern genre theory. [12] On the other hand, Westermann's judgment is lacking in nuance, especially with respect to Isa 63:7–64:11.

In this psalm, a lament that is arguably the composition's oldest section (63:15–19a) is the segue to the petition for a theophany (63:19b–64:4a). In order that the psalm might be penitential, the lament is not jettisoned, but certain of its expressions are embryonic confessions of sin. Specifically, the lament states that the LORD has caused the people to err and has hardened their hearts (63:17). In the context of a national catastrophe, i.e. the desecration of the sanctuary (63:18), the assertion that God has caused the people's wrongdoing amounts to a protest of innocence. This protest, as it throws blame on God, has led Timo Veijola to observe: "Although in the contemporary [exilic] psalms of lament the stubborn assertion of one's innocence occurs sporadically, there predominates in them yet the awareness of one's own sin which is to be perceived as the true reason for the catastrophe."[13] In analysis that is psychological as well as literary,

---

atonement held in the covenantal ceremony of *Berakhot* (cf. 1QS 1:24–2:1; CD 20:27–28)." In a footnote, Nitzan points to extant portions of words in the *Berkhot* fragments. Fragmentary lexemes such as יני, she suggests, witness to the communal confession formulated with expressions such as אבותינו or עוונו. "The Textual, Literary and Religious Character of *4QBERAKOT* (4Q286–290)," pp. 636–56 in *The Provo International Conference on the Dead Sea Scrolls* (ed. D. W. Perry and E. Ulrich; Leiden: Brill, 1999), 652.

[11] Westermann, *Praise and Lament in the Psalms*, 206.

[12] Chapter one (nn. 92,93) introduced Jakobson's concept of the dominant "as the focusing component of a work of art: it rules, determines and transforms the remaining components. It is the dominant which guarantees the integrity of the structure."

[13] "Obwohl in den damaligen Klageliedern sporadisch auch die sture Behauptung der eigenen Unschuld begegnet (Ps. xliv 18–23), überwiegt in ihnen doch das Bewußtsein der eigenen Schuld, die als eigentliche Ursache der Katastrophe empfunded wird." Timo Veijola, "Das Klagegebet in Literatur und Leben der Exilsgeneration am Beispiel einiger Prosatexte," *VTSup* 36 (1985): 305.

Veijola and others describe the emergence of the confession of sin within the lament as a complex of forces such as insight, denial and resistance.[14] Although not subject to strict verification, the views of these scholars remind us of the human context within which occur shifts in expression that call for theological interpretation. A shift in human awareness leading to self-reproach helps to explain an important literary development, namely how the confession of sin supplanted the lament as the element anterior to the petition in a psalm of communal lament.

The Motivating Element

In the psalms of communal lament, the petition to God for help is typically followed by an appeal to God's honor and name, which evildoers have besmirched (Pss 74:22, 79:9). Ideally, the prospects of reasserting the divine honor are used to motivate God to act on behalf of the petitioners. It is noteworthy that in the two post-exilic laments we have considered in this chapter, the most substantive confessions of sin occur immediately after the petition, where traditionally was found the appeal designed to motivate God to respond. Furthermore, these confessions of sin function motivationally, albeit indirectly and to a limited degree.

Isa 63:19b–64:4a petitions for a theophany reminiscent of Sinai, and 64:4b–6 is the prayer's most self-conscious attempt at confession. The latter section correlates references to sin and iniquity with the people's alienation from God. The terms for sin and iniquity are חטא (64:4b) and עון (64:5b,6b); God is described as one who is angry and not apt to save (64:4b), whose name and strength are no longer invoked (64:6), and who has become at best a hidden presence (64:6b). Human sin and God's lamentable remoteness are at the center of a complex, troubled relationship. The following section contains another confession of sin (64:8) that is patterned on Ps 79:8–9 but takes a much bleaker view of human iniquity, עון, as the spur to God's anger, קצף. Thus, Isa 63:7–64:11 reserves some of its strongest pentential language until after the petition has been issued. That this language intends to motivate God is not self-evident, but it is significant that 64:4b–6 meditates upon the basis of the difficulty. Mowinckel notes that in order to motivate God, a psalm may "call to mind the cause of the distress," i.e. the parties who have transgressed against the community.[15] In an unconventional way, 64:4b–6 performs this function. With the psalm from Trito Isaiah, the guilty party is the community itself, and its

---

[14] For example, Hans-Joachim Kraus deems it an "insight" when God's people see how their foes have wrought destruction and profaned God's honor. He maintains that "the confession of guilt is not toned down or restricted by this insight. The nation confesses its guilt, which is so deeply rooted in the events of past generations." *Theology of the Psalms* (Minneapolis: Augsburg, 1986), 99.

[15] Mowinckel, *The Psalms in Israel's Worship*, 1:206.

lament would induce God not to condemn it but to requite it, and to do so by the tenets of mercy (Isa 63:7 גְּמָלָם כְּרַחֲמָיו).

In another instance, Neh 9:6–37 follows the petition (9:32) with the prayer's most complex confession of sin, 9:33–35. The confession is built on a reversal of subjects that in turn redefines the binary opposition of צדיק and רשע as it is found in the communal laments. Among this prayer's several confessions of sin, 9:33–35 is unique. Unlike 9:16, 18, 26 and 29, only 9:33 asserts that God is righteous as well as merciful, וְאַתָּה צַדִּיק, thereby demonstrating that the people realize that their own evildoing is the root cause of their trouble. The key to the expression, however, is what it says about God, whose righteousness is not merely recalled as part of an honor motif. Rather, וְאַתָּה צַדִּיק invokes the justice of God in the manner of "an independent motivation for [God's] readiness to hear [the people's] prayers."[16]

Later in the Second Temple Period, at least four penitential prayers include motivational elements that incorporate the confession of sin. The Prayer of Manasseh blends together the petition and the motivation/confession:

> And now I am bending the knees of my heart before you;
> And I am beseeching your kindness.
> I have sinned, O Lord, I have sinned;
> and I certainly know my sins.
> I beseech you O Lord, forgive me! (vv. 11–12)

In Baruch, the penitential prayer (1:5–3:8) similarly interlaces petition and confession as a motivating element:

> Hear, O Lord, and have mercy
> For we have sinned before you. (3:2)

The following verse restates the petition and designates sin as the cause of the present calamity:

> O Lord Almighty, God of Israel, hear now the prayer of the dead of Israel
> And of the sons of those who sinned before thee,
> Who did not heed the voice of the Lord their God,
> So that calamities have clung to us. (3:3)

In Joseph and Aseneth, the principal female character, Aseneth, offers an extended prayer of contrition (chapters 12–13).[17] In her prayer, a close connection obtains between the petition and a motivational element forged with the confession of sin.

---

[16] Ibid., 1:205.
[17] The text of of this prayer, edited by C. Burchard, is available in *OTP*, 2:177–247.

> To you I will pour out my supplication,
> To you I will confess my sins.
> Spare me Lord,
> Because I have sinned much against you. (12:3–4)

Finally, the penitential prayer of Simon in 3 Maccabees presents the high priest's petition (2:13) followed by a disparate collection of appeals, one of which is penitential:

> Wipe out our sins, and disperse our offenses
> And show your pity at this moment. (2:19)

In sum, there is permanence to the form-critical development whereby the motivational element in a communal lament becomes a vehicle for the confession of sin. First evident in passages such as Isa 64:4b–6 and Neh 9:33–35, this transformation is attested in several prayers of the subsequent centuries. In every case, penitence affirms and endorses the petition that God help the people in their distress.

It is curious, nonetheless, that in several of the later prayers there are also post-petitionary expressions designed to motivate God to respond on the basis of divine attributes. That is, non-penitential motivational elements are equally attested. At one point the Prayer of Manasseh states: "I make my supplication before you, you will save me according to your mercies." (v. 13) Similarly, the prayer of Baruch asks: "Hear, O Lord, our prayer and our supplication, and for thy own sake deliver us." (2:14) In Aseneth's prayer, one petition reads: "Have mercy upon me, Lord, and guard me, a virgin, who is abandoned and an orphan, because you Lord are a sweet and gentle and good father." None of these appeals recommends itself through a confession of sin; rather the motivation offered to God is God's own reputation and honor, the standard formula for gilding a petition in the psalms of communal lament, as in Pss 74:22 and 79:9.

Moreover, there are other penitential prayers from the centuries following the post-exilic period that frame the petition with a motivational element unconnected to the confession of sins. For example, the Prayer of Azariah follows the petition "May we be accepted" with the following motivation: "Deliver us according to your marvelous works, and give glory to your name, O Lord." (Dan 3:16–20) Additional examples include Dan 9:17–18 and Ps Sol 9:8.[18] Thus, in the second and first centuries B.C.E., the composers of penitential prayers enjoyed at least two options when following a petition with a motivating element; one could employ either the ancient custom of appealing to God's honor or the post-exilic innovation in which a confession of sin heightens the plea for God's help. Both options were available to a people that no longer composed communal laments but followed some of the formal patterns initially associated with the genre.

---

[18] The text of these psalms, edited by R. B. Wright, is available in *OTP*, 2:639–70.

5.3 The Confession of Sin: A Lexical Typology

Just as the psalms of communal lament undergo transformations in structure, so their lexical elements evolve and become increasingly particularized in the course of history. Although individual lexemes do not represent structural data, in this section we will deal with clusters of terms that communicate concepts. As such, these lexical clusters are central to the composition and are in this sense diagnostic. This is especially true of four clusters that articulate the confession of sin. These four are appropriate for study because they provide the principal means whereby the confession of sin dominates the genre of the communal lament in the post-exilic period. The first of these four clusters involves three synonyms for sin.

עון פשע חטא

The conjoined admissions of iniquity, transgression and sin are well attested in the penitential prayers of this period. Although the triad עון פשע חטא is not found in the prayers we have so far studied,[19] it is attested in late biblical prayer (Lev 16:21) and non-biblical prayer (see below the sixth blessing of the *'Amîdah*), as well as in accounts of prayer from Qumran and the rabbinic sources (see above 1QS and *m.Yoma* 3:8, 4:2, 6:2). The triad of terms derives from a cultic context, where multiple categories of sin allowed one to differentiate deeds at the level of intention. That is to say, עון implies *willful* wrongdoing, פשע *purposeful* transgression, and חטא *unintentional* sin, with these denotations based on the legislation in Num 15:27–31.

Intention, however, is not always at issue,[20] and the terms may appear piecemeal rather than conjoined – as is the case with the three post-exilic prayers we have studied. Moreover, after the exile the expressions are sufficiently commonplace that their exact meaning is increasingly elusive. These circumstances underscore the challenge of adequately interpreting חטא and עון, פשע. In the post-exilic period, an interpretive key emerges. The meaning of such a term in a given psalm must ultimately be adduced through context as well as other, more specific penitential expressions elsewhere in the composition. As A. J. Avery-Peck has noted:

> While the distinctions ... in the meanings of the biblical terms [חטא, עון, פשע] used for sin are important, it must also be clear that in later biblical and post-

---

[19] Rather, in our previous chapters we have considered piecemeal the denotations and connotations of חטא (Isa 64:4; Neh 9:29), עון (Isa 64:5,6,8; Ezra 9:6,7,13), and רעים מעשים (Ezra 9:13; Neh 9:28).

[20] In certain exilic and post-exilic texts the three terms used conjointly point to "a more or less fixed liturgical formula." See Blenkinsopp, "The Second Temple as a House of Prayer," 119.

biblical texts these terms frequently are used to refer to sin in general. The distinctive connotations attributable to their root meanings and to their original uses often times appear to have been lost, so that in later contexts the words simply function as synonyms.[21]

Thus, the repeated use of עון or "iniquity" in Ezra 9:6–15 is simply a moralizing way to refer to the misdeed of intermarriage. Conversely, in Isa 64:5, 6, 8 עון directs attention to the people's strained relationship with God.

Subsequently, in the Hellenistic and Roman periods, generic articulations of sin in Jewish prayer continue to be shaded by other, more exact expressions as well as by context. For example, at Qumran it was believed that sin's deleterious effects are vast and far-reaching, and many of the scrolls present sin (חטא) as a condition into which people are born and against which they must struggle until death. The Hodayot speak of a human as "dust shaped with water, his base is the guilt of sin, vile unseemliness, source of impurity, over which a spirit of degeneracy rules." (1QH 5:20–21; cf. 1QS 11:9)[22] For the covenanters, atonement required a humble disposition, the confession of sins, a plea for mercy, a vow never to sin again, and a prayer for divine aid in the future (1QH^a 4:18–24; 6:17; 14:6; cf. CD 15:3). Clearly, at Qumran the lexeme חטא became synonymous with a person's lifelong struggle to avoid evil and do good. Throughout the Second Temple Period, a prayer's generic expressions of sin were informed by more particular turns of phrase elsewhere in the composition. We will study three such expressions that are especially illustrative of the link between the psalms of communal lament and the prayers that were modeled upon them.

ידה in *hitpa'el*

To interpret Neh 9:2,3, where the Israelites "*confess* their sins and iniquities" (וַיִּתְוַדּוּ עַל חַטֹּאתֵיהֶם וַעֲוֹנוֹת) and "*make confession*" (מִתְוַדִּים), one should focus on the expression "confess," ידה in *hitpa'el*. Such is the case as well for Ezra 10:1, where "Ezra prayed and *made confession,*" (עֶזְרָא וּכְהִתְפַּלֵּל וּכְהִתְוַדֹּתוֹ), an expression similar in kind to Neh 9:2,3. All three verses contain examples of a short confession that may be traced back to a priestly context in which the confession of sins constituted a part of the sacrificial rituals (Lev 5:1–6, Num 5:5–10). In approaching the cult, a person confessed when he or she felt guilt for deliberate, intentional sins; the confession, in Jacob Milgrom's opinion, converted the deliberate sins into "inadvertancies, thereby qualifying them for sacrificial expiation."[23] In this priestly formulation, ידה in *hitpa'el* was a simple and utilitarian means of rectifying sin.

---

[21] Avery-Peck, "Sin in Judaism," 1323.

[22] Elsewhere the Hodayot report that humans are "in sin from the maternal womb, and in guilty iniquity right to old age." (1QH 12:29–30; cf. 4Q507 1:2–3).

[23] Jacob Milgrom, *Leviticus 1–16*, 301–2.

With the post-exilic increase of prayer that is independent of the cult, the short confession accrued new meaning. In G. Mayer's view, ידה in *hitpa'el* connotes a private individual speaking for him or herself extemporaneously, as opposed to citing a complex composition within the cult.[24] This view helps to explain why ידה in *hitpa'el* appears adjacent to but never *within* the long penitential prayers we are studying. To confess sin in earnest, the long prayers use language distinct from the pithy sense of ידה in *hitpa'el*. Furthermore, Mayer notes a trend of the short confession framing such prayers, as with both Ezra 10:1 and Neh 9:2,3.[25] If this framing were the prevailing literary practice, it would further explain why ידה in *hitpa'el* is not attested in the prayers themselves, which reserve other language for the confession of sin.

Different in kind from Neh 9:2,3 and Ezra 10:1 is the case of Ezra 10:11, with the imperative "make confession to the LORD" (תְּנוּ תוֹדָה לַיהוָה). In chapter three we noted how Ezra 10:11 parallels the imperative to confess/praise in Josh 7:18–19, where Achan is commanded to glorify the Lord and to confess to the Lord his sin of appropriating devoted goods (שִׂים נָא כָבוֹד לַיהוָה אֱלֹהֵי יִשְׂרָאֵל וְתֶן לוֹ תוֹדָה). A sin against God, Achan's misdeed jeopardizes Israel's otherwise successful occupation of the land. Achan has brought misfortune upon his people, as do the mixed marriages in Ezra 9–10. Thus, both situations call for an admission of sin that is more substantive than the short confession exemplified in Neh 9:2,3 and Ezra 10:1. The action indicated in Ezra 10:11 is tantamount to the *todah,* the psalm type that corresponds to the thanksgiving sacrifice offered in the wake of distress. The *todah* "has the tendency to combine didactic messages with the retrospective descriptions of the distress and the occurrence of the turn of events."[26] Indeed Ezra 10:11 is a complex directive whose moralizing involves narrative and irony. Ezra recounts that the people by intermarriage have increased Israel's guilt and must therefore make confession and send away their foreign wives, in accord with God's will. ידה in *hitpa'el* is the catalyst of this complex directive. As well, ידה in *hitpa'el* anchors the pithy reference to confession in Ezra 10:1.

The post-exilic prayers, especially Ezra 9–10, illustrate how ידה in *hitpa'el* may function on two distinct levels. It may indicate a short confession offered extemporaneously, perhaps as part of the frame to a longer, more stylized prayer of confession. It may also indicate the *todah,* an integral response of confession and praise after specific transgressions of God's law have jeopardized the wellbeing of God's people. The duality of ידה in *hitpa'el* is not sheerly a literary phenomenon; it has antecedents in the cult. In fact, the literary evidence that we have drawn from a liturgical context parallels the sacrificial evidence from the cultic context. Recalling Milgrom's interpretation of Lev 5:1–6 and Num 5:5–10, where ידה in *hitpa'el* converted intentional sins into inadvertancies that may

---

[24] G. Mayer, *TDOT* 5:441.

[25] Ibid., 5:442.

[26] Hans-Joachim Kraus, *Psalms 1–59: A Commentary* (Minneapolis: Augsburg, 1988), 51.

then be expunged ritually, we should also consider Lev 26:40, which calls for the people to confess their iniquity וְהִתְוַדּוּ אֶת עֲוֹנָם. The confession, offered after God has scattered the people among the nations on account of their sins (26:36–39), causes God to remember the covenant with Abraham, Isaac and Jacob and restore the scattered people to the land (26:42). With this action, ידה in *hitpa'el* performs a dual function. As Werline observes: "It now provides both the legal means to reduce the nation's prolonged intentional sins to inadvertancies and a *method* to remove them!"[27]

The duality of ידה in *hitpa'el* that was established both cultically and literarily after the exile remains discernible in the penitential prayers of the Hellenistic and Roman periods. The short, pithy confession appears in Dan 9:4a and 9:20 to frame an extended prayer of penitence, Dan 9:4b–19a. Stereotypically, ידה in *hitpa'el* appears nowhere in the prayer proper. A Qumran manuscript, 4QDan[e], quite probably contained only the prayer proper excerpted from its literary context.[28] If it were fully intact, the manuscript could provide an indication of how integral the framework of ידה in *hitpa'el* (Dan 9:4a, 20) was to the prayer proper in the minds of those responsible for 4QDan[e]. Unfortunately, the manuscript lacks its beginning and ending verses with only portions of vv. 12–17 extant. Even a reconstruction of the text does not suggest whether or not Dan 9:4a, 20 were included in 4QDan[e].

From this period, the Greek translation of Daniel to be included in the Septuagint captured the short, pithy confession of 9:20 with the verb ἐξομολογέομαι. Across the Septuagint, the Greek verb could denote a simple confession of sin, as in Dan 9:20, or the act of giving thanks and praise, as in Gen 29:35 and 2 Sam 22:50. Moreover, the Septuagint uses ἐξομολογέομαι to translate Josh 7:19's imperative to confess/give thanks, as it is directed at Achan. Thus the Septuagint harmonizes the semantic differences of ידה in *hitpa'el* and does so principally through the term ἐξομολογέομαι.

The Psalms of Solomon, however, pairs ἐξομολογέομαι with a second verb to express the sort of distinction highlighted above with regard to Ezra 10:1 and 10:11. Ps Sol 9:6 reads:

> To whom will you be kind, O God, except the ones calling upon the Lord?
> He will cleanse a sinful soul by means of confession (ἐν ἐξομολογήσει)
>   with declarations (ἐν ἐξαγορίαις),
> Because shame falls upon us and our faces concerning quite all these
>   things.

The psalm nuances the Septuagint's standard expression for confession through the phrase ἐν ἐξομολογήσει ἐν ἐξαγορίαις. While the first term is familiar to

---

[27] Emphasis not added. Werline, *Penitential Prayer in Second Temple Judaism*, 49.

[28] Perhaps 4QDan[e] was a text used for devotional or liturgical purposes. Other examples of excerpted biblical prayers found at Qumran include 4QPss[g,h]. The critical edition of 4QDan[e] is available in *DJD* 16, 287-89.

us and here indicates the more substantive type of confession exemplified in Ezra 10:11 (δότε ὁμολογίαν Esdras A 9:8) and elsewhere, the second term references the pithy confession of sin previously noted in Ezra 10:1 (ἐξηγόρευσαν Esdras B 10:1) and Lev 5:5 (ἐξαγορεύσει LXX). Thus, the "confessions with declarations" stipulated in Ps Sol 9:6 captures the range of meaning available in biblical Hebrew's ידה in *hitpa'el*, "to confess."

Interestingly, in the first century B.C.E., when the Psalms of Solomon were composed, "with declarations" ἐν ἐξαγορίαις may have been synonymous with the excantation of a disease. The evidence for this includes the *Apotelesmatica* of Claudius Ptolemaeus, a work of the second century C.E.[29] In the context of Ps Sol 9:6, ἐν ἐξαγορίαις may denote the healing of a spiritual disease through confession of the sin that occasioned it. In short, the virtually limitless potential of ידה in *hitpa'el* to collect and communicate penitential nuance is especially well attested in Ezra 10:1,11 and extends into the post-biblical era when Greek expressions perpetuated the phenomenon.

Parallelism Involving מרה

We have observed that within the post-exilic penitential prayers, the historical prologue can be a serviceable vehicle for the confession of sin. A reference to misdeeds and iniquity, the confession may be in the first-person (Ezra 9:7–8) or third-person (Isa 63:10; Neh 9:16, 18, 26, 29). The latter are *de facto* confessions of sin because they involve a frank admission of guilt on behalf of the people. In two of the cases we have considered there is a striking lexical parallel between this sort of confession and the historical material found in Psalm 78:

וְהֵמָּה מָרוּ וְעִצְּבוּ אֶת רוּחַ קָדְשׁוֹ
= But they were obstinate and grieved his holy spirit (Isa 63:10a)

---

[29] H. G. Liddell and R. Scott define ἡ ἐξαγορία as "excantation of a disease, cure by confession" based upon Ptolemaeus's *Apotelesmatica* 3.15.5.9 (available in *Claudii Ptolemaei Opera quae exstant omnia* [ed. W. Hübner; Stuttgart: B.G. Teubner, 1998], 278); see LSJ 580. Further support for defining ἡ ἐξαγορία as "excantation" is found in Plutarch's *De Superstition* 168.D.7, which offers this remedy for someone who is in extreme affliction: "He is seated, wearing only a miserable cloak or wrapped in hideous rags, and often he rolls around in mire nude, confessing (ἐξαγορεύει) certain of his sins and errors, such as he ate or drank a given thing or chose a path forbidden to him by the god." The author's translation is based upon *De Superstition* in *Plutarque: Oeuvres Morales* (vol. 2; ed. J. Defradas et al.; Paris: Les Belles Lettres), 258. A modern editor of this passage remarks: "The verb ἐξαγορεύω, which expresses a self-accusation based in superstition, becomes in the Hellenistic period a quasi technical term that designates the confession of sin." G. Lozza, *De Superstitione* (Milan: Angelo Guerini, 1989), 124.

וַיַּמְרוּ וַיִּמְרְדוּ בָךְ
= Nevertheless they were rebellious and revolted against you
(Neh 9:26aα)

כַּמָּה יַמְרוּהוּ בַמִּדְבָּר יַעֲצִיבוּהוּ בִּישִׁימוֹן
= How often they rebelled against him in the wilderness and grieved him in the desert (Ps 78:40)

All of the citations match מרה with contemporary synonyms for sin, מרד (Neh 9:26aα) and עצב (Isa 63:10; Ps 78:40). The parallel verbs of Isa 63:10 and Ps 78:40 may represent a standardized expression; the verbs in Neh 9:26aα mimic the pattern but are themselves *sui generis*. Were we to broaden the survey, the triliteral root מרה appears predominantly (seven times) in Psalms 78 and 106, often parallel to a synonym of Dtr or sapiential origin, as in the three examples above. In post-exilic penitential compositions, parallelism involving מרה and a synonymous term becomes a literary convention. At the level of interpretation, it is worth recalling that forms of the root מרה from the post-exilic period represent Israel's rebelliousness in the face of God's public, historical deeds.[30] The term becomes synonymous with ingrates sinning in the wilderness.

Within the Bible, a historical section in Deuteronomy further confirms the link between the wilderness context and a parallel construction involving מרה. Moses rebukes the people:

וַתַּמְרוּ אֶת פִּי יְהוָה וַתָּזִדוּ וַתַּעֲלוּ הָהָרָה
= You rebelled against the Lord's command and acted insolently and went up into the hill country. (Deut 1:43)

In this instance, מרה is paired with זיד, the root for "to act insolently" prominent in Nehemiah 9 (9:10, 16, 29). At one point in that prayer, we will recall, the confession of sin is predicated on the reversal of the term זיד. In 9:10 it is said that Israel's foes, the Egyptians, acted insolently (הֵזִידוּ), but in time the Israelites themselves act insolently before God (9:16, 29).

In the post-biblical age, parallelism involving "rebel" became associated with the confession of sin for certain Greek-speaking Jews. Psalms of Solomon 9 begins:

> When they were carried off (ἐν τῷ ἀπαχθῆναι) into exile in a foreign land,
> When they were rebelling (ἐν τῷ ἀποστῆναι) against the Lord who had redeemed them,
> Israel was dispossessed of an inheritance that the Lord had given to them.
> (Ps Sol 9:1)

---

[30] Knierim, *TLOT* 2:688.

The aorist passive infinitive τῷ ἀπαχθῆναι, from ἀπάγω, connotes not only the passage into exile but deportation for wrongdoing. The aorist active infinitive τῷ ἀποστῆναι, from ἀφίστημι, has in this context a meaning of revolt. The parallel infinitives support a context of sinful Israel in transit, although here the wilderness wandering has been replaced by the exiles' trek to Babylon. In issuing its initial confession of sin, the psalm employs parallelism involving מרה (translated as τῷ ἀποστῆναι) while updating the geographical aspect of this literary convention.

The wilderness wandering is retained in 4Q504, the week-long collection of daily prayers, each beginning with a historical recollection. Keynoting day five are the ancestors who rebelled against God's command (בהמרותם את פיכה), a choice of words that closely reflects Deut 1:43 as cited above.[31] Unlike the verse from Deuteronomy, however, the reference to rebellion has no parallel verb. Elsewhere the ancestors are said to have angered God and required Moses to atone for their sins, yet these statements do not constitute parallelism, and it appears that the author or authors responsible for 4Q504 preferred a more oblique sort of wordplay involving מרה.

That is to say, the petition of the prayer from the day prior also refers to the rebellious lot:

המרו [...] וינ°כוה וימצאוכה [...] ר לו[וא] האמינו

= They rebelled ... and they poured it out as a libation ... and they found you ... they did not believe. (4Q504 frag.7, lines 14–16)

A lacuna in the text, whose translation is thus elusive, leaves open the possibility of the standard sort of parallelism between מרה and a synonymous verb. It is, however, unlikely that the petition invokes the penitential conventions that were well attested in the post-exilic prayers and Psalm 78. The penitents known to us through 4Q504 look to the rebellious ancestors not to claim solidarity in their guilt but to establish foils to the present generation, who are saved by a merciful God in large part because of their belief and their association with Sinai.

Esther Chazon has discerned this generational contrast based on the references to belief in 4Q504:

> The petitionary section of this prayer incorporates a reference to God's merciful forgiveness of the rebellious Israelites in the wilderness. In this statement, the supplicants not only appeal to God's mercy but also present themselves as more worthy of salvation than their rebellious forefathers. They accomplish this by disassociating themselves from those rebels "who did not believe" and by associating themselves with the Sinai covenanters to whom God revealed himself "so that they will believe."[32]

---

[31] In 4Q504, the reference is in frags. 1–2, col. 2, line 8.

[32] The unbelief of the ancestors is cited above (frag. 7, line 16). The belief of the Sinai generation is indicated slightly earlier in the prayer (frag. 3, col. 2, lines 12–13).

Thus, in an oblique and novel sense, parallelism involving מרה is attested at Qumran, but the second term, "belief," now *contrasts* with the first and serves to distinguish the more worthy penitents. While the Dead Sea community's own literature suggests that it would have considered itself more worthy, the parallelism operative here does not have the exclusive stamp of Qumran. As Nitzan notes:

> [In contrast to Isa 63, Neh 9] the system of remembrances in [4Q504] is two-directional, depicting situations of both punishment and recompense. To be more precise, it describes the curses and blessings of the covenant throughout the generations. ... However, the extreme deterministic-dualistic aspect found in the writings of the sect is absent, and is without its the [sic] literary flourish.[33]

Rather, the prayer reflects a basic principle of Deuteronomistic theology: punishment for those who violate the covenant and reward for those who uphold it. The author and his or her group confidently number themselves among the latter inasmuch as they identify with the Israelites who encountered God at Sinai.

Excursus: Sinai

In 4Q504, the Sinai legacy is associated with people of right belief who eschew rebellion. In addition, Sinai emphasizes covenant-making and direct revelation, as indicated by the phrase "eye to eye you have been seen in our midst" (עין [... בעין נראיתה בקרבנו]), a detail from the historical prologue to the prayer of the fourth day.[34] On this point, 4Q504 appropriates Sinai differently than do the post-exilic prayers we have studied to this point. We recall that in Neh 9:13a the reference to Sinai involves some circumlocution in order to maintain both God's immanence and transcendence: "You came down upon Mount Sinai, and spoke with them from heaven." The verse locates God on Sinai *and* in heaven, an apparent contradiction.[35] Sinai is again a vehicle of theophanic speculation in Deut 4:36: "From heaven he made you hear his voice to discipline you. On earth he showed you his great fire, while you heard his words coming out of the fire." We have noted that this verse rules out the possibility of seeing God, *contra* Gen 32:31 and Exod 33:20. Contact with the divine is now a matter of words issued from heaven.[36] However, the trajectory of

---

Like Chazon, we refer to the mountain of theophany as Sinai even though 4Q504 uses the alternative Horeb. See her "A Liturgical Document from Qumran, 17.

[33] B. Nitzan, *Qumran Prayer and Religious Poetry* (Leiden: Brill, 1994), 95, n. 25.

[34] In 4Q504, the reference is in frag. 3, col. 2, line 7.

[35] See n. 96 of chapter 4.

[36] The words that mediate between God and God's people are the commandments, which people encounter as proximate and in no way remote, according to Deut 30:11–14.

theophanic minimalism represented by Deut 4:36 and Neh 9:13a does not pass through 4Q504, which instead reports that God has been in the people's midst and that they have seen God "eye to eye." The prayer speaks of an immediate and vital relationship with God to be enjoyed only by those who partake of the Sinai covenant and eschew rebellion.

There is another sense in which the Sinai legacy articulated in 4Q504 is fuller than that of Neh 9:6–37. In the latter prayer, Sinai is at the center of the historical recital as a hinge and moral threshold. Sinai marks the new era after the law has been given, when it is possible to transgress its precepts and turn away from God. Not explicit in Neh 9:13 but central to Jewish belief is an additional dimension of Sinai. In addition to the law's establishment, Sinai represents the grounds of its fullfillment.[37] The law from Sinai is *the* counterforce to sin, and as such it changes peoples' natures and augers a refounding of God's people. Rebirth is at hand. When 4Q504 identifies God amid the people in the petition to day four, it draws attention to Sinai as the cradle of the people Israel. Faithfulness to the law of Sinai is the basis of this identification, which, as we saw in chapter two, may incorporate other *topoi*. Isa 63:19–64:4a combines the *topoi* of Sinai and of elemental creation in a post-exilic attempt to reestablish the greatness of Israel on a plane other than that of history. The great and awesome deeds of God the creator are associated with the events of Sinai in Trito-Isaiah's version of Israel's refounding.

For God's people, Sinai is a foundation and a *telos*. The point is made by Levenson in his work on Sinai. He notes that history is "the foreground" of Torah observance, but observance is the teleological end of history and the fundamental affirmation of the covenant.[38] Sinai thus represents the beginning and the end of Torah. Sinai is synonymous with the "glorious vision" beheld at the founding of the Qumran community and recounted in several of its prayers, including 1Q34[bis].[39] The prayer praises God for renewing the covenant so that

---

In Deuteronomy the waning of theophany coincides with the end of prophecy, and both are mitigated by assurances that the word of God remains securely in the possession of the hearer.

[37] In the rabbinic literature (*b. Šabb.* 145b–146a), the Israelites "who stood at Sinai" are said to be free of lust, which is moral shorthand for an inherited, corrupt nature. While Judaism has no concept of original sin, there is an analogous notion rooted in the lust that the snake imparted to Eve. The lust is remedied by the Israelites' standing at Sinai and, according to another opinion in the same source, by the merit of the ancestors. In addition to *b. Šabb.* 145b–146a, see *b. B. Bat.* 16a.

[38] Levenson, *Sinai and Zion*, 44.

[39] In 1Q34[bis] frag. 3, col. 2, line 6, God's renewal of the Sinai covenant with the Qumran community occurs in a "glorious vision" (במראת כבוד). See also 4Q509, frag. 97–98, col. 1, lines 7–8. 1Q34[bis] is found in *Discoveries in the Judaean Desert* 1 (ed. D. Bathélemy and J. T. Milik; Oxford: Clarendon Press, 1955), 154.

God's people might know "the foundations of glory [read: Sinai] and the steps toward eternity [read: the *telos*] (יסודי כבוד ומעשי עולם)."⁴⁰

רשע and צדיק as Binary Categories

In the post-exilic prayers of penitence, one of the most popular manners of confessing sin involves the binary categories of רשע and צדיק, or righteous and wicked. The terms are invoked in all three of the prayers we have studied, most notably in Neh 9:6–37. One verse in particular reverses the referents previously established for רשע and צדיק. In chapter four we looked carefully at the expression and structure of Neh 9:33:

9:33aα: You have been just וְאַתָּה צַדִּיק

9:33aβ: In all that has come upon us עַל כָּל הַבָּא עָלֵינוּ

9:33bα: For you have acted faithfully כִּי אֱמֶת עָשִׂיתָ

9:33bβ: Yet we have acted wickedly וַאֲנַחְנוּ הִרְשָׁעְנוּ

It is a reversal of sorts to call God just when the psalms of communal lament consistently portray God as culpably indifferent to the people's plight (Pss 44:9–14,19; 74:1,11,19–21; 77:9–10; 80:12–13). God, the people's *de facto* opponent, is not called righteous in the psalms. Moreover, the psalms of communal lament assert that the people have not failed God's covenant (Ps 44:17–18) and so are innocent. They are innocent and righteous. Declaring their

---

⁴⁰ 1Q34^bis frag. 3, col. 2, line 7. The notion that Sinai is a key to both the foundation and the telos of the community at Qumran has been explored by Adolfo Roitman in a paper delivered June 30, 2000, at the Israel Museum, Jerusalem. Roitman maintains that the people at Qumran wanted to accomplish and fulfill Exodus 19 as it both recalled the foundational terms of the covenant and pointed to the end times. "The *Endzeit* was like the *Urzeit*" for the community in the desert, according to Roitman (whose choice of words recalls the title of Gunkel's book *Schöpfung und Chaos in Urzeit und Endzeit*). In another study of the community at Qumran, George Brooke similarly maintains that "the community's *Endzeit* experience is to be an *Urzeit* realization." Brooke, however, holds that the view developed in reference to the primordial age that was *prior* to that of Sinai: "An appeal to the covenant at Sinai was clearly considered important, but it was felt necessary by some to look back before Sinai to explain the movement's unique place in the divine scheme of things." The positions of Roitman and Brooke are consistent inasmuch as they make the same point about exegesis at Qumran while citing different MSS that comment on different portions of scripture. See Brooke's "'The Canon Within the Canon' at Qumran and in the New Testament," pp. 242–66 in *The Scrolls and the Scriptures: Qumran Fifty Years After* (JSPSup 26; ed. S. E. Porter and C. A. Evans; Sheffield: Sheffield Academic Press, 1997), 251.

own wickedness in Neh 9:33bβ dramatically reverses the binary categories established in the psalms.

Like Neh 9:6–37, Ezra 9:6–15 asserts God's righteousness over and against the people's guilt. Like Neh 9:33, the prayer in Ezra does so through an envelope construction. In the prayer's first verse, 9:6, Ezra acknowledges his shame and disgrace and admits that, in solidarity with the people, he is guilty. The prayer's final verse, 9:15, exonerates and indeed glorifies God as just in the events God oversees. Because Ezra's prayer compounds the people's guilt with God's righteousness, it is a reversal of the lament theology established in the psalms through the terms רשע and צדיק. In a more subtle manner, Isa 63:7–64:11 as well recalibrates the binary opposition of רשע and צדיק so that the people may make a confession of sin. We will recall that Isa 64:5b reads: "And we have fallen like a leaf, all of us, and like the wind, our iniquities carry us away." The verse is based upon the distinction between the righteous and the wicked (צדיקים / רשעים) in Ps 1:6; the immediate source is Ps 1:3–4, a complex description of a leaf *not* withering and the wind driving away chaff. Unlike the psalm, Isa 64:5b applies both images, the leaf and the chaff, pejoratively. The leaf *does* wither and the chaff is scattered to imply that wickedness, specified as iniquity (עון), determines the direction of people's lives. The effects or consequences of human wrongdoing are emphasized in this novel usage of עון, which is a proxy for רשע as it is found in the psalter. The low opinion of humans in Isa 63:7–64:11 is shared by the post-exilic prayers of penitence in Ezra and Nehemiah, which further contrast the peoples' wickedness with the righteousness of God.

The binary designation of רשע and צדיק that appeared after the exile has had an enduring influence on Jewish penitential prayer, and Moshe Weinfeld notes that the present day service for Yom Kippur clearly echoes Neh 9:33: "For you [God] have acted faithfully, but we have acted wickedly."[41] He adds that the phrase "we have acted wickedly" is also attested in a prayer from Qumran, 4Q508 frag. 3, line 1.[42] While the manuscript does not complement this term with a reference to righteousness, we may recall the passage from 1QS discussed earlier in this chapter. 1QS 1:21–26 refers to God's "righteous acts" (צדקות אל) in contradistinction to the iniquities of the children of Israel, who with their forebears have acted wickedly (הרשענו), contradicting both truth and righteousness ([וצד] אמת). Contemporary with the first phase of the Qumran community is the penitential prayer from Daniel 9, which also invokes the binary designation of רשע and צדיק as it was construed after the exile. The petition to God in Dan 9:15–16 may be cited thus: "We have sinned, we have acted wickedly; O Lord, in all your righteousness turn your anger and your

---

[41] The Hebrew reads כי אמת עשית ואנחנו הרשענו, as quoted by Moshe Weinfeld in "Prayer and Liturgical Practice in the Qumran Sect," pp. 241–58 in *The Dead Sea Scrolls: Forty Years of Research* (ed. D. Dimant and U. Rappaport; Leiden: Brill, 1992), 247.

[42] Ibid., 246.

wrath away from your city Jerusalem."⁴³ Dan 9:15–16 follows Neh 9:32–33 in content and in form; structurally, both prayers frame the petition to God with a confession of sin keyed to the binary opposition of רשע and צדיק.

In the prayer from Qumran cited by Weinfeld, 4Q508, there is a reference to the just and the wicked, רשע and צדיק, (frag. 1, line 2) but the fragmentary nature of the text makes it virtually impossible to discern the referents to these terms.⁴⁴ The expression, however, is also contained in 1Q34^bis frag. 3, lines 5–6, where it is clear that both parties are humans: "Between the righteous and the wicked: of the wicked you will make our ransom, while for the upright you will destroy all our enemies."⁴⁵ The penitents identify with the righteous and cast their enemies in the role of the wicked. The designations represent a return to the pre-exilic perspective of the lament psalms, where the speaker is צדיק. The evidence from Qumran is thus mixed as it preserves different conceptions of רשע and צדיק. 1Q34^bis follows the older and decidedly plaintive model of the speakers identifying with the righteous, over and against their enemies, the wicked. 1QS, on the other hand, emphasizes that God is righteous and that a person enters God's covenant only after a thorough confession of his or her wickedness.

The Psalms of Solomon also present multiple perspectives on רשע and צדיק as binary categories.⁴⁶ In Psalm 9, righteousness and wickedness are indicated by terms such as just and the unjust (δίκαιος, ἄδικαιος). The psalm begins by defining the exile as an event that justified God in God's judgment of the people's lawless deeds (ἵνα δικαιωθῇς ὁ θεός ἐν τῇ δικαιοσύνῃ σου ἐν ταῖς ἀνομίαις ἡμῶν 9:2). Here the psalm opposes the people's wickedness/injustice with God's righteousness/justice. There follows, however, a meditation on injustice that reflects a belief in the freedom of the will (9:4–5).

While affirming God's justice, Ps Sol 9:4 states that to do justice and injustice "is in the works of our hands" (ἐν ἔργοις χειρῶν ἡμῶν), i.e. a matter

---

⁴³ The Hebrew of these verses reads: חָטָאנוּ רָשַׁעְנוּ אֲדֹנָי כְּכָל צִדְקֹתֶךָ יָשָׁב נָא אַפְּךָ וַחֲמָתְךָ מֵעִירְךָ יְרוּשָׁלַם

⁴⁴ The Hebrew reads (בין צד)יק לרשע. לדר(ע)[ה]. DJD 7, 177.

⁴⁵ The Hebrew reads בין צד[י]ק לרשע ונתתה רשעים [כ]ופרנו וב[ונ]דים [ ] [כלה בכל מעינו

⁴⁶ George Nickelsburg proposes that the roles of the righteous and sinners supply an organizing principle for a set of psalms within the collection (Psalms 3, 4, 6, 9, 10, 13, 14, 15, 16). See his *Jewish Literature between the Bible and the Mishnah: A Historical and Literary Introduction* (Philadelphia: Fortress, 1981), 209–12. P. N. Franklyn claims that in the Psalms of Solomon, the comparison of the pious and the godless is based not on early distinctions between the profane and the cultic, as with the righteous and the wicked of the psalms, but on "relational categories that nominalize concrete groups of people." We observed an earlier instance of this phenomenon through Albertz's observation that after the exile the accusation against the enemy comes to target those who foment social conflict, whereas earlier its objects were demonic powers. See n. 47 of chapter two and Franklyn's "The Cultic and Pious Climax of Eschatology in the Psalms of Solomon," *JJS* 18 (1987): 8–9.

of human choice. The following verse, 9:5, while affirming God's judgment, maintains that the person who does justice accrues life with God (θησαυρίζει ζωὴν αὐτῷ παρὰ κυρίῳ) while the one who acts unjustly is responsible for the ruin of his soul (αἴτιος τῆς ψυχῆς ἐν ἀπωλείᾳ). Ps Sol 9:4–5 locates רשע and צדיק primarily on the human plane. As for the divine, the psalm addresses God's providence by way of humans' free will. By affirming both providence and free will, the psalm provides a reckoning of the two concepts comparable to that of Josephus in his description of the Pharisees [47] and not unlike that found in select parts of the Hebrew Bible, notably Qohelet.[48]

Ultimately, the psalm's perspectives on רשע and צדיק represent two regnant paradigms derived from Nehemiah 9 and the psalms of communal lament, respectively. On the one hand, God is understood as righteous/just while humans are wicked/unjust (Ps Sol 9:2). On the other hand, certain persons are just because they choose to act justly while others are unjust based again on the actions they choose for themselves (9:4–5). The psalm indicates the breadth of thought then current with respect to רשע and צדיק as binary categories useful in confessing sin. This ferment, in turn, owed much to the contemporary deliberations on free will, such as the Pharisees' synthesis of free will and providence as well as Philo's asserting free will over and against the strict determinism of the Stoics.[49]

---

[47] The relevant texts are *J. W.* 2.162–66, *Ant.* 13.172 and *Ant.* 18.13. In presenting movements in Judaism as if they were schools of Greek philosophy, Josephus states that unlike the Sadducees, who privilege free will, and unlike the Essenes, who privilege fate, the Pharisees understand there to be a balance between fate and free will. *Ant.* 18.13 reads: "While thinking that all things are accomplished through fate, they [the Pharisees] do not discount the exercise of human will that is involved in that impetus [i.e. fate] that comes upon people. They think that by God a blending is achieved that joins the realm of fate and the human will with its virtue and vice." The author's translation is based upon the Greek text in *Josephus: Jewish Antiquities Books XVIII–XIX* (LCL 433; ed. L. H. Feldman; Cambridge, Mass.: Harvard University Press, 1965), 12–14.

[48] Examining texts from Genesis, Trito-Isaiah, Malachi and Proverbs, Peter Machinist maintains that the Bible offers no "easy and consistent" means of correlating fate and the concern for morally accountable action, both of which are proper to God. He proposes that Qohelet's applying human reason "to the perennial tension between fate and morally accountable action" results in an affirmation of fate over and against reason. "Fate, *miqreh,* and Reason: Some Reflections on Qohelet and Biblical Thought," pp. 159–75 in *Solving Riddles and Untying Knots: Biblical, Epigraphic and Semitic Studies in Honor of Jonas C. Greenfield* (ed. Z. Zevit et al.; Winona Lake, Ind.: Eisenbrauns, 1995), 164, 173.

[49] As John Dillon observes, Philo's position on free will and providence is rather equivocal. While Philo makes strong statements about the doctrine of free will (*Deus* 47–48) in order to resist the determinism of the Stoics, he elsewhere suggests that humans are bodies that God moves through divine providence (*Cher.* 128). Dillon concludes: "In truth Philo is neither a determinist nor a believer in absolute free will. He is caught between these two poles of opposition. Nor is his dilemma peculiar to himself. It is

5.4 Literary and Theological Summation

Through structural and lexical transformations, the penitential prayers of the Second Temple Period not only distinguish themselves from the psalms of communal lament but in certain cases later in the era reappropriate patterns that had predominated in the psalms. The oscillation begins in the Persian period when prayers such as Isa 63:7–64:11 and Neh 9:6–37 make innovative use of the lament psalms' form-critical repertoire; these prayers support their petition with elements such as a historical prologue, a penitential lament, and a confession of sin. All three elements become vehicles for the confession of sin, which in these prayers as well as Ezra 9:6–15 is articulated stereotypically in clusters of penitential words.

In the Hellenistic and Roman periods, the earlier transformations of the lament form continue to be attested in works such as Daniel, the prayers and manuals found at Qumran and the Jewish apocrypha and pseudepigrapha. In the penitential prayers of this time, however, a second set of developments arise to indicate a different kind of transformation. Structurally, 1 Maccabees, the Prayer of Manasseh and 4Q504 begin with a historical recital but do not infuse it with the confession of sin. In a related development, the prayers attributed to Manasseh, Baruch and Aseneth make a petition to God and key the subsequent element, the motivation, to God's attributes rather than the confession of sin. The penitential dimension of these six prayers is mitigated through shifts in structure as well as expression. Significantly, 4Q504 speaks of the wilderness generation's rebellion not to claim solidarity in their guilt but to establish ancient foils to the Qumran covenanters. In other texts from Qumran as well as in the Psalms of Solomon, the speakers suggest that they, like God, are righteous beings while it is their enemies who are wicked. These role designations retrieve a motif of the communal laments that had been rejected by Neh 9:33, whose declaration that God is just and the people wicked has been influential but not definitive.

By incorporating the confession of sin so significantly into both their structure and expression, Neh 9:6–37 and the other prayers of penitence from the Persian period represent a nadir in perceptions of the divine-human relationship.[50] The root of this development is the alienation that Jews experienced as a result of the exile and loss of sovereignty to the Babylonians

---

shared ... by all the Platonists of our period." *The Middle Platonists, 80 B.C to A.D. 220* (Ithaca, N.Y.: Cornell University Press, 1977), 168.

[50] These compositions may be included among Walter Brueggemann's psalms of disorientation, which reflect "the awareness that things between Yahweh and Israel are messed up. In the broadest sense, [these psalms] have one partner or the other speak about the 'disarray' into which the relationship has fallen. It is a disarray that concerns both partners in various ways." *The Message of the Psalms: A Theological Commentary* (Minneapolis: Augsburg, 1984), 58.

and then the Persians. Within the golah community, there was a connection between anticipating the next misfortune and perceiving the proximity of God, as Veijola notes: "On the one hand, the readiness to accept diverse forms of ruin had increased, but on the other hand it entailed the danger of objectifying God."[51] Veijola is commenting on Neh 9:33, a signature text for the post-exilic era when Jews confronted the loss of Israelite religion's important forms, such as the monarchy and the Solomonic temple. With the bond to the ancestors also undone (Isa 63:16), theological pessimism had taken root. In this period, some of the people sought consolation by invoking God personally as Father (Isa 63:16, 64:7) and patterning their religion on familial realities.[52]

Addressing God as father counters the alienation that the people experience and understand to be the result of their sin. Another such strategy in Trito-Isaiah is to supply a rationale (Isa 65:1–2) for God's denying the people a response: the severity of their sin has delayed any oracle. In both cases, the strategy offers the people who are confessing their sins the future possibility for renewed relationship with God. Eventually, these prospects attain their most mature form in the theology of *teshuvah*, the turning *from* evil and *toward* good. In the Hellenistic and Roman periods, there emerge noticeable impulses to found anew the covenant of divine-human relationship over and against sin and its effects. The impulses occur intermittently within a body of penitential prayers otherwise marked by theological pessimism. At Qumran the covenanters who confess their sin also identify with Israel at Sinai to claim for themselves a faith above that of common sinners. The Psalms of Solomon appeal to the Pharisaic doctrine of free will to imply that people who choose to do evil are truly wicked while those who strive to avoid evil and do good fall under a different designation. These and other strategies distill from the confession of sin some hope of a return to God. The texts in question document the emergence of the notion of *teshuvah*.

Our study has shown, indeed, that disparate streams of tradition developed in the wake of the psalms of communal lament. Across the prayers of the Second Temple Period, penitence is in no way univocal. Thus it is at this point premature to conclude that the grouping of prayers constitutes a new genre or even a homogeneous set.[53] To argue for a distinct organization of the penitential prayers from the Second Temple period, one must develop "a systematic consideration of how to classify and relate" the variety of texts within this

---

[51] "... auf der einen Seite die Bereitschaft, die verschiedenen Formen des Unheils zu akzeptieren, erhöhte, auf der anderen aber die Gefahr der Verobjektivierung Gottes nach sich zog...." Veijola, "Das Klagegebet," 304–5.

[52] See the observations of Albertz indicated in n. 30 of chapter two.

[53] Boda claims that "a specific *Gattung* ... called Penitential Prayers" comprises Ezra 9:6–15, Neh 9:6–37, Dan 9:4–19 as well as Psalm 106, Neh 1:5–11, 1 Kings 8, Bar 1:15–2:15 (–3:8), Dan 3:26–45 (LXX), 1QS, 4Q504. One might counter, however, that Boda's comparative analysis of form in Neh 9:6–37 and the other prayers points out enough differences to preclude a common genre designation. *Praying the Tradition*, 27, 28–41.

grouping.⁵⁴ It is now impossible to provide such a consideration with exactitude. Methodologically, it is more appropriate to define these texts as penitential prayers and to comment on features that establish a form-critical affinity to the psalms of communal lament or other genres, such as the Levitical sermon that has influenced Ezra 9:6–15. Such conclusions with regard to form may subsequently serve as the basis for studies of the prayer's tone and manner as well as its *Sitz im Leben*.

5.5 Manner and Tone: Prophecies of Warning

Our studies of Ezra 9:6–15 and Neh 9:6–37 led to the conclusion that aspects of both prayers display the tone and manner of a warning. The warning is that of the prophets, understood as spokespersons for both the law (Ezra 9:10–11) and for penitence (Neh 9:26). As living lawfully and turning back to God are central to these prayers, the references to the prophets are not made in passing. The gravity of the prophets' messages is not quantifiable, but it would seem that the prophetic function of warning is greater in Ezra 9:6–15 and Neh 9:6–37 than in the psalms of communal lament.⁵⁵ Discernible in the prayers of Ezra 9 and Nehemiah 9 are content and contextual features that point back to prophecies of warning and misfortune in Amos, Micah and Ezekiel.

In Amos, Micah and Ezekiel the prophet announces Israel's impending misfortune by way of a "preaching" that parallels his "prophesying" (Amos 7:16, Mic 2:6, Ezek 21:2,7). In these cases such preaching is designated by the root נטף in *hif'il,* which literally means "to drip." נטף in *hif'il* appears in none of the penitential prayers in our study, thereby ruling out a most direct link to the prophetic tradition of warning and misfortune. Nonetheless, there are significant points of contact between the prayers and the prophetic function in question.

First, we have noted in chapter three that common content brings into focus the details of the misfortune. The preaching of Mic 2:6 warns that the concomitant of wrongdoing is shame (כלם). Such content is also found in Ezra 9:6, where iniquities and guilt leave the speaker disgraced (וְנִכְלַמְתִּי) such that he cannot lift his face to God. In another vein, the prophet's preaching of misfortune may include graphic examples of destruction, typically by the sword (חֶרֶב). When Amos is warned not to preach (7:16), he prophesies that his adversary's children will be killed by the sword (7:17). On the other hand, when Ezekiel *is* told to preach (21:7), he announces that God will put down wicked and righteous people alike with a sword (21:8). Later, when Ezra 9:8 speaks of

---

⁵⁴ Hindy Najman indicates the importance of "a systematic consideration of how to classify and relate Second Temple texts" in her remarks on genre, found in her review of R. A. Argall, *1 Enoch and Sirach: A Comparative Literary and Conceptual Analysis of the Themes of Revelation, Creation and Judgment, HS* 40 (1999): 347–49.

⁵⁵ According to Gunkel, the threat as a prophetic genre is found only once in the entire psalter. He maintains that his example, Ps 53:6, is too brief and textually corrupt to sustain a comparison with the prophetic threat. See *Einleitung in die Psalmen,* 362–64.

the misfortune suffered on account of guilt and iniquity, the litany begins with the destruction by sword (בַּחֶרֶב) and proceeds to mention captivity, plunder and shame. More generally, the root חרב connotes destruction by any means. For example, in Isa 64:10 the destruction of the sanctuary's vessels is referred to as וְכָל מַחֲמַדֵּינוּ הָיָה לְחָרְבָּה, similar to Amos 7:9 concerning the sanctuaries of Israel being laid to waste, וּמִקְדְּשֵׁי יִשְׂרָאֵל יֶחֱרָבוּ.

Second, like the prophets of warning, the penitential prayers devise word plays involving expressions for deceit and general wrongdoing. The practice informs Mic 2:11:

לוּ אִישׁ הֹלֵךְ רוּחַ וָשֶׁקֶר כִּזֵּב אַטִּף לְךָ
לַיַּיִן וְלַשֵּׁכָר וְהָיָה מַטִּיף הָעָם הַזֶּה׃

The portion of the verse in direct speech indicates a man who deals in falsehood (וָשֶׁקֶר); the portion in indirect speech portrays the man preaching wine and strong drink (וְלַשֵּׁכָר). The mention of strong drink puns on the earlier reference to falsehood, whose Hebrew characters are nearly identical. In Isa 63:7,10, the root שקר is also subject to irony. At first (63:8), God claims the people as God's own and declares them incapable of deceit (לֹא יְשַׁקֵּרוּ). Specifically, dramatic irony is operative as שקר represents an impossibility to the speaker, but it has a darker meaning to those who understand the situation. The latter view surfaces in 63:10, which confirms that the people are imbued with שקר. They rebel and grieve God's holy spirit (וְהֵמָּה מָרוּ וְעִצְּבוּ אֶת רוּחַ קָדְשׁוֹ), with "spirit" (רוח) establishing another parallel back to Mic 2:11. Later in the Second Temple Period, שקר remains a lexical device to confront people with their wrongdoing.

In the Dead Sea Scrolls, שקר is generally synonymous with "falsehood" and "deceit,"[56] but in 1QpHab it points to the מטיף הכזב, or "spouter of lies (10:9)," who builds a community of deceit (עדה בשקר 10:11) and teaches its members acts of deceit (במע[ש]י שקר 10:12).[57] At Qumran, שקר had a historical referent, a man who spoke as if he were a prophet (נטף in hif'il) but issued falsehoods. These references to the false prophet or "spouter of lies" in column 10 of 1QpHab are followed by other polemics in column 11 against the wicked priest, who appears in conjunction with the interpretation of Hab 2:15. The biblical verse promises woe to anyone who makes a neighbor drunk in order to gaze upon the neighbor's nakedness: וְאַף שַׁכֵּר לְמַעַן הַבִּיט עַל מְעוֹרֵיהֶם. The interpretation of Hab 2:15 puns upon the words for nakedness (מְעוֹרֵיהֶם) and festival (מוֹעֲדֵיהֶם), to indict anyone who induces a neighbor to drink to excess and thereby fail to observe a festival. Although the interpretation of Hab 2:15 in 11:4–8 does not pun or otherwise play with שכר, the term for drunk,[58] it is more

---

[56] Cf. 1QS 4:21; CD 6:1; 11QH 5:27, 7:12; 11QT 61:9.

[57] The citation of 1QpHab cols. 10–11 are from Brownlee, *The Midrash Pesher of Habakkuk*, 7–8.

[58] According to Brownlee, the interpreter rather equates the Hebrew words for "drink," "swallow" and "destroy" to recall an occasion when the Wicked Priest tried to

than coincidence that the pesher would align references to שכר and שקר with the Righteous Teacher's two adversaries and denigrate the former as a lying prophet (נטף in *hif'il*).[59]

In summation thus far, there are points of contact between the prophetic warning and the penitential prayers of the Second Temple period. Because said contact is often indirect and oblique, however, we cannot assert a literary relationship between the prophetic warning and the penitential prayer. A missing link of sorts is available in Job 29, the first portion of a lament that extends from Job 29–31. In Job 29, Job recalls a glorious past in which he helped others to overcome their misfortune. Helmut Madl proposes that Job 29 is a key for interpreting the passages about prophecy and preaching in Amos, Ezekiel and Micah, and his suggestion merits consideration.[60]

The key to Madl's comparison is Job's statement in Job 29:22, "After I spoke, they did not speak again, and my word descended upon them":

אַחֲרֵי דְבָרִי לֹא יִשְׁנוּ וְעָלֵימוֹ תִּטֹּף מִלָּתִי׃

Thus נטף is attested both in the prophetic books and Job 29:22, and in both it denotes not mundane speech but oratory. Although the prophets use נטף in *hif'il* and Job employs *qal*, the change in *binyan* does not constitute a material difference. All of the uses are comparable syntactically as the prophetic passages never supply an accusative for נטף in *hif'il* and Job 29:22 is the Bible's only intransitive use of נטף in *qal*. Moreover, both Job and the prophets use the verb in the imperfect, except for the imperatives in Ezek 21:2, 7. In addition to these grammatical similarities, one might expect a relationship in tone between the prophets and Job 29:22. In fact, tonal indicators found in the prophets recur in Job but are applied differently. For example, adversaries admonish the prophet to silence (Amos 7:16, Mic 2:6) as part of their polemic. In Job 29:21–22, however, the people respond to Job in silence because they are receptive to his words (Job 29:21; cf. Lam 2:10, 18; 3:28 where silence [דמם] is a formal gesture of penitence). In sum, Job 29 is a post-exilic lament manifesting literary connections to the prophetic corpus. Specifically, Job 29:22 provides evidence that the prophetic function of warning had a bearing on the composition of laments after the exile and through the Second Temple period.

While Job 29 is shaped by the prophetic function of warning, it also is a lament that broadly parallels the penitential prayers of our study. By locating Job 29 among these prayers, we may highlight certain of their features that are

---

"swallow up" the Righteous Teacher and those who follow him. See his "Biblical Interpretation Among the Sectaries of the Dead Sea Scrolls," *BA* 14 (1951): 67–68.

[59] Maurya Horgan notes that there are lexical differences between this citation of Hab 2:15 and an allusion to the biblical verse in 1QH 4:11–12. Specifically, the word שכר is included in 1QpHab but left out of 1QH. See her *Pesharim: Qumran Interpretations of Biblical Books* (CBQMS 8; Washington: The Catholic Biblical Association, 1979), 48.

[60] Madl makes his proposal in the course of his article "נטף," *TDOT* 9:398–400.

consistent with the prophetic function of warning in the post-exilic period. First, Job 29 is oriented toward the righteous and the wicked. Specifically, Job dons righteousness (צֶדֶק) like a garment while justice is his robe and tartan (29:14).[61] In this apparel Job does the bidding of the blind, lame and poor (29:14–16); in turn he sets upon the wicked (עַוָּל 29:17). The binary opposition of righteous and wicked is central to Nehemiah 9's confession of sin, which asserts that God is righteous and the penitents wicked (9:33). More exactly, the chiastic construction of Neh 9:33, elaborated in chapter four, aligns with that of Job 29:14.[62] Also, Job 29:14 sheds light on Isa 64:5a, with its counterintuitive association of righteous deeds and a soiled garment. Job 29:14 equates righteousness with a garment, indicating the initial, ideal state of affairs before the people's wrongdoing has soiled the garment of their righteousness.

Second, Neh 9:33 refers to the binding relationship between justice and faith, which once obtained in people (Neh 9:8) but now is proper only to God (9:33). Job 29:24 also indicates the people's lack of faith אֶשְׂחַק אֲלֵהֶם לֹא יַאֲמִינוּ, an expression which David Noel Freedman translates: "I smile at those who lack confident faith." Freedman explains that the object of Job's "benign superiority" is people who lack faith or confidence but are not hopelessly downcast.[63] Job 29:24–25 indicate the people have accepted enlightenment from Job (אוֹר פָּנַי), a distinction in faith not unlike that claimed by the Qumran covenanters who are specially associated with the Sinai theophany (see above re. 4Q504 frag. 3, col. 2, lines 12–13). In this guise, the covenanters imply that they have greater faith than their rebellious ancestors. In both texts, the people who receive the prophetic warning are not perfect in their faith, nor are they the worst of sinners.

Finally, the structure of Job 29 has affinities with that of a lament psalm. Our comparison builds upon Westermann's suggestion that the compound theme of a felicitous past and woeful present played out in Job 29–31 has its clearest formulation in the laments of the community.[64] Following Westermann's suggestion, John Holbert has correlated sections of Job 29–31 to form-critical

---

[61] Noting that 29:14 is the pivotal verse of the chapter, Bruce Malchow compares Job's robing with justice as a virtue. He further notes that Job's possession of royal justice carries a possible allusion to kingly garb, and that the entire chapter may be based on a royal prototype. See his "A Royal Prototype in Job 29," pp. 178–84 in *The Psalms And Other Studies on the Old Testament Presented to Joseph I. Hunt* (ed. J. C. Knight and L. A. Sinclair; Nashotah, Wis.: Nashotah House Seminary, 1990), 179.

[62] Re. Job 29:14, David Noel Freedman observes that the chiastic structure joins the opening and closing words, מִשְׁפָּט and צֶדֶק, and that the two verbs of the first colon work with the two objects of the second colon, "interpreted severally." He also points out alliteration in the verse. See his review of *Job 29–31 in Light of Northwest Semitic: A Translation and Philological Commentary,* by A. R. Ceresko, *JBL* 102 (1983): 141–42.

[63] Ibid., 142.

[64] Specifically, Westermann maintains that the recollection of God's beneficence in Job 29 parallels Psalm 80. *Der Aufbau des Buches Hiob* (Stuttgart: Calwer Verlag, 1977), 59–65.

elements of the communal laments.⁶⁵ For example, Holbert identifies the address in Job 29 (29:2–5) as stylistically similar to those of the communal laments. Ideally, one would be able to demonstrate other affinities between the structural elements of Job 29 and the communal laments, but there are insurmountable difficulties involved in this task.

In summation, Job 29 is a link between the prophetic function of warning and the post-exilic prayers of penitence. On the one hand, the prophetic function of warning is attested explicitly in Job 29:22. On the other hand, despite the substantial differences between Job 29 and Isa 63:7–64:11, Ezra 9:6–15 and Neh 9:6–37, the latter three laments contain thematic and structural aspects of Job 29. That is to say, they have received the same prophetic deposit as has Job, but employ it for their own particular purposes. In all three prayers, prophetic preaching is a significant element, but it no longer requires נטף in hif'il. Rather, the erstwhile function of warning is presented as the priority of righteousness over evil, of faith over unbelief (Neh 9:33). Moreover, in Isa 63:7–64:11, Ezra 9:6–15 and Neh 9:6–37, the preaching of misfortune no longer foretells the future, as in Amos, Micah and Ezekiel. Rather, it recounts the past as a time of suffering in retribution for sins committed. If the preacher's audience heeds the recollection, they become disposed to repent and confess their sins.

5.6 Sitz im Leben

In the preceding chapters we considered the historical relationship between post-exilic penitential prayers and the liturgy of repentance. The liturgy of repentance was seen to be a logical setting for prayers that seek to console the unfortunate by allowing them to confess their sin. Begun at the time of the exile, the liturgy of repentance accentuated the twin themes of penitence for one's failings and resolve to amend one's ways.⁶⁶ Details of this liturgy are not extant, although it probably entailed fasting (Zech 7:3,5; 8:19), public mourning (Lam 2:10–11), and perhaps even self-laceration (Jer 41:5).⁶⁷ Regrettably, none of the exilic or post-exilic sources disclose as much as we would like about the penitential liturgy. Using what data the sources provide, we will selectively elaborate the liturgical record of the exilic and post-exilic periods in order to consider how historical situations may have influenced or been influenced by the language of Jewish penitence.

Some of the earliest evidence of penitential prayer arising from international developments in the Neo-Babylonian period is reflected in Jer 14:1–15:4. Here

---

⁶⁵ John Holbert, "The Rehabilitation of the Sinner: The Function of Job 29–31," ZAW 95 (1983): 235.

⁶⁶ As well, the liturgy allowed penitents to avow their loyalty to the past and their singular dependence upon divine grace. See Ackroyd, Exile and Restoration, 47.

⁶⁷ The liturgy may have included the following penitential practices, which are documented in Ezra 9–10 and Nehemiah 9: tearing clothes, pulling out hair, weeping, fasting, wearing sackcloth, and placing dust on the head.

is reported lamentation (14:17–18), confession of sin (14:20), and petition (14:21). In his analysis of this text, Boda identifies it as a "prophetic liturgy" that indicates the transition between "Classic Lament and [post-exilic] Penitential Prayer."[68] The reference to post-exilic penitential prayers includes the three prayers treated in this dissertation. Boda surmises that Jer 14:17–21 is a liturgy that was used during the siege of Jerusalem in 597 B.C.E., and that within ten years the verses were incorporated into a prayer (the present Jer 14:1–15:4) that was said during a drought occurring sometime during the reign of Zedekiah.[69] In Boda's reconstruction of events, the historical context of Jeremiah 14–15 also gives rise to Lamentations 3, an artistic prayer that issues a call to repentance and confession: "[Lam 3] represents the expression of the prophet after the experience of Jer 14–15. He recognizes God's hand against him due to his sin and calls the community to a depth of repentance that transcends mere words (Lam 3:40–41)."[70] In Boda's view, there is an "organic connection" between the book of Lamentations and the post-exilic penitential prayers.[71] He notes continuities between the two collections, such as common setting and common purpose, and he acknowledges fundamental differences as well.[72]

Penitential practices became increasingly commonplace in the exilic period, as indicated by the four days of fasting in Zech 8:19, in contrast to the one fast day, Yom Kippur, that is prescribed by biblical law.[73] Eventually, fasting became a fixture of Second Temple Judaism and a concomitant of its penitential prayer. Many of the extant prayers were said in the context of ritual fasts (Ezra 10:6; Neh 1:4, 9:1; Dan 9:3). Perhaps there existed other prayers linked to fasting and intended to end drought; drought was the occasion for the Jewish court to decree as many as 13 fast days, according to *m. Ta'an.* 1:6. Inasmuch as

---

[68] Mark Boda, "From Complaint to Contrition: Peering though the Liturgical Window of Jer 14,1–15,4," *ZAW* 113 (2001): 197. As a literary designation, "prophetic liturgy" is not problematic, but one must ask, To what historical *realia* does the text correspond? Where was this liturgy enacted and by whom? Elsewhere Boda offers a profile of the officiant ("The Priceless Gain of Penitence," 8), and admittedly the sources do not allow us to say much more about the worship.

[69] Ibid., 194–95.

[70] Boda, "The Priceless Gain of Penitence," 12.

[71] Ibid., 10.

[72] Ibid., 9.

[73] Regarding Yom Kippur, see Leviticus 23, esp. 23:27. Commentators suggest that Zech 8:19 correlates its four fasts to critical moments in Judah's demise. Thus, the fast in the fourth month marks when Jerusalem was successfully attacked, the fast in the fifth month recalls the destruction of the Temple in 587 B.C.E., the seventh-month fast indicates the death of the provisional governor, Gedaliah, and the tenth-month fast coincides with Nebuchadnezzar's laying siege to Jerusalem. These events are supplied by David L. Petersen, who also notes that the fast days, while commemorating hardship, are to become for Judah joyful celebrations. *Haggai and Zechariah 1–8: A Commentary* (Philadelphia: Westminster, 1984), 312.

the *Mishnah* derives from the religious practice of Second Temple Judaism,[74] it witnesses to that period's standard practices of penitence, such as frequent fasting and as well placing dust on the head (*m. Ta'an.* 2:1).

In the fifth century B.C.E., even after the completion of the Second Temple and the restoration of national rites, penitential practices remained vital to the local liturgy. The gathering of Judeans described in Nehemiah 8 is explicitly liturgical (8:6–7), and it is significant that the people are disposed to mourn and weep (8:9) and to grieve (8:11). The gathering in Nehemiah 8, it has been suggested, represents a penitential service initially associated with Sukkoth and later observed as Yom Kippur.[75] Another potential link to Yom Kippur is found in Nehemiah 9, which reports penitential practices such as fasting, sackcloth and dust on the head (Neh 9:1) as well as penitential language. In the remaining portion of this section, we will consider the evidence that links the prayer in Nehemiah 9 to the standing prayers or *'Amîdah* for both Yom Kippur and the daily liturgy.

The language of Nehemiah 9 may have influenced the synagogal prayers for Yom Kippur, according to Liebreich. He has suggested that the standing prayers for the Day of Atonement incorporate Neh 9:17b, the first three words of 9:19, and 9:33.[76] Liebreich also claims that 9:17b's mention of God's סְלִיחוֹת inspired the liturgical practice of reciting Exod 34:6–7 in the course of the prayers for forgiveness.[77]

The difficulty with Liebreich's claim is that the term סְלִיחוֹת does not appear in Exod 34:6–7; even if it did, a number of sources other than Neh 9:17b could supply a parallel.[78] When, however, one considers that in Nehemiah the term סְלִיחוֹת is part of a constellation of divine attributes that function as a refrain, Neh 9:17 stands "more closely to later liturgical formulae" such as the Thirteen Attributes of God, which are based on Exod 34:6–7, where Moses

---

[74] As stated in chapter one (n. 3), we hold the view associated with Heinemann and others that there was continuous development in Jewish liturgical thought throughout antiquity, from the early stages of prayer to the final, set formulations of prayer texts that postdate the fall of the Second Temple by several centuries. Thus, rabbinic sources can provide important data about Second Temple prayer. As Reif observes, gaining access to "the original evidence" can be challenging: "The problem for the researcher is that [liturgical] developments are not of course seen as such, or not at least described as such, in the relevant or in subsequent generations. Once new customs or rites are legitimately established, they are redefined in light of their new status and acquire an authority and history that cover the original evidence with layers of later deposits." *Judaism and Hebrew Prayer*, 20.

[75] Similarly, the weeping at the reading of the law in Nehemiah 8 has been associated with the ritual celebration of the New Year. See Norman Snaith, *The Jewish New Year Festival* (London: S.P.C.K., 1947), 151.

[76] "The Impact of Neh 9:5–37 on the Liturgy of the Synagogue," 236.

[77] Ibid.

[78] Among the likely sources are Isa 55:7; Jer 5:1, 5:7, 31:34, 50:20; and 2 Chr 7:14. The root סלח is also well attested in cultic contexts such as Lev 4:20, 5:10, 15:25, 19:22.

received the second set of tablets.⁷⁹ This insight of Newman requires the hindsight of the rabbinic commentators, whom Ismar Elbogen has also read carefully. He takes the view that סְלִיחוֹת and related descriptors of the divine are the "nucleus of all prayers for atonement."⁸⁰ Thus, in light of literary developments documented in the rabbinic period, Neh 9:17b is not an unlikely source for subsequent liturgical expressions involving the divine attributes. The influence may have occurred at almost any time in the Second Temple period. An early date is implied if with Lee Levine one associates the community gathering at the gate in Ezra-Nehemiah with proto-synagogal practice.⁸¹ Levine notes, however, that the "dramatic initiative" of introducing obligatory, public communal prayer takes place in the post-70 Palestinian synagogue.⁸²

The standing prayers or *'Amîdah* were not limited to Yom Kippur and were in fact a fixture of daily prayer by the time of the rabbis.⁸³ Also known as the 18 Benedictions or *Šemone Esre*, the standing prayers comprise 13 intermediate blessings that are preceded and followed by a series of three blessings. The influence of Nehemiah 9 is apparent in the first blessing, an extended invocation that refers to God as האל הגדול הגבור והנורא (Neh 9:32, from Deut 10:17).⁸⁴ Elsewhere the blessing cites God's loving kindness, גומל חסדים טבים, which Reuven Kimelman takes as an allusion to Isa 63:7, and the blessing speaks of God redeeming for the sake of God's name, למען שמו, which Kimelman links to Isa 63:16 and Ezek 20:9.⁸⁵ Thus there is prima facie evidence that blessings of

---

⁷⁹ The Thirteen Attributes are elaborated in *b. Roš Haš.* 17b. The link between divine attribute formula of Neh 9:17 and the talmudic text is suggested by Newman, *Praying By the Book*, 88–89.

⁸⁰ See his *Jewish Liturgy: A Comprehensive History* (Philadelphia: Jewish Publication Society, 1993 [1924]), 177.

⁸¹ Lee Levine, *The Ancient Synagogue: The First Thousand Years* (New Haven/London: Yale University Press, 2000), 30–32.

⁸² Regarding the *'Amîdah,* the contribution of the rabbis at Yavneh in 70 is the subject of much debate. While many scholars have long assumed that a public form of the *'Amîdah* existed before 70, certain scholars began in the 1980s to assert that no organized communal prayer existed until the rabbis at Yavneh devised them. We are inclined to follow Levine's mediating position: "There can be little doubt that obligatory daily prayer—both personal and communal – was conceived in the post–70 period under the auspices of Rabban Gamaliel. On the other hand, as noted, these prayers were not created *ex nihilo* There were many precedents, and the Yavnean *tannaim* incorporated earlier materials, reworking, reformulating, and restricting them so as to fashion a prayer which they sought to make obligatory for Jews everywhere, as a community and as individuals." Ibid., 503, 518.

⁸³ See *b. Ber.* 28b.

⁸⁴ Citations of the *'Amîdah* are from *Daily Prayers* (ed. M. Stern; New York: Hebrew Publishing Co., 1928), 50–52.

⁸⁵ "The Literary Structure of the Amidah and the Rhetoric of Redemption," pp. 171–218 in *The Echoes of Many Texts: Reflections on Jewish and Christian Traditions:*

the *'Amîdah* echo the post-exilic penitential prayers that are the basis of our study. The fifth blessing concerns returning to God or *teshuvah:*

השיבנו אבינו לתורתך
וקרבנו מלכנו לעבודתך
והחזירנו בתשובה שלמה לפניך

> Bring us back, O our Father, to your Torah,
> Draw us near, O our King, to your service,
> Bring us back, in full repentance, before You.

Kimelman maintains that the first strophe "is based on the parallel drawn by Nehemiah between 'returning ... to you' (Neh 9:26) and 'returning ... to your Torah' (9:29)."[86] Kimelman's point is that the return to God is said to be through Torah, and thus "the rhetoric of blessing is a rhetoric of return."[87] The argument is strengthened, Kimelman claims, when the third strophe uses the same term both for return and repentance, בתשובה. The blessing implies that "one need not start over to repent, only to recommit to what was once one's own."[88] Although the textual evidence linking Neh 9:26,29 to the fifth blessing is not overwhelming, both texts speak to the prospect of returning to Torah. The likelihood of such a return, however, appears significantly greater in blessing five of the *'Amîdah* than in Neh 9:26,29, where the people reject the prophets (9:26) and the God who sends the prophets (9:29).

The *'Amîdah's* sixth blessing, for forgiveness, is more formulaic. Confession of sin is expressed in phrases such as "we have sinned" חטאנו, "we have transgressed" פשענו. Although the first-person plural verbs recall Isa 64:4b וַנֶּחֱטָא and Neh 9:33 הִרְשָׁעְנוּ, one must take into account both the prevalence of these terms in Second Temple Judaism as well as their virtually limitless semantic field at the time (see footnote 20). Thus, if there were a literary relationship between blessing six of the *'Amîdah* and the prayers of our study, it could not be proven solely on the basis of פשענו and חטאנו. Nonetheless, the repetition of penitential vocabulary indicates that between the biblical prayers and the *'Amîdah* there is compatibility and perhaps a degree of confluence.

It is difficult to determine how or when a confluence may have taken place between the penitential prayers and the *'Amîdah*, and on this matter scholarly opinion is mixed. Earlier in this century, Elbogen and Kaufmann Kohler took seriously the talmudic dictum (*b. Ber.* 33a) that the *'Amîdah's* origins go back to the time of the Great Assembly, which Jewish historiography describes as an assembly of 120 rabbis that ruled in the period after the time of the prophets up

---

Essays in Honor of Lou H. Silberman (ed. W. G. Dever and J. E. Wright; BJS 313; Atlanta: Scholars Press, 1997), 200.

[86] Ibid., 188.
[87] Ibid.
[88] Ibid.

to the start of rabbinic Judaism in 70 C.E. The אנשי כנסת הגדלה are dated no earlier than the fifth century B.C.E. Thus, both Elbogen and Kohler attempted to date the *'Amîdah* in the first half of the Second Temple period. Elbogen located certain of the benedictions at the beginning of the Hellenistic period,[89] and Kohler dated the *'Amîdah's* initial composition earlier, among "the older generations of the elders" who succeeded Ezra.[90] It is intriguing to imagine the persons first responsible for the *'Amîdah* drawing on prayers attributed to Ezra and Nehemiah only a generation or so after these historical figures passed from the scene. But the evidence for this scenario is not compelling, and while certain scholars continue to work under the type of assumptions that Elbogen and Kohler made, currently most would date the *'Amîdah* to second half of the Second Temple period. Based on the prayers' form and content, some date the *'Amîdah* to the final quarter of the first century C.E. (see footnote 82).

For example, Ezra Fleischer argues that the *'Amîdah* "was designed to institute a new form of divine service, to restore the relationship between God and the Jewish people, rent by the destruction of the [Second] Temple."[91] Fleischer understands the prayer to be supplications by a people moving toward their "eschatological redemption."[92] This view is close to that of Kimelman, who holds that "the Amidah turns out to be a remarkable orchestration of redemptive motifs."[93]

The focus that Fleischer brings to the *'Amîdah* leads him to read blessings five and six as part of an eschatological concatenation. "Were they granted the knowledge [of blessing four], they would realize that their iniquities caused their punishment and they would repent; by the merit of their repentance God would make atonement for their iniquities and forgive them."[94] Fleischer reminds readers that blessings five and six, for repentance and atonement, are simply the prelude to redemption, God's decisive action on behalf of the people. As Moshe Weinfeld has demonstrated, the prayers for knowledge, return and forgiveness are comparable to "prayers for admission" and as such merely establish a person's initial willingness to abandon evil and "return" to God.[95] It is telling that the scholars cited here do not compare the *'Amîdah* to Ezra 9:6–15, Neh 9:6–37 or Isa 63:7–64:11. When the *'Amîdah* is given a late date after 70 C.E.,

---

[89] *Jewish Liturgy*, 29.

[90] Kaufmann Kohler, "The Origin and Composition of the 18 Benedictions," *HUCA* 1 (1924): 389.

[91] Fleischer "The *Shemone Esre* – Its Character, Internal Order, Content and Goals," *Tarbiz* 63 (1993): vi.

[92] Ibid.

[93] "The Literary Structure of the Amidah," 214.

[94] "The *Shemone Esre*," 198.

[95] "The Prayer for Knowledge, Repentance and Forgiveness in the 'Eighteen Benedictions' – Qumran Parallels, Biblical Antecedents, and Basic Characteristics," *Tarbiz* 48 (1979): 187.

the influence of the post-exilic penitential prayers appears at best remote and diffuse.

5.7 Conclusion

The work of Fleischer and Weinfeld draws attention to a certain pattern vis-à-vis the confession of sin in Second Temple Judaism. Although the confession of sin becomes one of the best attested prayer forms in the Second Temple Period and serves as a hallmark of post-exilic piety, its predominance waxes and wanes. Chapters two, three and four examined penitential prayers of the post-exilic period, when Persia ruled over a once autonomous Judea. In the prayers of this period, the confession of sin permeates many of the form-critical elements drawn from the psalms of communal lament and incorporated into prayers such as Isa 63:7–64:11, Ezra 9:6–15 and Neh 9:6–37. The present chapter, in contrast, has shown that the confession of sin, while still a fixture of Second Temple prayer, becomes less conspicuous in the Hellenistic and Roman eras. Differences in literary structure and expression have combined to indicate a less dominant role for the confession of sin in both prayers and penitential texts.

Structurally, the review of history is attested in penitential prayers throughout the Second Temple period, but its post–exilic function of fostering penance via the confession of sin is at times abandoned, as in 4Q504. In that text and others, the forebears are exemplars whom penitent sinners are to emulate rather than models of moral failure. Related to structure, the motivational element that follows a petition to God is often a confession of sin, per post-exilic practice, but several of the later prayers include post-petitionary expressions that would motivate God to respond on the basis of divine attributes. Our examples have been drawn from the prayers offered by Manasseh, Baruch and Aseneth as well as the standing prayers of Yom Kippur, which highlight the attribute of סְלִיחוֹת.

Another divine attribute is צדקה, and it too offers insight into the confession of sin's diminished role in later prayers. In the post-exilic prayers, the binary categories of רשע and צדיק were applied invariably to God and to humans, respectively. 1Q34 [bis], however, retrieves an older and more plaintive scenario in which צדיק may apply to humans as well as God. An individual is said to be righteous over and against a wicked enemy. In turn, the increased focus on one's enemy as the party at fault for a given misfortune mitigates any self-accusation. For example, we noted that 1QpHab applies the term for deceit, שׂקר, not to members within its own group, as does Isa 63:7–10, but to the enemy without, the "spouter of lies" who rivals the Righteous Teacher. In light of these developments, it is not surprising that the prayers for forgiveness and atonement are not dominant in the 'Amîdah, which is characterized rather by a theme of redemption or more simply return, תשובה.

As the confession of sin becomes less acute and less pervasive, there begins a divide between the lament of the community and the individual; in the words of August Strobel, with the Judaism of the New Testament era "we differentiate the collective and the individual prayer of penitence."[96] Prescinding from this later development, we may conclude by recalling that which is common to both the collective and personal modes of penitential expression. Theologically, both collective and personal penitence concern themselves with fundamental perception as to the relationship of God and humankind.[97] After the exile, when this relationship appeared increasingly vulnerable and remote to the people descended from Israel, the children of the exile sought a refounding of the nation not limited by history and a renewed relationship with God emphasizing penitence and the confession of sin. In subsequent centuries, *teshuvah* no longer epitomized this relationship and came to connote something broader. *Teshuvah*, however, remained a significant part of the Jewish way to God throughout the period of the Second Temple.

---

[96] "Im Judentum des neutestamentlichen Zeitalters geht beides deutlich nebeneinander her: das Eingeständnis der Gemeinschaftsschuld und das persönaliche Sündenbekenntnis. Wir underscheiden das kollektive und das individuelle Bußgebet." August Strobel, *Erkenntnis und Bekenntnis der Sünde in neutestamentlicher Zeit* (Stuttgart: Calwer Verlag, 1968), 11.

[97] "Was in ältester Zeit vor allem Erfahrung des Volkes war und in späterer Zeit sogar mehr und mehr auch Erfahrung des einzelnen Frommen, wird gelegentlich zu einer grundsätzlichen erkenntnis über das Verhältnis von Gott und Mensch." Ibid.

SELECTED BIBLIOGRAPHY

Achtemeier, Elizabeth. *The Community and Message of Isaiah 56–66.* Minneapolis: Augsburg, 1982.
Ackroyd, Peter. *The Chronicler in his Age.* JSOTSup 101. Sheffield: Sheffield Academic Press, 1991.
———. *Exile and Restoration: A Study of Hebrew Thought of the Sixth Century B.C.* Philadelphia: Westminster, 1968.
———. *I & II Chronicles, Ezra, Nehemiah.* London: S.C.M. Press, 1973.
Albertz, Rainer. *A History of the Israelite Religion in the Old Testament Period.* 2 vols. Louisville: Westminster John Knox, 1994 (1992).
———. "Le Milieu des Deutéronomistes." Pages 377–407 in *Israël construit son Histoire.* Edited by A. de Pury, et al. Geneva: Labor et Fides, 1996.
Albeck, Chaim, ed. *Mishnah.* Tel Aviv: Dvir, 1959.
Anderson, Carl R. "The Formation of the Levitical Prayer of Nehemiah 9," Th. D. diss., Dallas Theological Seminary, 1987.
Baillet, Maurice, ed. *Discoveries in the Judaean Desert 7.* Oxford: Clarendon Press, 1982.
Balentine, Samuel. *Prayer in the Hebrew Bible: The Drama of Divine-Human Dialogue.* OBT. Minneapolis: Augsburg Fortress, 1993.
———. *The Torah's Vision of Worship.* OBT. Minneapolis: Fortress, 1999.
Batten, L. W. *A Critical and Exegetical Commentary on the Books of Ezra and Nehemiah.* ICC. Edinburgh: T & T Clark, 1913.
Begrich, Joachim. "Das priesterliche Heilsorakel." *ZAW* 52 (1934): 81–92.
Bellinger, W. H., Jr. *Psalmody and Prophecy.* JSOTSup 27. Sheffield: JSOT Press, 1984.
Berquist, Jon L. *Judaism in Persia's Shadow: A Social and Historical Approach.* Minneapolis: Fortress, 1995.
Beuken, W. A. M. "The Main Theme of Trito-Isaiah: 'The Servants of Yahweh'." *JSOT* 47 (1990): 67–87.
Bickerman, Elias. *From Ezra to the Last of the Maccabees: Foundations of Post-biblical Judaism.* New York: Schocken Books, 1962.

Blenkinsopp, Joseph. *Ezra-Nehemiah: A Commentary.* OTL. Philadelphia: Westminster, 1988.

———. *A History of Prophecy in Israel.* Louisville: Westminster John Knox, 1996 (1983).

———. "The Judaean Priesthood during the Neo-Babylonian and Achaemenid Periods: A Hypothetical Reconstruction." *CBQ* 60 (1998): 25–43.

———. "The Narrative in Genesis-Numbers: A Test Case." Pages 84–115 in *Those Elusive Deuteronomists: the Phenomenon of Pan-Deuteronomism.* JSOTSup 268. Edited by L. Schearing and S. McKenzie. Sheffield: Sheffield Academic Press, 1999.

———. *The Pentateuch: An Introduction to the First Five Books of the Bible.* New York: Doubleday, 1992.

———. "Prophecy and Priesthood in Josephus." *JJS* 25 (1974): 239–62.

———. "The Prophetic Reproach." *JBL* 90 (1971): 267–78.

———. "The Second Temple as a House of Prayer," Pages 190–222 in *Où demeures-tu?* Edited by J. C. Petit. Quebec: Éditions Fides, 1994.

———. "The Servant and Servants in Isaiah and the Formation of the Book." Pages 155–75 in *Writing and Reading the Scroll of Isaiah: Studies of an Interpretive Tradition.* Edited by C. Broyles and C. Evans. Leiden/New York/Cologne: Brill, 1997.

———. "The Structure of P." *CBQ* 38 (1976): 275–92.

———. "Temple and Society in Achaemenid Judah." Pages 22–53 in *Second Temple Studies 1: Persian Period.* Edited by D. J. A. Clines. Sheffield: JSOT Press, 1991.

Boda, Mark J. *Praying the Tradition: The Origin and Use of Tradition in Nehemiah 9.* BZAW 277. Berlin/New York: Walter de Gruyter, 1999.

Boeker, Hans. *Redeformen des Rechtslebens im Alten Testament.* WMANT 14. Neukirchen-Vluyn: Neukirchener, 1964.

Botterweck, G. J., and H. Ringgren, eds. *Theological Dictionary of the Old Testament.* Translated by J. T. Willis, G. W. Bromiley and D. E. Green. 8 vols. Grand Rapids, Mich.: Eerdmans, 1974–.

Brettler, Marc Z. *The Creation of History in Ancient Israel.* London/New York: Routledge, 1998 (1995).

Bright, John. *A History of Israel.* Philadelphia: Westminster, 1981 (1959).

Brownlee, William H. *The Midrash Pesher of Habakkuk.* SBLMS 24. Missoula: Scholars Press, 1979.

Brueggemann, Walter. *The Message of the Psalms: A Theological Commentary.* Minneapolis: Augsburg, 1984.

Buis, Pierre. "Notification de jugement et confession nationale," *BZ* nf 11 (1967): 193–205.

Burrows, Millar, ed. *The Dead Sea Scrolls of St. Mark's Monastery.* Vol. 1. New Haven: ASOR, 1950.

Carroll, Robert P. *When Prophecy Failed: Cognitive Dissonance in the Prophetic Traditions of the Old Testament.* New York: Seabury, 1978.

Charlesworth, James H., ed. *Old Testament Pseudepigrapha.* 2 vols. New York: Doubleday, 1985.

Chazon, Esther. "A Liturgical Document from Qumran and Its Implications: 'Words of the Luminaries' (4QDibHam)." Ph. D. diss., The Hebrew University of Jerusalem, 1991.

Clifford, Richard. "In Zion and David a New Beginning: An Interpretation of Psalm 78." Pages 121–41 in *Traditions in Transformation: Turning Points in Biblical Faith.* Edited by B. Halpern and J. D. Levenson. Winona Lake, Ind.: Eisenbrauns, 1981.

Clines, David J. A. *Ezra, Nehemiah, Esther.* NCB. Grand Rapids, Mich.: Eerdmans, 1984.

Cody, Aelred. *A History of the Old Testament Priesthood.* Rome: Pontifical Biblical Institute, 1969.

Collins, John J. *Isaiah.* Collegeville, Minn.: The Liturgical Press, 1986.

Colson, F. H., ed. *Philo VII.* LCL 341. Cambridge, Mass.: Harvard University Press, 1939.

Cross, Frank Moore. "A Reconstruction of the Judean Restoration." *JBL* 94 (1975): 4–18.

Culley, Robert. *Oral Formulaic Language in the Biblical Psalms.* Toronto: The University of Toronto Press, 1967.

Delitzsch, Franz. *Commentar über Das Buch Jesaia.* Leipzig: Dörffling & Franke, 1889.

Dillard, Raymond B. "Reward and Punishment in Chronicles: The Theology of Immediate Retribution." *WTJ* 46 (1984): 164–72.

Dillon, John. *The Middle Platonists, 80 B.C to A.D. 220.* Ithaca, N.Y.: Cornell University Press, 1977.

Dubrow, Heather. *Genre.* London/New York: Methuen, 1982.

Dyck, Jonathan. *The Theocratic Ideology of the Chronicler.* Leiden/Boston/Cologne: Brill, 1998.

Eichrodt, Walter. *Theology of the Old Testament.* OTL. 2 vols. Philadelphia: Westminster, 1961–67 [1933–39].

Elbogen, Ismar. *Jewish Liturgy: A Comprehensive History.* Philadelphia: Jewish Publication Society, 1993 (1924).

Elliger, Karl. *Die Einheit des Tritojesajas.* BWANT 45. Stuttgart: Kohlhammer, 1928.

Emmerson, Grace I. *Isaiah 56–66.* Sheffield: Sheffield Academic Press, 1992.

Engnell, Ivan. "Methodological Aspects of Old Testament Study," pp. 13–30 in *Congress Volume : Oxford 1959.* VTSup 7. Ed. G. W. Anderson et al. Leiden: E. J. Brill, 1960.

Falk, Daniel K. *Daily, Sabbath, and Festival Prayers in the Dead Sea Scrolls.* STDJ 27. Leiden/Boston/Cologne: Brill, 1997.

Feldman, Louis H., ed. *Josephus: Jewish Antiquities Books XVIII-XIX.* LCL 433. Cambridge, Mass.: Harvard University Press, 1965.

Fensham, F. C. *The Books of Ezra and Nehemiah.* Grand Rapids, Mich.: Eerdmans, 1982.

———. "Neh. 9 and Pss. 105, 106, 135 and 136: Post-exilic Historical Traditions in Poetic Form," *JNSL* 9 (1981): 35–51.

Ferris, Paul Wayne, Jr. *The Genre of Communal Lament in the Bible and the Ancient Near East.* SBLDS 127. Atlanta: Scholars Press, 1992.
Fishbane, Michael. *Biblical Interpretation in Ancient Israel.* Oxford: Clarendon Press, 1985.
———. *The Exegetical Imagination: On Jewish Thought and Theology.* Cambridge, Mass.: Harvard University Press, 1998.
Fischer, Irmtraud. *Wo ist Jahwe? Das Volksklagelied Jes 63,7–64,11 als Ausdruck des Ringens um eine gebrochene Beziehung.* Stuttgart: Verlag Katholisches Bibelwerk GmbH, 1989.
Fleischer, Ezra. "The *Shemone Esre*—Its Character, Internal Order, Content and Goals," *Tarbiz* 63 (1993): 179–223. (Hebrew)
Fowler, Alastair. *Kinds of Literature: An Introduction to the Theory of Genres and Modes.* Cambridge, Mass.: Harvard University Press, 1982.
Franklyn, P. N. "The Cultic and Pious Climax of Eschatology in the Psalms of Solomon." *JJS* 18 (1987): 1–17.
Frye, Northrop. *Anatomy of Criticism.* Princeton: Princeton University Press, 1957.
Galling, Kurt. *Die Bücher der Chronik, Esra, Nehemia.* Göttingen: Vandenhoeck & Ruprecht, 1954.
Geissler, Johannes. *Die literarischen Beziehungen der Esramemoiren insbesondere zur Chronik und den hexateuchischen Quellschriften.* Chemnitz: Pickenhahn, 1899.
Gerstenberger, Erhard S. "The Lyrical Literature." Pages 409–44 in *The Hebrew Bible and Its Modern Interpreters.* Edited by D. A. Knight and G. M. Tucker. Minneapolis: Fortress, 1985.
———. *Psalms, Part 2, and Lamentations.* FOTL 15; Grand Rapids, Mich.: Eerdmans, 2001.
Gilbert, Maurice. "La place de la Loi dans la prière de Nèhèmie 9." Pages 307–16 in *De la Tôrah au Messie.* Edited by M. Carrez et al. Paris: Desclée, 1981.
Goulder, Michael D. *The Psalms of Asaph and the Pentateuch: Studies in the Psalter, III.* JSOTSup233. Sheffield: Sheffield Academic Press, 1996.
Grabbe, Lester. *Ezra-Nehemiah.* London/New York: Routledge, 1998.
———. *Judaism from Cyrus to Hadrian.* Minneapolis: Fortress, 1992.
Gunkel, Hermann. *Einleitung in die Psalmen: Die Gattungen der religiösen Lyrik Israels.* Edited by Joachim Begrich. Göttingen: Vandenhoeck & Ruprecht, 1933.
———. "Die Psalmen." Pages 4:1609–27 in *Die Religion in Geschichte und Gegenwart: Handwörterbuch für Theologie und Religionswissenschaft.* Edited by H. Gunkel and L. Zscharnack. 6 vols. 2nd ed. Tübingen: Mohr, 1927–31.
Gunneweg, Antonius H. J. *Esra.* KAT 19.1. Stuttgart: Gerd Mohn, 1985.
———. *Nehemia.* KAT 19.2. Stuttgart: Gerd Mohn, 1987.
Halpern-Amaru, Betsy. *Rewriting the Bible: Land and Covenant in Postbiblical Jewish Literature.* Valley Forge, Pa.: Trinity, 1994.

Hanson, Paul D. *The Dawn of Apocalyptic: The Historical and Sociological Roots of Jewish Apocalyptic Eschatology.* Philadelphia: Fortress, 1979 (1975).
Heinemann, Joseph. *Prayer in the Period of the Tanna'im and the Amora'im: Its Nature and Its Patterns.* Jerusalem: Magnes, 1966.
Hempel, Johannes. *Gebet und Frömmigkeit im Alten Testament.* Göttingen: Vandenhoeck & Ruprecht, 1922.
Horgan, Maurya P. *Pesharim: Qumran Interpretations of Biblical Books.* CBQMS 8. Washington: The Catholic Biblical Association, 1979.
In der Smitten, Wilhelm T. *Esra; Quellen, Überlieferung und Geschichte.* SSN 15. Assen: Van Gorcum, 1973.
Jakobson, Roman. "The Dominant." Pages 82–87 in *Readings in Russian Poetics: Formalist and Structuralist Views.* Edited by L. Matejka and K. Pomorska. Cambridge, Mass.: The MIT Press, 1971.
Japhet, Sara. *The Ideology of the Book of Chronicles and Its Place in Biblical Thought.* Frankfurt: Peter Lang, 1989.
———. *I & II Chronicles.* OTL. Louisville: Westminster/John Knox Press, 1993.
Jenni, Ernst, and Claus Westermann, eds. *Theological Lexicon of the Old Testament.* Translated by M. E. Biddle. 3 vols. Peabody, Mass.: Hendrickson, 1997.
Joüon, Paul. *A Grammar of Biblical Hebrew.* Revised by T. Muraoka. Rome: Pontifical Biblical Institute, 1991 (1923).
Kautzsch E., ed. *Gesenius' Hebrew Grammar.* 2nd ed. Oxford: Clarendon Press, 1910.
Kellermann, Ulrich. *Nehemia; Quellen, Überlieferung und Geschichte.* BZAW 102. Berlin: Töpelmann, 1967.
Kelly, Brian. *Retribution and Eschatology in Chronicles.* JSOTSup 211. Sheffield: Sheffield Academic Press, 1996.
Kimelman, Reuven. "The Literary Structure of the Amidah and the Rhetoric of Redemption." Pages 171–218 in *The Echoes of Many Texts: Reflections on Jewish and Christian Traditions: Essays in Honor of Lou H. Silberman.* BJS 313. Edited by W. G. Dever and J. E. Wright. Atlanta: Scholars Press, 1997.
Knohl, Israel. *Sanctuary of Silence: The Priestly Torah and the Holiness School.* Minneapolis: Augsburg Fortress, 1995.
Koehler, Ludwig, and Walter Baumgartner, eds. *Lexicon in Veteris Testamenti libros.* 2nd ed. Leiden: Brill, 1958.
Kraus, Hans-Joachim. *Psalms 1–59: A Commentary.* Minneapolis: Augsburg, 1988.
———. *Theology of the Psalms.* Minneapolis: Augsburg, 1986.
———. *Worship in Israel: A Cultic History of the Old Testament.* Richmond: John Knox, 1965 (1954).
Kugel, James. *The Idea of Biblical Poetry: Parallelism and Its History.* New Haven/London: Yale University Press, 1981.

Kühlewein, Johannes. *Geschichte in den Psalmen*. Stuttgart: Calwer Verlag Stuttgart, 1973.
Lacoque, André. "The Land in 'D' and 'P'," Pages 91–100 in *"Dort ziehen Schiffe dahin ...."* Edited by M. Augustin and K.-D. Schunck. Frankfurt: Lang, 1996.
Lauterbach, J. Z., ed. *Mekhilta of Rabbi Ishmael*. 3 vols. Philadelphia: Jewish Publication Society of America, 1976.
Lemaire, A. "Populations et territoires de Palestine à l'époque perse." *Transeu* 3 (1990): 31–73.
Levenson, Jon. *Sinai and Zion: An Entry into the Jewish Bible*. New York: Harper & Row, 1985.
Levine, Lee I. *The Ancient Synagogue: The First Thousand Years*. New Haven/London: Yale University Press, 2000.
Liebreich, Leon. "The Impact of Nehemiah 9:5–37 on the Liturgy of the Synagogue." *HUCA* 32 (1961): 227–37.
Liddell Henry G., et al., eds. *A Greek-English Lexicon*. 9th ed. Oxford: Clarendon Press, 1996.
Lipinski, Edward. *La Liturgie Pénitentielle dans la Bible*. Paris: Les Éditions du Cerf, 1969.
———. "Marriage and Divorce in the Judaism of the Persian Period." *Transeu* 4 (1991) 63–71.
Machinist, Peter. "Fate, *miqreh,* and Reason: Some Reflections on Qohelet and Biblical Thought." Pages 159–75 in *Solving Riddles and Untying Knots: Biblical, Epigraphic and Semitic Studies in Honor of Jonas C. Greenfield*. Edited by Z. Zevit et al. Winona Lake, Ind.: Eisenbrauns, 1995.
Mason, Rex. *Preaching the Tradition: Homily and Hermeneutics After the Exile Based on 'Addresses' in Chronicles, the 'Speeches' in the Books of Ezra and Nehemiah and the Post-Exilic Prophetic Books*. Cambridge: Cambridge University Press, 1990.
McCarthy, Dennis J. "Covenant and Law in Chronicles–Nehemiah." *CBQ* 44 (1982): 25–44.
McKenzie, Steven L., and M. Patrick Graham, eds. *The Chronicler as Author: Studies in Text and Texture*. JSOTSup 263; Sheffield: Sheffield Academic Press, 2000.
Milgrom, Jacob. *Leviticus 1–16*. AB 3. New York: Doubleday, 1991.
Miller, Patrick D. *They Cried to the Lord: The Form and Theology of Biblical Prayer*. Minneapolis: Fortress, 1994.
Mowinckel, Sigmund. *The Psalms in Israel's Worship*. 2 vols. New York: Abingdon, 1992 (1962).
Muilenburg, James. "Form Criticism and Beyond." *JBL* 88 (1969): 1–18.
Myers, Jacob M. *Ezra. Nehemiah*. AB 14. Garden City, N.Y.: Doubleday, 1965.
Nasuti, Harry. *Defining the Sacred Songs: Genre, Tradition and the Post-Critical Interpretation of the Psalms*. JSOTSup 218. Sheffield: Sheffield Academic Press, 1999.

Neusner, Jacob, et al., eds. *Encyclopedia of Judaism*. 3 vols. New York: Continuum, 1999.

———. *The Idea of Purity in Ancient Judaism*. Leiden: Brill, 1973.

Newman, Judith H. *Praying by the Book: The Scripturalization of Prayer in Second Temple Judaism*. SBLEJL 14. Atlanta: Scholars Press, 1999.

Nickelsburg, George W. E. *Jewish Literature between the Bible and the Mishnah: A Historical and Literary Introduction*. Philadelphia: Fortress, 1981.

Niditch, Susan. *Oral World and Written Word*. Louisville: Westminster John Knox Press, 1996.

Nitzan, Bilhah. *Qumran Prayer and Religious Poetry*. Leiden: Brill, 1994.

———. "The Textual, Literary and Religious Character of *4QBERAKOT* (4Q286–290)." Pages 636–56 in *The Provo International Conference on the Dead Sea Scrolls*. Edited by D. W. Perry and E. Ulrich. Leiden: Brill, 1999.

Oswalt, John. *The Book of Isaiah: Chapters 40–66*. Grand Rapids, Mich.: Eerdmans, 1998.

Petersen, David L. *Haggai and Zechariah 1–8: A Commentary*. OTL. Philadelphia: Westminster, 1984.

———. *Late Israelite Prophecy: Studies in Deutero-Prophetic Literature and in Chronicles*. SBLMS 23. Missoula: Scholars Press, 1977.

Petuchowski, J. J., and E. Fleischer, eds. *Studies in Aggadah, Targum and Jewish Liturgy*. Jerusalem: Magnes Press, 1981.

Plöger, Otto. "Reden und Gebete im deuteronomistischen und chronistischen Geschichtswerk." Pages 35–49 in *Festschrift für Günther Dehn zum 75 Geburstag*. Edited by W. Schneemelcher; Neukirchen-Vluyn: Neukirchener Verlag, 1957.

Pröbstl, Volker. *Nehemia 9, Psalm 106 und Psalm 136 und die Rezeption des Pentateuchs*. Göttingen: Cuvillier Verlag, 1997.

Von Rad, Gerhard. "The Form-Critical Problem of the Hexateuch." Pages 1–78 in *The Problem of the Hexateuch and Other Essays*. New York: McGraw-Hill, 1966.

———. "The Levitical Sermon in I and II Chronicles." Pages 267–80 in *The Problem of the Hexateuch and Other Essays*. New York: McGraw-Hill, 1966.

———. *Theologie des Alten Testaments*. 2 vols. Munich: Chr. Kaiser Verlag, 1968-69 (1957).

Rehm, Martin. "Nehemias 9," *BZ* nf. 1 (1957): 57–67.

Reif, Stefan C. *Judaism and Hebrew Prayer: New Perspectives on Jewish Liturgical History*. Cambridge: Cambridge University Press, 1993.

Reventlow, Henning Graf. *Gebet im Alten Testament*. Stuttgart/Berlin/Cologne/Mainz: Kolhammer, 1986.

Römer, Thomas, and Marc Z. Brettler. "Deuteronomy 34 and the Case for a Persian Hexateuch." *JBL* 119 (2000): 401–19.

Rofé, Alexander. "The Piety of the Torah-Disciples at the Winding-Up of the Hebrew Bible: Josh 1:8; Ps 1:2; Isa 59:21." Pages 78–85 in *Bibel in jüdischer und christlicher Tradition: Feststschrift für Johann Maier*. Edited by H. Merklein et al. Athenüms Monografien Theologie 88. Frankfurt: Hain, 1993.

Rudolph, Wilhelm. *Esra und Nehemia samt 3 Esra.* HAT 20. Tübingen: J. C. B. Mohr (Paul Siebeck), 1949.

Simon, M., and I. Epstein, eds. *Hebrew-English Edition of the Babylonian Talmud.* London: Soncino, 1960.

Smith, Morton. *Palestinian Parties and Politics that Shaped the Old Testament.* London: SCM, 1987 (1981).

Steck, Odil. *Studien zu Tritojesaja.* BZAW 30. Berlin/New York: Walter de Gruyter, 1991.

———. "Tritojesaja Im Jesajabuch." Pages 361–406 in *The Book of Isaiah Le Livre D'Isaïe: Les Oracles et leurs Relectures Unité et Complexité de l'Ouvrage*. Edited by J. Vermeylen. Leuven: Leuven University Press, 1989.

Strobel, August. *Erkenntnis und Bekenntnis der Sünde in neutestamentlicher Zeit.* Stuttgart: Calwer Verlag, 1968.

Sweeney, Marvin A. *Isaiah 1–39.* FOTL 16. Grand Rapids, Mich.: Eerdmans, 1996.

Throntveit, Mark A. *Ezra-Nehemiah.* Louisville: John Knox, 1992.

Torrey, C. C. *The Compositional and Historical Value of Ezra-Nehemiah.* Giessen: Riokersche Buchhandlungen, 1896.

Van Seters, John. *In Search of History: Historiography in the Ancient World and the Origins of Biblical History.* New Haven/London: Yale University Press, 1983.

VanderKam, James C. "Ezra-Nehemiah or Ezra and Nehemiah?" Pages 55–75 in *Priests, Prophets and Scribes: Essays on the Formation and Heritage of Second Temple Judaism in Honour of Joseph Blenkinsopp.* Edited by E. Ulrich et al. JSOTSup 149. Sheffield: Sheffield Academic Press, 1992.

Veijola, Timo. "Das Klagebet in Literatur und Leben der Exilsgeneration am Beispiel einiger Prosatexte." VTSup 36 (1985): 286–307.

Weinfeld, Moshe. *Deuteronomy and the Deuteronomic School.* Oxford: Oxford University Press, 1972.

———. "Prayer and Liturgical Practice in the Qumran Sect." Pages 241–58 in *The Dead Sea Scrolls: Forty Years of Research.* Edited by D. Dimant and U. Rappaport. Leiden: Brill, 1992.

———. "The Prayer for Knowledge, Repentance and Forgiveness in the 'Eighteen Benedictions'—Qumran Parallels, Biblical Antecedents, and Basic Characteristics." *Tarbiz* 48 (1979): 186–200. (Hebrew)

Weiser, Artur. *The Psalms: A Commentary.* 2 vols. Philadelphia: Westminster, 1962.

Welch, Adam C. "The Source of Nehemiah ix." *ZAW* 47 (1929): 130–37.

Werline, Rodney A. *Penitential Prayer in Second Temple Judaism: The Development of a Religious Institution.* SBLEJL 13. Atlanta: Scholars Press, 1998.
Westermann, Claus. *Basic Forms of Prophetic Speech.* Louisville: Westminster/John Knox, 1991.
———. *Elements of Old Testament Theology.* Atlanta: John Knox, 1982.
———. *Isaiah 40–66.* OTL. Philadelphia: Westminster, 1969.
———. *Praise and Lament in the Psalms.* Atlanta: John Knox, 1981.
———. *The Praise of God in the Psalms.* Richmond: John Knox, 1965 (1953).
Whybray, R. N. *Isaiah 40–66.* NCB. Grand Rapids, Mich.: Eerdmans, 1981.
Williamson, H. G. M. *Ezra, Nehemiah.* WBC 16. Waco: Word Books, 1985.
———. "Isaiah 63:7–64:11: Exilic Lament or Post-Exilic Protest?" *ZAW* 102 (1990): 48–58.
Wimsatt, William K., Jr., and Monroe C. Beardsley. "The Intentional Fallacy." Pages 945–51 in *Critical Theory Since Plato.* Edited by H. Adams.Orlando: Harcourt, Brace, Jovanovich, 1992. Repr. from William K. Wimsatt. *The Verbal Icon: Studies in the Meaning of Poetry.* Lexington. Ky.: University Press of Kentucky, 1954.

AUTHOR INDEX

A

Aberbach, Moses 131
Achtemeier, Elizabeth 35, 49, 62
Ackroyd, Peter 5, 25, 86, 109, 122, 135, 165
Aharoni, Yohanon 47
Albertz, Rainer ...39, 41, 46, 55, 56, 59, 60, 63, 112, 126, 127, 157, 160
Amit, Yaira................................. 58
Andersen, Francis...................... 109
Anderson, Carl 9, 10, 127
Auld, A. Graeme 94
Avery-Peck, Alan ..4, 140, 146, 147

B

Baer, Seligmann 113
Baillet, Maurice........................ 140
Balentine, Samuel 23, 78
Batten, L. W. 8, 109
Beardsley, M. C. 22
Begrich, Joachim...................41, 42
Bellinger, W. H., Jr. 6, 16, 118
Ben Zvi, Ehud 11, 12
Bentzen, Aage 42
Berquist, Jon.........................24, 63
Beuken, W. A. M. 47
Bickerman, Elias 98, 99
Biddle, Mark 127
Blenkinsopp, Joseph.......4, 8, 9, 14, 21, 38, 46, 47, 57, 62, 67, 69, 73, 85, 86, 87, 88, 89, 91, 93, 94, 95, 96, 106, 107, 108, 109, 113, 115, 122, 123, 125, 129, 133, 135, 136, 146
Boda, Mark 9, 10, 11, 21, 107, 126, 160, 166, 167
Boecker, Hans........................... 120
Brettler, Marc.............81, 100, 127, 134, 135
Bright, John................................26
Brooke, George........................ 155
Brown, Laurence..........................62
Brownlee, William.............. 19, 162
Brueggemann, Walter . 16, 118, 159
Buis, Pierre 20, 125
Burchard, C............................... 144
Burrows, Millar........ 31, 52, 53, 141

C

Carroll, Robert 44
Charlesworth, James 139
Chazon, Esther....... 5, 140, 152, 153
Chrostowski, Waldemar.... 124, 126
Clifford, Richard..... 38, 51, 57, 114
Clines, David 26, 79
Cody, Aelred............................. 132
Cook, Stephen............................56
Cross, Frank Moore 31, 67
Culley, Robert.......... 15, 16, 22, 138

D

Dahood, Mitchell 53
de Solms, E. 121
de Vaux, Roland 70
Delitzsch, Franz 51
Dillard, Raymond 98
Dillon, John 158
Drijvers, Pius 119
Dubrow, Heather 17, 83
Dyck, Jonathan 100

E

Eichrodt, Walter 6
Elbogen, Ismar 168, 169, 170
Elliger, Karl 45, 63
Emmerson, Grace 38
Engnell, Ivan 8

F

Falk, Daniel 140
Fensham, F. C. ..8, 73, 79, 109, 110
Fernández, Andrés 77
Ferris, Paul 116, 117
Fischer, Irmtraud 35, 41, 46
Fishbane, Michael ... 19, 23, 71, 73, 76, 77, 82, 91, 97
Fitzmyer, Joseph 50
Fleischer, Ezra 170, 171
Floyd, Michael 12
Fowler, Alastair 17, 79, 83, 84
Franklyn, P. N. 157
Freedman, David Noel 109, 164
Frye, Northrop 13

G

Galling, Kurt 8
Geissler, Johannes 125
Gerleman, G. 124
Gerstenberger, Erhard 36
Gilbert, Maurice 130
Gosse, Bernard 95
Goulder, Michael 25, 36
Grabbe, Lester ... 19, 20, 69, 90, 136
Grimme, Hubert 94
Gunkel, Hermann 12, 13, 14, 16, 20, 24, 25, 35, 36, 72, 74, 83, 111, 116, 117, 137, 138, 155, 161
Gunneweg, Antonius H. J. ... 72, 75, 98, 109

H

Halpern-Amaru, Betsy 20, 71, 88
Hanson, Paul 37, 38, 49, 61, 62
Heinemann, Joseph 2, 167
Herbert, A. S. 54
Hildebrand, David 63
Holbert, John 164, 165
Horgan, Maurya 163

I

Illman, K.-J. 25
In der Smitten, Wilhelm 8

J

Jakobson, Roman 21, 143
Janzen, J. Gerald 19
Japhet, Sara 20, 43, 44, 91, 94, 96, 98, 100, 124, 125
Joüon, Paul 53
Judge, H. G. 132

K

Kaufmann, Yehezkel 4
Kellerman, D. 75
Kellermann, Ulrich . 8, 92, 106, 109
Kelly, Brian 43, 44, 99
Kimelman, Reuven 168, 169, 170, 171
Klopfenstein, M. A. 50
Knierim, Rolf 4, 17, 49, 75, 83, 84, 117, 151
Knohl, Israel 5, 25, 131, 133
Koch, K. 51
Kohler, Kaufmann 169, 170
Kook, A. I. 3
Kraus, Hans-Joachim .. 20, 143, 148
Kugel, James 10, 19, 109
Kühlewein, Johannes 37, 111, 114, 115
Kutscher, E. Y. 31

L

Lacocque, André 127, 132
Lemaire, Andre 70
Levenson, Jon.....................38, 154
Levine, Lee.............................. 168
Liebreich, Leon 109, 167
Lipinski, Edward...........69, 70, 111
Lozza, G. 150

M

Machinist, Peter....................... 158
Madl, Helmut 163
Maimonides.................................. 3
Malchow, Bruce 164
Mannati, Marina....................... 121
Mason, Rex 79, 81, 83
Mathias, Dietmar....................... 79
Mayer, G. 108, 148
McCarthy, Dennis 95
Melugin, Roy............................. 17
Milgrom, Jacob 2, 76, 147, 148, 149
Miller, Patrick 41
Mowinckel, Sigmund............14, 20, 21, 24, 25, 35, 36, 39, 45, 49, 73, 111, 115, 116, 117, 118, 119, 143
Muilenburg, James 18
Muraoka, T................................. 53
Myers, Jacob 8, 67

N

Najman, Hindy 161
Nasuti, Harry............................. 118
Nelson, Richard D. 126
Neusner, Jacob 52
Newman, Judith..............10, 11, 22, 104, 110, 117, 125, 126, 168
Nickelsburg, George.......10, 70, 157
Niditch, Susan 72
Nitzan, Bilhah 141, 142, 153

O

Oeming, Manfred..................... 129
Oesterley, W. O. E 6

Olmstead, Albert........................ 24
Oswalt, John 51, 61

P

Pardes, Ilana.............................. 113
Person, R. F. 56
Petersen, David 124, 166
Plöger, Otto............... 17, 18, 81, 92
Porten, Bezalel........................... 70
Preuss, H. D. 128
Pritchard, James........................ 77
Pröbstl, Volker.............................. 9
Puech, Émile 140

R

Rad, Gerhard von 6, 17, 43, 59, 79, 80, 82, 83, 85, 88, 90, 110, 129
Rehm, Martin.................. 109, 110
Reif, Stefan 134, 167
Reventlow, Henning Graf.......3, 16
Robinson, T. H............................. 6
Rofé, Alexander........................ 74
Roitman, Adolfo 155
Römer, Thomas......... 127, 134, 135
Rudolph, Wilhelm............ 8, 66, 67, 104, 107

S

Schwienhorst, L. 49, 50
Seebass, Horst........................... 128
Silberman, Lou 1
Smith, Morton............................58
Smolar, Leivy 131
Snaith, Norman 26, 167
Sommer, Benjamin 22
Steck, Odil 40, 41, 42, 43, 44, 47
Strobel, August 171
Sweeney, Marvin 26
Szörényi, Andreas.......................72

T

Talmon, Shemaryahu..................31
Tam, Jacob ben Meir 39
Throntveit, Mark............... 113, 122

Todorov, Tzvetan 17
Torrey, C. C. 96
Trebolle Barrera, Julio 130
Tulli, A. 69

U

Ulrich, Eugene 31, 66, 67

V

Van Seters, John 80
VanderKam, James 92
Veijola, Timo 142, 143, 160
Vermes, Geza 19
Volz, Paul 40

W

Wagner, S. 43, 74, 90
Weinfeld, Moshe 57, 58, 60, 89, 126, 129, 130, 156, 157, 170, 171
Weiser, Artur 52
Wellhausen, Julius 20, 43
Werline, Rodney ... 10, 19, 38, 55, 56, 149
Westermann, Claus 7, 16, 21, 24, 35, 39, 42, 45, 116, 118, 119, 120, 123, 142, 164
Whybray, R. N. 8, 32, 35, 40, 41, 47, 51
Williamson, H. G. M. 38, 61, 66, 72, 73, 87, 93, 94, 95, 106, 115
Wilson, Robert 15
Wimsatt, W. K. 22
Wright, R. B. 145

Y

Yardeni, Ada 70
Young, Edward 51

Z

Ziegler, Joseph 32

SCRIPTURE INDEX

Genesis

Genesis 1–11	56
Gen 1:1	128
Gen 1:2	128
Gen 1:28	132
Gen 2:2–3	131
Gen 6:5	43
Gen 8:21	140
Gen 15:6	120, 129, 141
Gen 15:6a	129
Gen 15:6b	129
Gen 15:18	129
Gen 17:5	128
Gen 17:7	129
Gen 19:31–38	91
Gen 21:10–14	71
Gen 21:23	50
Genesis 22	19
Gen 29:35	149
Gen 31:43–50	70
Gen 32:31	130, 153
Gen 35:2–5	127
Gen 41:45	71
Gen 43:9	51
Genesis 46	93
Gen 46:21	93
Gen 46:32	48

Exodus

Exod 5:3	88
Exod 14:6	116
Exod 15:15	53
Exod 16:3	88
Exod 16:4	116
Exod 16:23	131
Exod 18:11	121
Exodus 19	155
Exod 19:4	57
Exod 19:4–6a	57
Exod 19:16–25	38, 59
Exod 20:11	131
Exod 21:14	121
Exod 22:7–8	120
Exod 27:19	87
Exod 31:12–18	131
Exodus 32	131
Exodus 32–34	55
Exod 32:1–6	131
Exod 32:4	131
Exod 32:4a	131, 132
Exod 32:4b	131, 132
Exod 32:35	131
Exod 33:20	130, 153
Exod 34:6–7	104, 167
Exod 34:14	58
Exod 35:1–3	131

Exod 35:18 87

Leviticus

Lev 4:20 167
Lev 5:1–6 .... 108, 147, 148
Lev 5:5 150
Lev 5:10 167
Lev 7:4 129
Lev 7:18 129
Lev 8:1–13 .... 10, 25
Leviticus 10 25
Lev 10:1–3 .... 10, 25
Lev 15:25 167
Leviticus 16 122
Lev 16:21 146
Lev 16:29 122
Lev 16:31 .... 23, 122
Leviticus 18 88
Lev 18:5 .... 125, 133
Lev 18:24–30 .... 69, 80
Lev 18:26–29 71
Lev 18:26–30 .... 88, 91
Lev 19:22 167
Lev 22:14–16 .... 75, 76
Lev 22:16a 75, 76, 80
Lev 23:3 131
Lev 23:27 .... 23, 122, 166
Lev 23:32 .... 23, 122
Lev 25:23 132
Lev 25:51 125
Lev 26:3–13 133
Lev 26:3–45 .... 21, 113
Lev 26:14–45 133
Lev 26:36–39 149
Lev 26:40 149
Lev 26:41–43 135
Lev 26:42 149

Numbers

Numbers 3 93
Num 3:1–13 .... 10, 25
Num 3:37 87
Num 5:5–10 .... 108, 147, 148
Num 5:6 3
Num 11:25 136
Num 12:1–8 71

Num 14:4 124
Num 14:11–25b 59
Num 14:13–19 104
Num 14:17–19 59
Num 14:19 59
Num 15:27–31 146
Num 16:1–50 .... 10, 25
Num 18:27 129
Num 22:24 77
Num 25:1–18 71
Num 26:38–41 93
Num 28:9–10 131
Num 29:7 .... 23, 122

Deuteronomy

Deuteronomy 88, 127
Deut 1:1–3:29 139
Deut 1:19–40 59
Deut 1:31 57
Deut 1:34–35 59
Deut 1:38–39 89
Deut 1:43 .... 121, 139, 151, 152
Deuteronomy 4 10
Deut 4:1 132
Deut 4:5 132
Deut 4:10 58
Deut 4:26 58
Deut 4:35 128
Deut 4:36 .... 130, 153, 154
Deut 4:37 128
Deut 5:9 58
Deut 5:26 58
Deut 5:28 130
Deut 6:1 130
Deut 6:2 58
Deut 6:4 128
Deut 6:11 .... 88, 133
Deut 6:13 58
Deut 6:15 58
Deut 6:18 132
Deut 6:24 58
Deut 7:1 .... 88, 132
Deut 7:1–3 .... 71, 80, 88
Deut 7:2 87
Deut 7:3 .... 89, 107, 108
Deut 7:6 76

Deut 7:6–8 128
Deut 7:8 128
Deut 7:11 130
Deut 8:1 132
Deut 8:2–3 60
Deut 8:4 104
Deut 8:6 58
Deut 8:16 61
Deuteronomy 9 131
Deut 9:1 132
Deut 9:3 132
Deut 9:5 .... 129, 132
Deut 9:12 58
Deut 9:16 58
Deut 9:20 25
Deut 10:12 58
Deut 10:14 128
Deut 10:17 .... 110, 168
Deut 10:20 58
Deut 10:21 59
Deut 11:8 .... 89, 132
Deut 11:10 132
Deut 11:28 58
Deut 11:29 132
Deut 11:31 132
Deuteronomy 12 87
Deut 12:5 .... 87, 128
Deut 12:11 87
Deut 12:14 .... 87, 128
Deut 12:29 132
Deut 13:5 58
Deut 14:2 .... 76, 128
Deut 14:21 76
Deut 14:23 58
Deut 17:13 121
Deut 17:19 58
Deut 18:6–8 25
Deut 18:9 88
Deut 18:20 121
Deut 21:18–21 49
Deuteronomy 23 91
Deut 23:3 107
Deut 23:3–6 .... 71, 80
Deut 23:3–7 88
Deut 23:4a 91
Deut 23:6 89

Deut 25:1 120
Deut 26:19 .... 57, 76
Deuteronomy 28–30 10
Deut 28:9 76
Deut 28:21 132
Deut 28:58 58
Deut 28:63 132
Deut 29:25–27 88
Deut 29:4 104
Deut 30:11–14 153
Deut 30:15–20 133
Deut 30:16 .... 132, 133
Deut 30:17–18 88
Deut 31:12 58
Deut 31:13 58
Deut 31:16 89
Deut 31:17 60
Deut 31:18 60
Deut 31:20 89
Deut 31:29 58
Deut 32:5–6 57
Deut 32:6 57
Deut 32:6b 41
Deut 32:11 57
Deut 32:15 133
Deut 32:16 58
Deut 32:20 60
Deut 32:21b 58
Deut 32:22 48
Deut 34:1b 127
Deut 34:11 116
Deut 34:7–9 127

Joshua

Joshua 88
Josh 1:5–9 82
Josh 1:8 74
Josh 1:11 132
Josh 5:11 133
Josh 5:12 133
Joshua 7 94
Josh 7:1 94
Josh 7:18–19 .... 94, 108, 148
Josh 7:19 .... 94, 149
Josh 7:20 108

Josh 11:20 .... 87, 133
Josh 14:1 132
Josh 14:2 132
Josh 14:3 132
Josh 18:1 132
Josh 18:3 132
Josh 19:51 132
Josh 21:4 132
Josh 21:13 132
Josh 22:17 125
Joshua 24 .... 127, 134
Josh 24:12 135
Josh 24:18 .... 134, 135
Josh 24:25 134
Josh 24:26 134

Judges

Judges 88
Judges 2 .... 113, 114
Judg 2:1 89
Judg 2:11–23 .... 56, 86, 113, 125
Judg 5:4–5 38

1 Samuel

1 Sam 9:1–2 93
1 Sam 14:27 76
1 Sam 14:29 76
1 Sam 14:49 93
1 Sam 15:29 49

2 Samuel

2 Sam 3:3 71
2 Sam 7:23 59
2 Sam 22:50 149

1 Kings

1 Kings 117
1 Kgs 2:4 129
1 Kgs 3:8 128
1 Kgs 6:1–8:11 129
1 Kgs 6:11–13 129
1 Kgs 6:12 129
1 Kings 8 160
1 Kgs 8:20 129
1 Kgs 8:31 120
1 Kgs 8:48 126

1 Kgs 11:1–8 69
1 Kgs 11:39 60
1 Kings 12 131
1 Kgs 12:15 129
1 Kgs 12:26–32 131
1 Kgs 12:28 132
1 Kgs 14:9 .... 104, 117
1 Kgs 14:28–29 91
1 Kgs 15:19 89
1 Kgs 16:31–32 69
1 Kgs 18:18 87
1 Kgs 19:10 117
1 Kgs 19:14 117

2 Kings

2 Kgs 12:22 91
2 Kgs 16:3 88
2 Kgs 17:16 87
2 Kings 19 128
2 Kgs 19:3 .... 117, 131
2 Kgs 19:15 128
2 Kgs 21:2 88
2 Kgs 23:8 25
2 Kgs 23:9 25
2 Kgs 23:20 25

Isaiah

Isaiah 31, 35, 36, 40, 42, 43, 44,
    47, 53, 54, 56, 61
Isa 1:7 .... 39, 60
Isa 1:26–27 40
Isa 1:30 52
Isa 3:12 58
Isa 5:1–7 123
Isa 5:5 77
Isa 6:5 52
Isa 8:17 53
Isa 9:15 58
Isa 22:3 87
Isa 30:9 50
Isa 34:4 52
Isa 42:13–16 .... 38, 52
Isa 46:3 41
Isa 49:15 41
Isa 51:9–11 .... 38, 52

SCRIPTURE INDEX

Isa 51:17 ... 47
Isa 51:22 ... 47
Isa 54:2 ... 87
Isa 54:8 ... 53
Isa 55:7 ... 167
Isaiah 56–66 ... 62
Isa 56:1–8 ... 45
Isa 58:3 ... 123
Isa 58:3–9 ... 123
Isaiah 59 ... 47
Isa 59:1–15 ... 54
Isa 59:5–8 ... 54
Isa 59:9–15a ... 47
Isa 59:10 ... 43
Isa 59:13–15a ... 54
Isa 59:15b–21 ... 47
Isa 59:16a ... 47
Isa 59:16b ... 47
Isa 59:17 ... 47
Isa 59:21 ... 74
Isaiah 60-62 ... 47
Isa 60:12 ... 46
Isa 62:2 ... 60
Isaiah 63 ... 153
Isaiah 63–65 ... 40
Isa 63:1–6 ... 46, 47
Isa 63:1–65:12 ... 46
Isa 63:3 ... 47
Isa 63:4 ... 47
Isa 63:5a ... 47
Isa 63:5b ... 47
Isa 63:7 ... 29, 32, 40, 55, 57, 62, 144, 162, 163, 168
Isa 63:7–10 ... 35, 49, 50, 54, 75, 171
Isa 63:7–14 ... 35, 36, 37, 48, 49, 56, 57, 61, 139
Isa 63:7–15 ... 26
Isa 63:7–64:11 ... 3, 5, 8, 9, 10, 12, 22, 26, 27, 29, 31, 32, 33, 35, 36, 37, 38, 39, 41, 42, 43, 45, 46, 47, 48, 49, 51, 54, 55, 56, 57, 61, 62, 137, 139, 141, 142, 143, 153, 156, 159, 165, 170, 171
Isa 63:7–64:14 ... 32
Isa 63:7–65:7 ... 44, 45
Isa 63:7–65:12 ... 47
Isa 63:7b–9 ... 57
Isa 63:8 ... 29, 48, 49, 50, 55, 74, 115, 139, 162
Isa 63:9 ... 29, 32, 33, 57, 59
Isa 63:9b ... 57
Isa 63:10 ... 29, 32, 33, 37, 43, 48, 49, 55, 115, 117, 139, 150, 151, 162
Isa 63:10a ... 57, 150
Isa 63:10b ... 57
Isa 63:11 ... 22, 29, 32, 33, 48
Isa 63:11–12 ... 61
Isa 63:11–14 ... 35
Isa 63:12 ... 29, 32, 33, 47, 48
Isa 63:13 ... 30, 32, 33
Isa 63:14 ... 30, 32, 33
Isa 63:15 ... 22, 30, 32, 33, 34, 37, 40, 48, 58, 60
Isa 63:15–19 ... 35
Isa 63:15–19a ... 26, 35, 36, 37, 48, 58, 60, 142
Isa 63:15–64:4a ... 35
Isa 63:15–64:11 ... 37
Isa 63:16 ... 26, 30, 32, 34, 36, 37, 39, 41, 48, 57, 58, 60, 61, 62, 156, 160, 163, 167
Isa 63:17 ... 30, 32, 34, 37, 38, 43, 48, 58, 142
Isa 63:17a ... 58
Isa 63:17b ... 26, 58, 60
Isa 63:18 ... 30, 32, 34, 37, 43, 58, 61, 62, 142
Isa 63:18–64:3 ... 38
Isa 63:18a ... 58
Isa 63:19 ... 29, 30, 34, 38
Isa 63:19–64:4a ... 38
Isa 63:19a ... 37, 62
Isa 63:19b ... 62
Isa 63:19b–64:3 ... 38, 113
Isa 63:19b–64:4a ... 26, 35, 36, 38, 46, 48, 59, 61, 62, 142, 143, 154
Isaiah 64 ... 42
Isa 64:1–12 ... 35
Isa 64:1 ... 22, 29, 30, 32, 34, 38, 48
Isa 64:2 ... 30, 34, 48, 59
Isa 64:3 ... 30, 32, 34

Isa 64:4 .... 30, 32, 34, 146
Isa 64:4b 39, 50, 55, 59, 143, 169
Isa 64:4b–6 ... 26, 35, 36, 39, 48, 50, 53, 54, 59, 61, 113, 143, 145
Isa 64:4b–7 35
Isa 64:4b–8 35
Isa 64:4b–11 61
Isa 64:5 ... 30, 32, 34, 38, 39, 51, 59, 60, 62, 146, 147
Isa 64:5a 50, 51, 52, 164
Isa 64:5b 50, 51, 55, 143, 156
Isa 64:6 .... 30, 32, 34, 50, 62, 143, 146, 147
Isa 64:6a 52, 55
Isa 64:6b 50, 53, 55, 143
Isa 64:7 .... 30, 34, 38, 39, 41, 46, 49, 57, 60, 62, 156, 160
Isa 64:7–8 ...... 35, 36, 39, 48, 60, 61
Isa 64:8 .... 30, 34, 38, 39, 49, 54, 60, 143, 146, 147
Isa 64:8–12 .... 35, 48
Isa 64:9 .... 30, 32, 35, 39, 48
Isa 64:9–10 .... 26, 35, 36, 39, 48, 60,
Isa 64:9–11 35
Isa 64:10 .... 31, 32, 35, 74, 162
Isa 64:11 .... 22, 31, 36, 40, 41, 42, 44, 48, 60, 61, 62
Isa 64:11–65:1 42
Isa 64:11–65:2 44
Isaiah 65 .... 42, 43, 44
Isa 65:1 .... 43, 46
Isa 65:1–2 .... 43, 45, 48, 56, 160
Isa 65:1–7 .... 42, 43
Isa 65:1–12 .... 46, 47
Isa 65:1–16a 42
Isa 65:1a 43
Isa 65:1b 43
Isa 65:2 43
Isa 65:3 44
Isa 65:3–4 44
Isa 65:3–7 44
Isa 65:5 44
Isa 65:6 60
Isa 65:6–7 44

Isa 65:8 .... 46, 48
Isa 65:8–12 .... 42, 44, 46, 47
Isa 65:9 46
Isa 65:10 46
Isa 65:11 40
Isa 65:12 .... 46, 48
Isa 65:13–25 42
Isaiah 66 .... 42, 43, 44
Isa 66:1–4 42
Isa 66:2 .... 69, 85
Isa 66:5 .... 69, 85
Isa 66:5–24 42
Isa 66:13 41

Jeremiah

Jer 2:3 75
Jer 2:4–13 123
Jer 3:4 41
Jer 3:19 41
Jer 3:25 90
Jer 4:27 133
Jer 5:1 167
Jer 5:7 167
Jer 5:18 133
Jer 8:13 52
Jer 13:11 57
Jeremiah 14 119
Jeremiah 14–15 166
Jer 14:1–15:4 166
Jer 14:4 74
Jer 14:17–18 166
Jer 14:17–21 166
Jer 14:20 166
Jer 14:21 166
Jer 20:4 .... 87, 97
Jer 24:4–7 46
Jer 24:8–10 46
Jer 25:15 47
Jer 30:11 133
Jer 31:19 .... 74, 90
Jer 31:34 167
Jer 32:6–25 123
Jer 32:17–22 123
Jer 32:17–24 123
Jer 32:18 110

Jer 32:23–24 123
Jer 32:42–44 123
Jer 33:5 53
Jer 33:8–9 57
Jer 33:9 57
Jer 41:5 .... 122, 165
Jer 41:9 53
Jer 44:17 111
Jer 46:28 133
Jer 49:23 53
Jer 50:20 167

Ezekiel

Ezekiel 84, 85, 161, 163, 165
Ezek 16:61 126
Ezek 16:63 126
Ezek 18:9 126
Ezekiel 20 .... 123, 124, 126, 139
Ezek 20:1–38 112
Ezek 20:5–10 112
Ezek 20:7–8 87
Ezek 20:8 139
Ezek 20:8b 124
Ezek 20:9 168
Ezek 20:11 .... 125, 133
Ezek 20:11–26 112
Ezek 20:13 .... 133, 139
Ezek 20:13b 124
Ezek 20:16 139
Ezek 20:21 139
Ezek 20:21b 124
Ezek 20:27–30 112
Ezek 20:33–34 124
Ezek 21:2 .... 15, 84, 161, 163
Ezek 21:7 .... 15, 84, 85, 161, 163
Ezek 21:8 .... 85, 161
Ezek 23:35 .... 104, 117
Ezek 35:12 117
Ezek 39:23 53
Ezek 39:24 53
Ezek 39:29 53
Ezek 44:6 25
Ezek 47:12 52

Hosea

Hos 4:12 58
Hos 9:10 .... 87, 123

Joel

Joel 2 41
Joel 2:12–13 123
Joel 2:19–20 41

Amos

Amos 84, 85, 165, 161
Amos 2:4 58
Amos 2:9–11 123
Amos 4:6–12 123
Amos 5:18 123
Amos 7 86
Amos 7:9 162
Amos 7:16 .... 15, 85, 161, 163
Amos 7:17 .... 85, 161
Amos 21:7 83
Amos 21:8 83
Amos 21:9 83

Obadiah

Obad 1:1–14 47

Micah

Micah 85, 161, 163, 165
Micah 2 84
Mic 2:2 84
Mic 2:4b–5 84
Mic 2:6 .... 15, 84, 85, 161, 163
Mic 2:11 162
Mic 3:4 53
Mic 3:5 58
Mic 4:14 88
Mic 6:3–5 123
Mic 7:11 77
Mic 7:14–20 56

Habakkuk

Hab 2:15 .... 162, 163

Haggai

Hag 2:10–19 63
Hag 2:13 63
Hag 2:13–14 .... 52, 63
Hag 2:14 63

Zechariah

Zech 1:1–6 .... 10, 86
Zech 7:1–8:23 10
Zech 7:3 .... 122, 165
Zech 7:5 .... 122, 165
Zech 8:19 .... 122, 165, 166
Zech 11:10–14 89

Malachi

Malachi 70
Mal 2:10 70
Mal 2:10–16 70
Mal 2:11 .... 70, 162
Mal 2:14 70
Mal 2:15–16 70

Psalms

Psalm 1 119
Ps 1:2 74
Ps 1:3–4 .... 52, 156
Ps 1:6 156
Psalm 3 157
Psalm 4 157
Psalm 6 157
Psalm 9 157
Ps 9:4–5 157
Ps 9:11 77
Psalm 10 .... 119, 157
Psalm 11 119
Psalm 13 .... 76, 157
Ps 13:2 53
Ps 13:4b 76, 78
Ps 13:5–6 76
Ps 13:22 166
Ps 13:25 166
Psalm 14 157
Psalm 15 157
Psalm 16 157
Ps 16:10 77
Ps 17:15 53
Ps 22:2 77
Ps 22:25 53
Ps 27:9 53
Ps 29:3–10 56
Ps 35:4 74
Ps 35:26 74
Ps 36:3 51
Psalm 37 119
Ps 37:25 77
Psalm 44 .... 24, 36, 50, 53, 56,
   74, 116, 119, 120, 126
Ps 44:1–8 .... 35, 138
Ps 44:9–14 .... 120, 155
Ps 44:9–22 35
Ps 44:10 85
Ps 44:10–17 111
Ps 44:10–20 74
Ps 44:16 .... 74, 77, 126
Ps 44:17–18 .... 119, 155
Ps 44:18 .... 48, 50, 55, 74
Ps 44:19 .... 120, 155
Ps 44:20 111
Ps 44:23 .... 52, 74
Ps 44:23–25 111
Ps 44:23–26 35
Ps 44:24 .... 53, 55, 60
Ps 44:25 110
Psalm 50 24
Ps 51:7 14
Ps 51:9 14
Psalm 52 119
Psalm 53 119
Ps 53:6 161
Ps 58:7–9 1120
Psalm 60 120
Ps 60:3–5 111
Ps 60:12 111
Psalm 66 56

Ps 66:6	37
Psalm 68	37, 56
Ps 68:11–31	56
Psalm 69	41, 75
Ps 69:33	41
Ps 69:6	75
Ps 69:8	53
Ps 71:13	74
Psalm 73	119
Psalm 73–83	24
Psalm 74	21, 24, 36, 56, 116, 119, 120, 128
Ps 74:1	120, 155
Ps 74:2	48, 110
Ps 74:3	142
Ps 74:3–9	142
Ps 74:4	142
Ps 74:4–11	111
Ps 74:11	120, 155
Ps 74:12	39
Ps 74:12–15	37, 138
Ps 74:18	110, 142
Ps 74:19–21	155
Ps 74:19a	110
Ps 74:20–23	45
Ps 74:20b	110
Ps 74:22	142, 143, 145
Ps 74:22–23	45
Ps 74:23	110
Psalm 75	119
Ps 75:1	52
Psalm 77	35, 56
Ps 77:9–10	119, 155
Ps 77:16-20	37
Ps 77:17	48
Ps 77:19	15, 22
Ps 77:20	48
Psalm 78	24, 35, 36, 49, 50, 56, 110, 113, 114, 115, 116, 117, 121, 128, 138, 148, 151, 152
Ps 78:8	49
Ps 78:9–11	138
Ps 78:11	116
Ps 78:12–32	51, 57, 112
Ps 78:13	48, 112, 116
Ps 78:13–24	56
Ps 78:13–32	113
Ps 78:14-24	112
Ps 78:17	48, 49, 50
Ps 78:17–19	138
Ps 78:25	116
Ps 78:32	51, 60, 138
Ps 78:32–39	51
Ps 78:33–39	114
Ps 78:33–40	51
Ps 78:39	52, 60
Ps 78:40	48, 49, 116, 117, 121, 151
Ps 78:40–64	113
Ps 78:43	116
Ps 78:44-51	112
Ps 78:44–55	57
Ps 78:44–72	112
Ps 78:50	78, 87
Ps 78:52–53	112
Ps 78:54–55	112
Ps 78:56	49
Ps 78:56–58	138
Ps 78:56–72	56
Ps 78:61–62	87, 97
Ps 78:65	52
Ps 78:65–72	38, 114
Psalm 79	24, 36, 54, 116, 120, 128
Ps 79:1	48
Ps 79:1–4	110, 111
Ps 79:5	110
Ps 79:6	52, 55
Ps 79:8	48, 55, 60, 110
Ps 79:8–9	54, 119, 143
Ps 79:9	55, 110, 143, 145
Ps 79:9b	46, 51, 60
Ps 79:10	16, 22, 45, 46
Ps 79:10–12	45
Ps 79:13	41, 46
Psalm 80	24, 36, 53, 78, 116, 120, 128, 164
Ps 80:2	110
Ps 80:5–7	110, 111
Ps 80:8	110
Ps 80:8–16	77, 78
Ps 80:12–13	129, 155
Ps 80:13	77, 111

Ps 80:15	15, 22, 48
Ps 80:17–19	77
Ps 80:18	52
Ps 80:19	53, 55, 60
Psalm 83	120
Ps 83:5–8	45
Ps 83:19	128
Ps 86:10	128
Ps 88:8	60
Ps 88:15	53
Psalm 89	120
Ps 89:3	56
Ps 89:34	48, 49, 55
Psalm 94	119
Ps 94:1–2	110
Psalm 96	96
Ps 99:6	52
Ps 102:3	53
Psalm 105	37, 56, 95, 96, 108, 110, 112
Ps 105:1	52
Ps 105:8–11	95
Ps 105:8–15	112
Ps 105:28–37	112
Ps 105:43	112
Ps 105:44–45	112
Psalm 106	37, 49, 56, 96, 110, 114, 115, 117, 151, 160
Ps 106:4	114
Ps 106:7	49
Ps 106:8–12	112
Ps 106:13–34	112
Ps 106:19–20	114
Ps 106:22	59
Ps 106:33	49
Ps 106:35–43	112
Ps 106:43	49
Ps 106:47	114
Ps 108:13	41
Ps 109:29	74
Psalm 114	56
Ps 114:3–5	37
Ps 116:4	52
Ps 116:13	52
Ps 116:17	52
Psalm 125	119
Psalm 127	119
Ps 132:1–18	56
Psalm 135	37, 56, 110, 112
Ps 135:7	56, 112
Ps 135:8–9	112
Ps 135:10–11	112
Psalm 136	37, 56, 110, 112
Ps 136:1–9	56
Ps 136:4–9	110, 112
Ps 136:10–15	112
Ps 136:16	112
Ps 136:20–24	112
Ps 143:7	53
Ps 144:12–15	41

Job

Job	13
Job 8:4	53
Job 29	163, 164
Job 29–31	163, 164
Job 29:2–5	165
Job 29:14	164
Job 29:14–16	164
Job 29:17	164
Job 29:21	159
Job 29:22	163, 165
Job 29:24	164
Job 29:24–25	164

Proverbs

Proverbs	166
Prov 2:19	133
Prov 5:6	133
Prov 6:23	133
Prov 10:17	133
Prov 15:24	133
Prov 24:31	77

Ruth

Ruth 1:4	71

Qohelet

Qohelet 158

Lamentations

Lamentations 21, 83
Lam 1:8 48
Lam 1:10 48
Lam 1:11 48
Lam 2:4 48
Lam 2:10 163
Lam 2:10–11 .... 122, 165
Lam 2:18 163
Lamentations 3 .... 81, 166
Lam 3:1–18 83
Lam 3:19–20 83
Lam 3:21–24 83
Lam 3:26–41 83
Lam 3:28 163
Lam 3:40–41 166
Lam 3:42 83
Lam 3:60 43
Lam 3:61 43
Lam 4:22 47

Esther

Est 8:3 43
Est 9:25 43

Daniel

Dan 3:16–20 145
Dan 3:26–45 160
Dan 4:1–9 9
Daniel 9 156
Dan 9:3 .... 132, 166
Dan 9:4 .... 108, 110, 147
Dan 9:4–19 160
Dan 9:4a 149
Dan 9:4b–19a 149
Dan 9:6 111
Dan 9:8 111
Dan 9:15–16 .... 156, 157
Dan 9:17–18 145
Dan 9:20 .... 108, 149
Dan 9:21 5
Dan 11:3 87
Dan 11:24 43

Ezra

Ezra 1:3 81
Ezra 2:63 136
Ezra 3:2 81
Ezra 4:1 81
Ezra 4:1–2 62
Ezra 4:2–6 66
Ezra 4:3 81
Ezra 4:4–16 45
Ezra 4:6 81
Ezra 4:9–11 66
Ezra 4:13 111
Ezra 4:21 81
Ezra 5:1 81
Ezra 5:12 82
Ezra 5:17–6:5 66
Ezra 5:3–17 45
Ezra 6:14 81
Ezra 6:21 63
Ezra 6:22 81
Ezra 7:1–10:44 23
Ezra 7:1–5 93
Ezra 7:6 81
Ezra 7:7–8 26
Ezra 7:15 81
Ezra 7:24 111
Ezra 7:26a 23
Ezra 8:25 81
Ezra 9 .... 7, 10, 71, 72, 85, 86,
   89, 91, 92, 95, 98, 107, 16
Ezra 9–10 .... 69, 70, 71, 72, 91,
   92, 93, 94, 95, 99, 100, 107, 108,
   109, 122, 146, 148, 165
Ezra 9:1 .... 69, 70, 91
Ezra 9:1–2 107
Ezra 9:1–5 .... 92, 108
Ezra 9:1–15 96
Ezra 9:1–10:19 71
Ezra 9:2 .... 69, 70, 76
Ezra 9:3–5 .... 100, 107

Ezra 9:4 ....69, 81
Ezra 9:5 5
Ezra 9:6 ....65, 66, 68, 70, 72, 73, 74, 81, 90, 96, 115, 126, 146, 161
Ezra 9:6–7 ....73, 89, 139
Ezra 9:6–15 ..... 5, 8, 12, 16, 23, 25, 27, 65, 66, 67, 68, 71, 72, 73, 77, 78, 79, 80, 81, 82, 83, 84, 86, 89, 90, 91, 92, 96, 97, 98, 99, 100, 107, 135, 136, 137, 139, 147, 153, 156, 159, 160, 161, 170, 171
Ezra 9:6a 73, 74, 78, 81, 82
Ezra 9:6b 75, 82
Ezra 9:6b–7 ....75, 73, 79, 80, 83
Ezra 9:7 ....65, 68, 72, 79, 82, 86, 87, 89, 90, 97, 99, 109, 146
Ezra 9:7–8 150
Ezra 9:7–9 ....72, 77
Ezra 9:7b 96, 99
Ezra 9:8 ....65, 67, 68, 72, 76, 78, 81, 85, 87, 99, 139, 161
Ezra 9:8–9 ....73, 89, 96
Ezra 9:9 ....23, 65, 67, 68, 76, 77, 78, 81, 82, 87, 89
Ezra 9:9–11 82
Ezra 9:10 ....65, 68, 72, 81, 87, 89
Ezra 9:10–11 ....69, 161
Ezra 9:10–12 ....72, 73, 79, 83, 89
Ezra 9:10–13 78
Ezra 9:10–14 73
Ezra 9:11 ......65, 68, 71, 82, 87, 88, 89, 91, 99
Ezra 9:11–12 ....71, 80, 88, 89, 90
Ezra 9:12 ....65, 68, 72, 82, 89, 97, 98, 99, 107
Ezra 9:12b 99
Ezra 9:13 ......65, 67, 68, 73, 75, 77, 78, 82, 89, 98, 99, 146
Ezra 9:13–14 ....72, 80
Ezra 9:14 ......65, 67, 68, 69, 71, 73, 81, 82, 89
Ezra 9:15 ....66, 67, 68, 73, 74, 79, 81, 83, 89, 90, 99
Ezra 10 95

Ezra 10:1 .... 97, 107, 108, 147, 148, 149, 150
Ezra 10:1–8 ....92, 108
Ezra 10:2 ....69, 81
Ezra 10:3 .... 69, 71, 85, 107, 108
Ezra 10:3–5 .... 71, 94, 95, 108
Ezra 10:4 ....69, 98
Ezra 10:6 166
Ezra 10:9 ....94, 95
Ezra 10:11 .... 93, 94, 108, 148, 149, 150
Ezra 10:15 69
Ezra 10:18–44 69
Ezra 10:19 76

Nehemiah

Neh 1:4 166
Neh 1:4–5 110
Neh 1:5–11 ....9, 92, 160
Neh 5:4 111
Neh 7:4 106
Neh 7:5–10:40 106
Neh 7:5b–72a 106
Neh 7:65 136
Neh 7:72–8:12 66
Neh 7:72b 106
Nehemiah 8 .... 4, 72, 167
Nehemiah 8–9 .... 122, 127
Neh 8:1–12 108
Neh 8:1–18 23
Neh 8:6–7 167
Neh 8:9 ....67, 167
Neh 8:11 167
Neh 8:17–18 127
Neh 8:18 .... 121, 134
Nehemiah 9 .... 4, 7, 110, 122, 123, 124, 125, 126, 127, 129, 134, 151, 153, 158, 161, 164, 165, 167, 168
Nehemiah 9–10 .... 107, 108, 109, 112, 135
Neh 9:1 23, 121, 122, 123, 162, 167
Neh 9:1–5 108
Neh 9:1–37 107
Neh 9:2 .... 108, 147, 148

SCRIPTURE INDEX

Neh 9:3 .... 108, 145, 147, 148
Neh 9:4–5 107
Neh 9:5 107
Neh 9:6 .... 101, 104, 105, 107, 111, 112, 125, 126, 134, 156
Neh 9:6–7 109
Neh 9:6–15 123
Neh 9:6–16 113
Neh 9:6–31 .... 110, 112, 113, 114, 115, 116, 118, 127, 134, 139
Neh 9:6–37 .... 5, 8, 9, 10, 11, 12, 16, 17, 20, 25, 26, 27, 101, 104, 105, 108, 109, 110, 112, 114, 115, 116, 118, 119, 121, 123, 124, 125, 126, 127, 132, 133, 134, 135, 136, 137, 144, 151, 152, 154, 155, 156, 159, 160, 161, 165, 170, 171
Neh 9:6a 118, 127
Neh 9:7 .... 101, 105, 125, 126, 128, 134
Neh 9:7–8 .... 111, 112
Neh 9:8 .... 19, 101, 105, 120, 126, 129, 132, 133, 134, 164
Neh 9:9 101
Neh 9:9–11 .... 110, 112, 114, 116
Neh 9:10 .... 101, 116, 120, 126, 151
Neh 9:11 .... 101, 116, 126
Neh 9:12 .... 101, 126
Neh 9:12–21 112
Neh 9:13 .... 101, 126, 129, 151, 154
Neh 9:13–14 .... 110, 129, 130, 131, 134
Neh 9:13a 130, 153, 154
Neh 9:14 .... 102, 125, 126, 130, 135
Neh 9:15 .... 102, 116, 126, 133, 156
Neh 9:15–19 116
Neh 9:15a 109
Neh 9:16 .... 102, 113, 115, 116, 119, 126, 144, 150, 151
Neh 9:16–17 .... 113, 117, 123
Neh 9:17 .... 102, 104, 105, 121, 124, 133, 167, 168
Neh 9:17–31 .... 113, 115
Neh 9:17a 116

Neh 9:17b 114, 167, 168
Neh 9:18 .... 102, 105, 113, 116, 117, 126, 131, 132, 134, 144, 148, 150
Neh 9:19 ... 102, 105, 121, 126, 167
Neh 9:19–20 114
Neh 9:20 .... 102, 136
Neh 9:21 .... 102, 104, 105, 126
Neh 9:22 .... 102, 105
Neh 9:22–31 .... 111, 112
Neh 9:23 .... 102, 105, 126
Neh 9:24 .... 102, 105, 124, 126, 132, 133, 135
Neh 9:24a 132
Neh 9:25 .... 102, 105, 126, 133
Neh 9:26 .... 102, 104, 105, 106, 113, 114, 116, 117, 124, 133, 136, 139, 144, 150, 161, 163, 169
Neh 9:26–31 113
Neh 9:26a 117, 121, 151
Neh 9:26b 117
Neh 9:27 .... 103, 121, 126
Neh 9:27b 114
Neh 9:28 ... 103, 106, 125, 126, 146
Neh 9:28b 114
Neh 9:29 .... 103, 106, 113, 116, 117, 120, 124, 125, 126, 133, 134, 136, 144, 146, 150, 151, 163, 169
Neh 9:29a 133
Neh 9:30 ... 103, 121, 124, 133, 136
Neh 9:31 .... 103, 104, 106, 133
Neh 9:31a 114
Neh 9:32 .... 103, 110, 111, 113, 116, 119, 121, 125, 126, 139, 144, 168
Neh 9:32–33 157
Neh 9:32–37 .... 79, 110, 111, 114, 115, 117
Neh 9:32a 110, 111, 115, 118
Neh 9:33 .... 103, 106, 111, 115, 117, 119, 120, 121, 126, 144, 156, 159, 160, 164, 167, 169
Neh 9:33–35 .... 39, 111, 116,

118, 119, 121, 134, 144, 145, 155, 165
Neh 9:33a 119, 120, 155
Neh 9:33b 119, 120, 155, 156
Neh 9:34 .... 103, 111, 124, 126, 133
Neh 9:34–35 121
Neh 9:35 .... 103, 106, 126
Neh 9:36 .... 103, 106, 111, 124, 133
Neh 9:36–37 .... 111, 115, 118, 121, 135
Neh 9:37 .... 103, 106, 124, 133
Neh 9:38 107
Neh 10:1 108
Neh 10:1–27 107
Neh 10:2 136
Neh 10:28 107
Neh 10:28–30 107
Neh 10:29 108
Neh 10:29–30 107
Neh 10:30 107
Neh 10:31 107
Neh 10:31–39 107
Neh 10:39 107
Neh 11:1 106
Neh 11:10–11 93
Neh 11:23 108
Neh 12:27a 106
Neh 12:31 106
Nehemiah 13 107
Neh 13:12 107
Neh 13:15–22 107
Neh 13:23 69
Neh 13:23–29 107
Neh 13:25 71

1 Chronicles

1 Chronicles 79, 96
1 Chronicles 2–9 96
1 Chr 2:3–4:23 93
1 Chr 2:7 .... 94, 95, 108
1 Chr 2:25–33 93
1 Chr 2:34–41 93
1 Chr 5:27–41 93
1 Chr 6:1–15 93
1 Chr 6:34–38 93
1 Chr 6:5–11 93
1 Chr 7:6–12 93
1 Chr 8:1–28 93
1 Chr 8:29–40 93
1 Chr 9:10–11 93
1 Chr 9:32 135
1 Chr 9:35–44 93
1 Chronicles 16 .... 95, 96
1 Chr 16:8–36 95
1 Chr 16:15–18 .... 93, 95
1 Chr 21:3 94
1 Chr 22:13 97
1 Chr 23:31 135
1 Chr 28:2–10 79
1 Chr 28:8–10 97
1 Chr 28:9 96
1 Chr 28:9b 98
1 Chr 28:10 97
1 Chr 28:20 97
1 Chr 29:10 107
1 Chr 29:18 43

2 Chronicles

2 Chronicles 79, 96
2 Chr 2:3 135
2 Chr 7:12–22 99
2 Chr 7:14 .... 43, 167
2 Chr 8:13 135
2 Chr 11:17 98
2 Chronicles 12 98
2 Chr 12:1–2 98
2 Chr 12:5 96
2 Chr 12:13b 91
2 Chr 15:2 96
2 Chr 15:13 43
2 Chr 19:6–7 79
2 Chr 19:7 79
2 Chr 19:9–11 79
2 Chr 19:11 97
2 Chr 20:5–12 17
2 Chr 23:4 135
2 Chr 23:8 135
2 Chr 24:2 96
2 Chr 24:18 96
2 Chr 24:26 91
2 Chr 28:10 96

2 Chr 28:13 96
2 Chr 29:5–11 79
2 Chr 29:6–9 79
2 Chr 29:9 87
2 Chr 30:15 74
2 Chr 31:3 135
2 Chr 32:7 97
2 Chr 33:23 96
2 Chr 34:4 66
2 Chronicles 35–36 66
2 Chr 36:15–23 135
2 Chr 36:22–23 135
2 Chr 36:20 135

Baruch

Bar 1:5–3:8 144
Bar 1:15–2:15 144
Bar 2:14 145
Bar 3:2 144
Bar 3:3 144

Judith

Jdt 9:1 5

1 Maccabees

1 Macc 2:49 139
1 Macc 2:49–70 139
1 Macc 2:52 19
1 Macc 2:62–63 139
1 Maccabees 155

Sirach

Sir 44:16 71

Tobit

Tob 3:14 140

Wisdom

Wis 44:20 19

Luke

Luke 15:7 1

Acts of the Apostles

Acts 10:30 5

www.ingramcontent.com/pod-product-compliance
Lightning Source LLC
Chambersburg PA
CBHW021841220426
43663CB00005B/349